Monitoring Penal Policy in Europe

The process of judicial control over institutions is often described as growing socio-legal trend which impacts the development of modern societies. This is particularly the case for prisons and other penal institutions, as international bodies and the courts have tried to influence prison policies since the 1960s. This book addresses this dynamic situation by focusing on European monitoring as a major influence on penal and prison policies within, between and across nation states.

Bringing together experts from around Europe, this book actively contributes to debates and analysis within penal and prison policy studies by shedding lights on the impacts of monitoring, and demonstrates how the study of penal and prison reform in different European countries can contribute to building a clearer and more precise picture of European legal systems.

This book will be of interest to researchers in the fields of prisons, penology and punishment, as well as policymakers and professionals working for national Ministries of Justice and for prison department and national human rights institutions, as well as those working for INGOs and NGOs.

Gaëtan Cliquennois is senior fellow for the French National Centre for Scientific Research at the University of Strasbourg. He is affiliated with the Centre for the Study of Penal Law at the University of Louvain-la-Neuve and has been visiting scholar at the University of Cambridge, the London School of Economics, the European University Institute and the College of Europe.

Hugues de Suremain is researcher in law and barrister. He is an expert of prisoners' rights and prison litigation before the European Court of Human Rights. He was formerly responsible officer of the legal and litigation section of the International Prison Observatory (OIP) in France. He is co-founder and leader of the NGO "Prison Litigation Network" that is funded by the European Commission.

Routledge Frontiers of Criminal Justice

www.routledge.com/Routledge-Frontiers-of-Criminal-Justice/book-series/RFCJ

41 **Transforming Summary Justice**
Modernisation in the lower criminal courts
Jennifer Ward

42 **Stop and Search and Police Legitimacy**
Ben Bradford

43 **Young Offenders and Open Custody**
Tove Pettersson

44 **Restorative Responses to Sexual Violence**
Legal, social and therapeutic dimensions
Edited by Estelle Zinsstag and Marie Keenan

45 **Policing Hate Crime**
Understanding communities and prejudice
Gail Mason, JaneMaree Maher, Jude McCulloch, Sharon Pickering, Rebecca Wickes and Carolyn McKay

46 **The Special Constabulary**
Historical context, international comparisons and contemporary themes
Edited by Karen Bullock and Andrew Millie

47 **Action Research in Criminal Justice**
Restorative justice approaches in intercultural settings
Edited by Inge Vanfraechem and Ivo Aertsen

48 **Restoring Justice and Security in Intercultural Europe**
Edited by Brunilda Pali and Ivo Aertsen

49 **Monitoring Penal Policy in Europe**
Edited by Gaëtan Cliquennois and Hugues de Suremain

Monitoring Penal Policy in Europe

Edited by Gaëtan Cliquennois
and Hugues de Suremain

Routledge
Taylor & Francis Group
LONDON AND NEW YORK

First published 2018 by Routledge

2 Park Square, Milton Park, Abingdon, Oxon OX14 4RN
605 Third Avenue, New York, NY 10017

Routledge is an imprint of the Taylor & Francis Group, an informa business

First issued in paperback 2021

Publisher's Note

The publisher has gone to great lengths to ensure the quality of this reprint but points out that some imperfections in the original copies may be apparent.

British Library Cataloguing-in-Publication Data
A catalogue record for this book is available from the British Library

Library of Congress Cataloging-in-Publication Data
Names: Cliquennois, Gaëtan, editor. | Suremain, Hugues de, editor.
Title: Monitoring penal policy in Europe / edited by Gaëtan Cliquennois and Hugues de Suremain.
Description: Abingdon, Oxon [UK] ; New York, NY : Routledge, 2017. | Series: Routledge frontiers of criminal justice ; 49 | Includes bibliographical references and index.
Identifiers: LCCN 2017017920 | ISBN 9781138688063 (hardback) | ISBN 9781315542034 (ebook)
Subjects: LCSH: Prisons—Law and legislation—Europe. | Imprisonment—Europe.
Classification: LCC KJC9769 .M66 2017 | DDC 344.403/5—dc23
LC record available at https://lccn.loc.gov/2017017920

ISBN: 978-1-138-68806-3 (hbk)
ISBN: 978-0-367-22810-1 (pbk)

Typeset in Times New Roman
by Apex CoVantage, LLC

Contents

Illustrations

Figure

Tables

Contributors

Giuseppe Caputo is post-doctoral researcher at the Department of Law, University of Florence in Italy. He is also a former lawyer and legal adviser. His interests are European prison law and European human rights. He is a member of the NGO for prisoners' rights 'L'altro diritto', Centre of Studies on Prison, Deviance, Marginalisation.

Sofia Ciuffoletti is academic researcher at the Department of Law, University of Florence, Florence, Italy. She is also a former lawyer and legal adviser. Her interests are European prison law and international human rights. She is a member of the NGO for prisoners' rights 'L'altro diritto'.

Leonidas Cheliotis is an Associate Professor of Criminology at the Department of Social Policy, London School of Economics and Political Science. He is also Co-Director of LSE's Mannheim Centre for Criminology, as well as an Editor and Book Review Editor of the British Journal of Criminology. In recognition of his research, he has received the 2016 Adam Podgòrecki Prize by the International Sociological Association's Research Committee on Sociology of Law, the 2015 Outstanding Critical Criminal Justice Scholar Award by the Critical Criminal Justice Section of the American Academy of Criminal Justice Sciences, and the 2013 Critical Criminologist of the Year Award by the Division on Critical Criminology of the American Society of Criminology.

Gaëtan Cliquennois works as senior fellow for the French National Centre for Scientific Research at the University of Strasbourg. He is affiliated with the Centre for the Study of Penal Law at the University of Louvain-la-Neuve and has been a visiting scholar at the University of Cambridge, the London School of Economics, the European University Institute and the College of Europe. In 2015, he has won the call for special issue launched by the European Law Journal.

Simon Creighton works for Bhatt Murphy Solicitors and has a considerable case load of public law challenges and applications to the European Court of Human Rights. Formerly, Simon has practised in prison law since 1993 when he was appointed as the first solicitor to the Prisoners' Advice Service. He is regularly asked to comment in the media on issues affecting prisoners.

Hugues de Suremain is researcher in law and barrister. He is an expert of prisoners' rights and prison litigation before the European Court of Human Rights. He was formerly the responsible officer of the legal and litigation section of the International Prison Observatory (OIP) in France. He is co-founder and leader of the NGO "Prison Litigation Network" that is funded by the European Commission.

Frieder Dünkel is professor emeritus in law and criminology at the University of Greifswald. He was president of the European Society of Criminology until 2016. Since 1994 he has co-ordinated several Tempus-projects funded by the European Union with Siberian law faculties. Furthermore he co-ordinates Erasmus exchange programmes with about 35 universities in Western and Eastern Europe and teaches, as guest professor, courses in German, English and French in several European universities

Corentin Durand is PhD candidate in sociology and temporary lecturer and researcher at the Ecole des hautes études en sciences sociales (Centre d'Etude des Mouvements Sociaux and Centre Maurice Halbwachs) in Paris. He is working on French prisoners' litigation and has been an active member of the prison litigation network funded by the European Commission. From September to December 2016, he was visiting scholar at the University of Cambridge.

Nicolas Ferran has a PhD in legal studies. He is the responsible officer of the legal and litigation section of the International Prison Observatory (OIP) since January 2011. As a lawyer, he successfully fought several cases in front of the European Court of Human Rights. He has notably co-organised the conference "Legal defence of prisoners" that took place in January 2013 at the French Senate (High Chamber).

Pauline Jacobs is Assistant Professor in criminal law and criminal procedure at the W.P.J. Pompe Institute for Criminal Law and Criminology of Utrecht University (the Netherlands). She is affiliated with the Montaigne Centre for Judicial Administration and Conflict Resolution of the same university.

Lauri Koskenniemi works currently as a research assistant at the Institute of Criminology and Legal Policy, where he has engaged in research on comparative criminal policy and prison conditions in Europe. He holds a law degree (2016) from the University of Helsinki and his prior research focused on the history of psychiatric and psychological expertise in the criminal process.

Tapio Lappi Seppälä is the Director General of the Institute of Criminology and Legal Policy. Alongside his current position he has been acting as a part-time professor in criminology and sociology of law at the University of Helsinki. He has actively taken part in international co-operation in criminal justice issues at the Scandinavian Research Council for Criminology, Council of Europe, the International Penal and Penitentiary Foundation (Vice President since 2005), and the European Society of Criminology (Member of the Board since 2008)

Christine Morgenstern is researcher in criminology at the University of Greifswald (Department of Criminology, Criminal Law, Criminal Procedure and Comparative Criminal Law and Justice). Since July 2016, she is a scientific co-coordinator of the EU project 'Towards pre-trial detention as ultima ratio' (funded by the European Commission).

Nicola Padfield is Reader at the Law Faculty, University of Cambridge, and Master of Fitzwilliam College in Cambridge. She has held a number of posts in the College including President, Director of Studies and Admissions Tutor. She was a Recorder (part-time judge) in the Crown Court 2002-2014, is a Bencher of the Middle Temple and served as the University Advocate for several years. She has been active in a number of pan-European research networks and was editor of the criminal practitioners' monthly 'Archbold Review' from 1996-2013.

Rosaria Pirosa is attorney and post-doctoral researcher at the Department of Law, University of Florence. Her research interests are European prison law and international human rights. She has contributed to the Prison litigation network (EU grant) as a member of the Italian team and is member of Altro Diritto, Centre of Studies on Prison, Deviance, Marginalisation.

Esther Pascual Rodriguez holds a PhD in law and works as a lawyer and mediator on penitentiary and criminal-related issues. She is a founding member and President of the Association for Mediation and Pacification. Dr. Pascual lectures a number of postgraduate courses in various Spanish Universities and is the author of several publications on restorative justice and mediation.

Clara Réy Sanchez is PhD candidate in international law at the University Jaume I of Castellón. She recently worked as a trainee for the European Commission (criminal justice division). She has also contributed to the Prison litigation network (EU grant) as a member of the Spanish team and to the EU grant "Armed Conflicts, Peacekeeping and Transitional Justice: Law as Solution".

Jonathan Simon is Adrian A. Kragen Professor of Law and Director, Center for the Study of Law and Society at the Berkeley Law faculty. Professor Simon's scholarship concerns the role of crime and criminal justice in governing contemporary societies. His past work includes two award winning monographs *Poor Discipline: Parole and the Social Control of the Underclass* (University of Chicago 1993, winner of the American Sociological Association's sociology of law book prize, 1994), and *Governing through Crime: How the War on Crime Transformed American Democracy and Created a Culture of Fear* (Oxford University Press 2007, winner of the American Society of Criminology, Hindelang Award 2010).

Sappho Xenakis is a Senior Lecturer in Criminology at Birkbeck Law School, University of London, where she has also founded and directs the MSc Global Criminology programme. She is also Founding Co-Director of the Birkbeck Centre for Political Economy and Institutional Studies (CPEIS). She is currently a Book Review Editor for Critical Criminology and sits on the editorial board of the British Journal of Criminology.

Anton Van Kalmthout is emeritus professor at Tilburg University (the Netherlands). He is a member of the European Committee for the Prevention of Torture and Inhuman or Degrading Treatment or Punishment (CPT) of the Council of Europe.

Foreword

Slowly, and with halting progress across the globe, the project of protecting the human dignity of prisoners is penetrating and transforming the national legal systems in which prisons find their authority and seek legitimacy. No place on the globe offers a more compelling picture of what that project looks like in fleshed out institutional form than the Europe Member States (virtually all 47 Member States) under the jurisdiction of the European Convention on Human Rights and its institutional infrastructure. Europe is the strongest example of an attempt to protect dignity through a regime of continuous standard setting and monitoring. This book presents the European monitoring of penal and prison policies as a spreading socio-legal trend which is contributing to the development of modern societies over time. This has been claimed, by some learned observers, to be the basis of a distinctive European penal sensibility tending toward leniency and minimisation of prison sentences although, of course, many other differences set Europe aside from common comparison cases and striking differences in respect for human dignity exist within the European penal space.

Even within the human rights world, monitoring is often ignored in favour of the grand pronouncements of national high courts and human rights courts, but the long history of struggles to protect dignity has demonstrated that the often monotonous work of monitoring is crucial both to defining the rights articulated in those grand decisions, and in implementing them. This book addresses precisely this dynamic situation by focusing on European monitoring as a major shaper and influencer of penal and prison policies within, between and across nation states. The accounts from twelve countries not only show the impact of European monitoring locally but also the interplay between the local and European policy spaces. The book actively contributes to debates and analysis within penal and prison policy studies by shedding lights on the impacts of European monitoring, and on how it operates in and through a range of different legal and political traditions. Importantly the book provides grounded empirical accounts of how a range of nation states across Europe have reacted to the common practices of monitoring and standard setting within European institutions. It is these reactions, as much as positive law itself, that determine the future of the European prison experience.

Collectively, this is therefore an outstanding contribution to socio-legal and criminological studies not only of penal and prison matters, but of processes of legal and political change in multi-state frameworks. While there has been growing attention to the idea of a European penal sensibility, there is no book that really engages with this major monitoring process within penal and prison policies in Europe. This book fills a significant gap in the literature and has the potential to be a resource for researchers, students and practitioners and policymakers. Such a book is necessary because current debates about penal and prison policies in a European context have been progressively influenced by the Council of Europe and the European Union. In particular, the Committee of Ministers and the European Court of Human Rights have engaged with common reform processes (standards, procedural obligation on the burden of national states) but there is no work that actively analyses the diverse responses and reactions from national states.

This book makes an important contribution to the penal and prison studies literatures in general. European structures of control conceived as a whole through their potential effects in terms of shaping and monitoring penal and prison policies remains woefully understudied and could form the basis for global comparisons. Very little has been written on the combination of oversight by the Council of Europe and the European Union, the coherence of the supervision exercised by these institutions, the often increasingly tight control of these bodies over Member States or legal, political and organisational reactions (as refusal, deterrence, resistance, curb, acceptance, cooperation, etc.) from national administrations. In organizing a series of national studies in a regional framework, this book initiates what must become an international comparative project. This book moves us forward by presenting studies of these dynamics in the most developed system of penal monitoring and prison standard setting in the world. As such, it offers a critical opportunity to raise the visibility of these little studied but crucial socio-legal processes in a wider community of stakeholders and researchers, and constitutes legal, criminological and socio-legal research.

By Professor Jonathan Simon

1 Introduction

The European monitoring of national penal and prison policies: Influence and shaping

Gaëtan Cliquennois

Introduction

The process of judicial control over many institutions and sectors is often described as an influential and spreading socio-legal trend, which is contributing to the development and the reform of modern societies. This particularly seems to be the case for prisons and other penal institutions, as international bodies and the courts have tried to influence prison policies since the 1960s at least. European judicial and inspectorate bodies that share the general principles and aims of what is now commonly referred to as 'global justice' have gained increasing prominence in the fields of penal and prison policy and practice in recent years, and each of those bodies is working in their diverse capacities to ensure that European human rights legislation is observed inside the borders of individual nation-states. National penal policies and prison policies are, in Europe, increasingly controlled and monitored by both the Council of Europe and the European Union. The influence of this European monitoring seems to be deep and broad, resulting from the interaction between, and the mutual reinforcement of, three distinct organs: the European Court of Human Rights ('ECtHR'), the Committee for the Prevention of Torture ('CPT') and the Committee of Ministers ('CM').

Despite the long-term development of the European monitoring of penal policies and some legal studies of this phenomenon (Belda, 2010), little empirical research has been done into their influence over penal and prison policies. The existing studies have mainly focused on some Recommendations of the Council of Europe (adopted by the CM and the CPT) and European Court of Human Rights jurisprudence (Rodley and Pollard, 2009; Van Zyl Smit and Snacken, 2009; Foster, 2011; Simon, 2011). They essentially underline the process of interpretation applied by the ECtHR without really paying attention to the evolution of European structures of judicial and institutional control (Foster, 2011). Indeed, scholars have assumed that the ECtHR used a bold, dynamic approach to develop legal standards adapted to the composite face of the person deprived of liberty, mobilising a range of interpretative methods, which simultaneously reflect both the fundamental objectives pursued by the judge and the contextual constraints imposed on him/her (Follesdal et al., 2013; Simon, 2011 and 2014; Van Zyl Smit and Snacken, 2009). In this manner, the margins of interpretation used by the

ECtHR and their socially desirable results have been stressed by judges. In contrast, the scope of the influence exerted by the ECtHR (as a CoE body) on penal policies through its constitutional structures and its interactions with other institutional and regional bodies (such as the EU) have been understated, and even neglected to date (Lambert-Abdelgawad, 2013). Instead, the few large-scale studies on the judicial monitoring of prison policies have focused on showing the effects of the rights granted to prisoners on national penal budgets and on the "humanisation" of certain aspects of prison life (Feeley and Rubin, 1998; Feeley and Van Swearingen, 2004; Snacken and Dumortier, 2012; van Zyl Smit and Snacken, 2009); on the weakness of the prison legal framework (Herzog-Evans, 2012) and on the growth of the prison population (Guetzkow and Schoon, 2015; Schoenfeld, 2010) and risk management techniques (Cliquennois and Champetier, 2013; Cliquennois, 2013), without highlighting the development of a control exerted by European organisations (Abels, 2012; Van Zyl Smit, 2010).

Therefore, little attention has been paid to the overall European structures of control and their effect on the shaping and monitoring of penal and prison policies. Very little has been written on the combination of oversight by the Council of Europe and the European Union, the often increasingly tight control of these bodies over Member States, or legal, political and organisational reactions (as refusal, deterrence, resistance, curb, acceptance, cooperation . . .) from national administrations. This is why contributors to this book insist and detail the content of the obligations imposed progressively by the ECtHR on human rights and the CM on national states. In this way, our book considers how these procedural obligations imposed by the Strasbourg Court could potentially impact and change penal and prison policies. Importantly, this book provides accounts of how this European monitoring is being engaged within a range of nation states across Europe (including Nordic and Southern countries), and draws on research in penal and prison policies to illuminate and develop analysis about the significance of studying the national and local reactions to this European influence. However, the European institutions' approach to criminal issues, including from a human rights perspective, is ambivalent. In this respect, the impact of the European standards on national policies, and above all those resulting from EU legislation, which impose a certain level of severity with regard to a number of infringements, would request a study as such, which the present work is not intended to produce.

Regarding the development of this European control over penal and prison policies, we question whether the establishment and strengthening of the relationship between the control of prisons ensured by the European organs of control has contributed to the shaping of prison policies and the creation of a monitoring system based on human rights, which has forced national prison administrations to develop political, legal and organisational responses. Indeed, this 'panopticon' based on human rights seems to be inverted in the sense that the supervision exerted by the European judicial and institutional bodies over the prison administrations is influenced by the complaints by prisoners and NGOs to them. In other words, is there any evidence in addition to the constant multifaceted supervision of prisoners (as in the hypothesis of Foucault, 1975), that national Ministers of

Justice and prison administrations are now also monitored and supervised by the European bodies? In this perspective, this book will present, on the one hand, the monitoring of penal policies and prisons by the European bodies (1), and, on the other hand, the reactions and responses from the national prison administrations to this European inverted panopticon (2).

1 The growing obligations imposed by the European bodies on national states

The Council of Europe and, to a lesser extent, the European Union have increasingly monitored national penal and prison policies over time. This process was achieved through a reinforcement of the power of the Strasbourg Court and the obligations it imposes on national states (1.1) and a new oversight exerted by the European Union in partnership with the CoE (1.2). The impacts of European monitoring, therefore, have been increased on domestic penal policies (1.3).

1.1 The reinforcement of the power of the ECtHR

The ECtHR has played an increasingly prominent role in the course of its history although its authority is challenged in a growing number of States, leading to a greater attention to the principle of subsidiarity (Spano, 2014). It has progressively applied a more expansive approach to human rights that pushes against the boundaries of state sovereignty to exert judicial control over Member State governments and their prison administrations (Follesdal et al., 2013). In this sense, the ECtHR has defended the civil and human rights of prisoners held in the Member States by issuing judgments that have the force of *res judicata* and that are binding on Member State governments. It can force Member State governments found guilty of breaching the European Convention on Human Rights ("ECHR") to take immediate corrective action and to amend their national legislation to prevent recurrences if the breach was due to commonly used legislation or practice (Christoffersen and Madsen, 2011). A case brought against one Member State government may have deep implications for other Member State governments (Follesdal et al., 2013), as the national authorities and courts tend to recognise ECtHR judgments as having *de facto erga omnes* effect.

In this respect, the ECtHR has increased its focus over time on the effectiveness[1] of the implementations of the ECHR on national laws (Christoffersen and Madsen, 2011). Since the *Belgium linguistic* case,[2] the ECtHR has extended the obligations of the Member States to include not only negative obligations (e.g. to refrain from breaching human rights) but also positive obligations, requiring them to take steps to protect the human rights covered by the ECHR (Tulkens, 2007). These positive obligations have enabled the ECtHR to strengthen, and sometimes extend, the substantive requirements of the ECHR and to link them to procedural obligations. This, in turn, has led to legal, administrative, judicial and practical changes, as well as legislation, to enforce the implementation of the ECHR (Popelier et al., 2011) which means that the ECHR's universality has been exemplified at the national level (Andenas and Bjorge, 2013). Many European countries, including France, Germany and Belgium have passed national prison laws[3] that are influenced by European standards, even though a significant part of the Belgian Prison Law of 12 January 2005 has not been implemented and the French Prison Law of 24 November 2009 merely enacts unchanged the provisions of Presidential decrees and looks like an attempt to comply with European standards in words only (Herzog-Evans, 2012). In addition, the French Council of State and the German Constitutional Court have also integrated a significant portion of ECtHR's case law into their national jurisprudence.

This trend has been reinforced by the ECtHR's use of pilot and quasi-pilot judgments ("Article 46 judgments") since 2004, supported by the Member States and by the CoE.[4] These pilot judgments allow the ECtHR to handle issues which come before it repeatedly, and to answer structural or large-scale systemic breaches of the ECHR caused by non-compliant legislation in certain Member States by ordering their governments to implement effective redress mechanisms and pass new legislation which is compliant with the ECHR (Sadurski, 2009: 447–431). Among others, Germany, the UK and Italy,[5] have been the subjects of pilot judgments. For its part, Belgium has had several quasi-pilot judgments made against it in particular, related to its lack of domestic remedies for prisoners and its prison overcrowding.[6] It also required Italy, on the one hand, to adopt new penal policies of deflation, increased parole and decriminalisation,[7] with a view to reducing overcrowding in its prisons and, on the other hand, to establish a combination of preventive and compensatory remedies to improve the living conditions in remand prisons. The preventive remedies had to make it possible for detainees to obtain prompt and effective examination of their complaints by an independent authority or court empowered to order remedial action. The compensatory remedies should provide redress, including a reduction of sentence or monetary compensation in an amount comparable to the ECtHR's awards in similar cases, to detainees held in inhuman or degrading conditions pending trial. The aim of such preventive remedies is to provide in Italy conditions of detention that are decent and that respect the human rights enshrined in the 1950 ECHR. For its part, the UK was condemned by the ECtHR and the CM (when supervising the execution of ECtHR judgments) to implement new legislation granting prisoners the right to vote,[8] despite successive UK governments having opposed this change.

Additionally, the architecture of the ECtHR has been redesigned over time to expand its scope of intervention, to transform it into a quasi-constitutional court and to facilitate the increasing number of individual applications, through the reform of its original control machinery by Protocol 11 of 11 May 1994 (which entered into force in late 1998). Between the signing of the ECHR in 1955 and 1998, the European Commission of Human Rights ("ECoHR") operated a complaint screening mechanism to filter individual complaints against the Member States. If the ECoHR ruled that a complaint was admissible, it was referred either to the CM for a 'political' settlement or to the ECtHR for a judicial settlement. Under this system, the Member States retained control of the cases brought before the ECtHR because the members of the ECoHR were appointed by the Ministers of Justice of the Member States, which meant that the Member States concerned acted as both judge and defendant (Blackburn and Polakiewicz, 2001). Additionally, decisions by the ECoHR to refer complaints to the ECtHR due to breaches of the ECHR (in its "Article 31" reports) had to be approved by a two-thirds majority. This meant that only 10.6 per cent of complaints were declared admissible by the ECoHR between 1955 and 1998 (Bond, 2013: 24). Protocol 11 put an end to this filtering mechanism by creating a single permanent court with full jurisdiction to replace both the ECoHR and the ECtHR. Protocol 11 set up a full quasi-constitutional review structure with a Grand Chamber (which renders leading judgments) and the right for applicants to request referral of a case decided by a Chamber to the Grand Chamber (Follesdal *et al.*: 13). Protocol 11 also reinforced the role of individual applicants (Bates, 2010). Within this system, individual applicants can now lodge complaints against a Member State directly with the ECtHR, whose rulings apply not only to that particular application, but also to other applicants in similar situations. This explains why most of the ECtHR's rulings regarding prisons have been made after these reforms[9].

The power of the ECtHR was further reinforced in January 2011 by the establishement of a new single-judge filtering section of the ECtHR's registry, following a suggestion made at the Interlaken Conference. The selection of cases by this filtering section so far, coupled with an amendment to the ECtHR's rules in June 2009 concerning the order in which it deals with cases,[10] have shown that the ECtHR's priority is less individual cases than wider systemic issues including:

(i) urgent complaints related to the right to life or health (Article 2 ECHR), the risk of torture or inhuman and degrading treatment (Article 3 ECHR) and to the right to legal detention (Article 5 ECHR);
(ii) complaints with the potential to affect the effectiveness of the ECHR or which raise questions of general interest;
(iii) complaints arising from pilot/leading judgments, such as repetitive and systemic breaches of human rights resulting in large-scale systemic breaches of the ECHR due to non-compliant legislation or practices in the Member States (Cameron, 2013: 42–43).

The outcome of the reforms introduced by Protocol 14 has been to deepen the influence of the ECtHR on national law and administrative practice in the Member States (Keller and Stone Sweet, 2008) and on prisoners in penal matters. In this sense, and thanks to its new quasi-constitutional architecture, the ECtHR has become an approximate equivalent at a pan-European level of the US Supreme Court (Alkema, 2000; Christoffersen, 2011; Follesdal et al., 2013; Sadurski, 2009), although the primary purpose of the Convention system is to provide individual relief.

The Court considers that, in principle, a wide margin of appreciation is given to the Member States in the field of prison and penal policy.[11] It is well-established in the Court's case law that a State's choice of a specific criminal justice system, including sentence review and release arrangements, is in principle outside the scope of the supervision exerted by the Strasbourg Court. Member States must be allowed a margin of appreciation when deciding on the appropriate length of prison sentences for particular crimes. As the ECtHR has stated, it is not its role to decide on the appropriate term of detention applicable to a particular offence or to pronounce on the appropriate length of detention or other sentence which should be served by a person after his conviction by a national court.[12] The analysis of the case-law reveals, however, the tendency of the Court to see in situations of prison overcrowding a circumstance limiting, in the name of the inviolability of the prohibition under Article 3, the margin of appreciation given to the Member States.

In this regard, the ECtHR has imposed uniform rules on Member States which have been obliged to substantially amend their penal (with regard to pre-trial detention and in some circumstances adjustment of sentences) and prison legislation. For instance, many Member States have been forced to amend national laws which breached the ECHR, such as Germany, which had to change its legislation on indeterminate preventive detention[13] and several countries which had to create a mechanism guaranteeing regular judicial reviews for prisoners serving life/ inderminate sentences.[14]

1.2 The new EU oversight of penal and prison policies

The EU also exerts some control over penal and prison policies since the EU and the CoE increased their dialogue on human rights, fundamental freedoms and the rule of law, by developing several forms of co-operation. This co-operation covers the establishment of a co-ordination committee responsible for setting standards[15] and the use of specialised bodies, such as the Venice Commission, the CoE's advisory body on constitutional matters in charge of providing legal advice to Member States and helping them to make their legal and institutional structures compliant with European human rights standards.[16]

In particular, the European Parliament is very active in the prison field by drafting and adopting resolutions, recommendations and reports on prisons in the EU, such as its resolution of 7 December 2011[17] (following its resolution of 18 January 1996 on poor conditions in prisons in the EU[18] and its resolution of 17 December 1998 on prison conditions in the EU: improvements and alternative penalties[19]) on detention conditions in the EU, which highlights the problems of prison overcrowding, an increase in the prison population, a rise in the number of foreign nationals being held, excessive numbers of pre-trial detainees, large numbers of detainees with mental and psychological disorders and numerous deaths and suicides in custody. With regard to these issues, which were also highlighted by the European Commission in its green paper of 2011,[20] the European Parliament recommended the Member States to take urgent measures to ensure that the fundamental rights of prisoners are protected by:

(i) allocating additional resources for the restructuring and modernisation of prisons and providing them with appropriate technical equipment and space;
(ii) enhancing prisoners' right to security;

(iii) rehabilitating and preparing inmates for their release and social integration;
(iv) developing probation measures as an alternative to imprisonment;
(v) providing the police and prison staff with training based on contemporary prison management practices and European human rights standards;
(vi) monitoring prisoners suffering from mental and psychological disorders;
(vii) limiting the use of pre-trial detention;
(viii) taking action to prevent suicides in custody and carrying out in-depth and impartial investigations into deaths in custody;
(ix) creating a specific EU budget to fund such projects.

In the same sense, the European Parliament also calls on the European Commission and the Fundamental Rights Agency to monitor detention conditions in the EU, to draft a legislative proposal on the rights of prisoners and to implement minimum standards for prison and detention conditions.[21] In its resolution for the Stockholm programme,[22] in its February 2011 Written Declaration on infringement of the fundamental rights of detainees in the European Union[23] and its resolution of 2 April 2014 on the mid-term review of the Stockholm Programme,[24] the European Parliament had already urged the European Commission to construct an EU criminal justice system through minimum standards for prison and detention conditions and a common set of prisoners' rights in the EU. Prior to this Written Declaration, the European Parliament had already recommended (in its recommendation on 24 February 2004[25] on the rights of prisoners in the EU) that the European Council draft a European Prisons Charter that recognises the fundamental rights of inmates (including the right to mental and physical safety and to rehabilitation and reintegration) and that it also assess the Member States' legislation in accordance with the standards set up by the CoE, the CPT and the ECtHR. In the same way, the European Council recently encouraged and invited the European Commission to support alternatives to custody, the exchange of best practices in prison management and the implementation of the European Prison Rules approved by the CoE.[26]

In addition, the European Parliament, through its Committee on Civil Liberties, Justice and Home Affairs[27] is responsible for the protection within the territory of the EU of citizens' rights, human rights and fundamental rights, as laid down in the Charter of Fundamental Rights of the EU, and the establishment and development of police and judicial co-operation in criminal matters. The Committee also monitors prison matters through sending delegations to inspect prisons and issuing regular reports on the situation of prisons in the Member States, especially those subject to hostile judgments from the ECtHR. For instance, a Committee delegation recently visited several Italian prisons[28] and released a report denouncing the situations of their inmates[29] following the *Torregiani v. Italy* case, where the ECtHR's judgment denounced excessive prison overcrowding and inhumane treatment of prisoners in Italy.[30]

The co-operation between the EU and the CoE has also been reinforced since they jointly established an active network of National Preventive Mechanisms to co-ordinate the fight against torture and inhumane treatment in Europe.[31] This co-operation has also been improved since secret prisons programmes set up by the CIA in Europe were scrutinised by both the European Parliament and the CoE. On behalf of the CoE and the European Parliament, several reports, recommendations and resolutions on the alleged transportation and illegal detention of prisoners in European countries by the CIA have been released by the Parliamentary Assembly of the CoE[32] and two committees of the European Parliament,[33] alleging breaches of human rights in the secret detention facilities and during the secret transfer of prisoners inside and outside Europe. The cases mentioned by the CoE and the EU were subsequently reported to the ECtHR, which had also issued hostile judgments against Italy[34] based on reports released and resolutions adopted by the European Parliament and the CoE.

On its side, the Court of Justice of the European Union (CJEU) has delivered its judgment on 5 April 2016 in Joined Cases Aranyosi and Căldăraru,[35] which relays and gives more strength to the protection of fundamental rights and the requirements imposed by the Strasbourg Court. In this regard, the CJEU introduced a two-step test, which the executing authority must conduct when it is in the possession of evidence of a 'real risk' of inhuman and degrading treatment of detainees in the issuing Member State. During the first step, the executing authority must initially rely on 'objective, reliable, specific and properly updated' information on the prevailing detention conditions in the issuing Member State that demonstrate the existence of deficiencies, 'which may be systemic or generalised, or which may affect certain groups of people, or which may affect certain places of detention'. Several sources can be used, such as the decisions of the ECtHR, the decisions of courts of the issuing Member State or reports drawn up by the organs of the Council of Europe or the UN. As a second step, the executing authority must also ascertain whether in the specific case the requested person would face a 'real risk' of inhuman or degrading treatment. To this end, the executing authority must request the provision of additional information from the issuing authority, which must provide this information within the time fixed in such a demand. In this manner, the CJEU endorses not only the ECtHR criteria on bad and degrading treatments but gives more power to the ECtHR judgments in the case of systemic and structural issues by putting an end to the principle of cooperation and mutual trust (recognised by the European Council) between the EU Member States in penal and prison matters.

1.3 The reinforcement of the European monitoring imposed on national states

The Council of Europe has required national states faced with massive prison overcrowding to change their penal policies through the development of alternative responses to incarceration.[36] In this regard, several states, among which are Italy[37] and Belgium,[38] have been condemned by the European Court due to their prison overcrowding and their very poor and inhumane conditions of detention. According to the Strasbourg Court, these Sates have committed on a large scale systemic and structural violation of Article 3 of the European Convention.

However, the Court considers that the process of reducing prison population raises a number of complex legal and practical issues which go, in principle, beyond the Court's judicial function.[39] Even in the framework of the pilot-judgment, it states that it does not have the capacity to involve itself in these kinds of reforms along with the CM or to order a specific general measure to be adopted in that process by the respondent State. According to the Strasbourg Court, the CM is better placed and equipped to monitor the measures that need to be adopted.[40] Moreover, judgments are declaratory in nature and it is for the State to choose, under the control of the CM, the means of fulfilling its legal obligation to eradicate the violation.

Nevertheless, this limitation does not prevent it from giving indications to States on the choices which States may make to resolve the systemic problems encountered, with varying degrees of precision and insistence according to the sections of the Court (Suremain, 2013).

Among the causes of prison overcrowding, the European Court retains the elements that follow in the list and also the best ways of alleviating them:

(i) Many national penal policies are deemed to be too harsh and repressive. According to the European Court, penal policies are supposed to be important leverage for decreasing prison population. This is why the Strasbourg Court approved, for instance, Italy's decision to pass less restrictive legislation in drug cases (considered partly responsible for prison overcrowding) in the context of the Torregiani case[41].[42] The Strasbourg Court also ascribes and promotes alternatives to custody such as probation, electronic monitoring and surveillance. However, the alternative measures can have negative effects as they sometimes enlarge penal intervention without leading to a decrease in the prison population. This process is called the penal net-widening effect.[43]

(ii) Minimal prison cell space imposed on states.[44]

(iii) Establishing the maximum capacity for each facility and giving the prison governors the power to decline detainees when beyond the prison capacity.[45]

(iv) An increase of prison capacity as requested in the Sulejmanovic v. Italy case,[46] renovation of old prisons, the replacement of old prisons with new ones and the construction of other kinds of facilities such as psychiatric facilities for mentally ill offenders, social defense institutions, medical facilities, and so on.[47]

(v) Decriminalization of illegal immigration is approved by the Court to get this population (partly responsible for prison overcrowding) out of prison.[48]

(vi) The development of effective domestic remedies is also required by the European Court[49] in order to ensure respect for human rights; although, a margin of appreciation is granted to national states to choose and implement them.

The European national cases subjected to European monitoring and presented in this book have been selected in order to represent the most important European countries in terms of funding of the Council of Europe and the European Union (the UK, France, Italy and Germany), countries of the main European legal traditions (the Roman-law, Common-law and German-law systems) and a diversity of territories (Western, Southern and Nordic states) and political models (Liberal, Social-democratic, Corporatist and Mediterranean). In this manner, we will show how these diverse legacies mediate the processes of European monitoring shaping.

2 Responses from national states to the European monitoring

We consider in this book how procedural obligations imposed by the Strasbourg Court could potentially impact and change penal and prison policies and lead to varied responses from national states. Despite some limits of the strategy pursued by the Council of Europe, the positive and procedural obligations imposed by the European Court of Human Rights on the Member States could have led to legal, administrative, judicial and practical changes such as the adoption of domestic penal and prison legislations enforcing the effective implementation of death prevention in custody, the provision of healthcare services, the assessment of prisoners' ability to serve custodial sentences and their right to apply for parole, limitations to overcrowding and improvements in conditions of detention, the right to effective remedies and compensation, the enhancement of rehabilitative programs and the development of family visits. In this perspective, each chapter presents a set of particular reactions from main national states to the European monitoring.

2.1 Cooperation with the council of Europe but with sometimes some opposition and passive resistance

The first part presents national reactions mainly based on peaceful cooperation and acceptance to this European monitoring from countries such as Germany, France and the Netherlands, since these countries have partially served as judicial model for the Council of Europe monitoring. Conversely, these countries have globally accepted the European monitoring at least on a political level by trying to integrate its requirement into their national system but sometimes with some passive resistance, opposition and even refusal.

For many years, European influence, notably the ECtHR jurisprudence, has been of minor importance to the German penal law and prison administration, according to Frieder Dünkel and Christine Morgenstern. This changed considerably in 2009 with the M. vs. Germany case by which the ECtHR condemned German legislation for having enabled courts to retrospectively order indeterminate preventive detention. This was seen as a breach of Articles 5 and 7 of the Convention by the ECtHR, although the German Constitutional Court argued differently. This decision by the ECtHR had enormous impact on the legislation governing preventive detention and its practical implementation in Germany. The ECtHR's case law, which is notably related to fair trial aspects and lengths of proceeding, has also required Germany to establish a remedy or a combination of remedies to secure adequate and sufficient redress for excessive long proceedings. In addition, the Federal Constitutional Court has recently not only sought to incorporate the ECtHR's jurisprudence, also related to conditions of detention, into its arguments but also its 'soft law' recommendations, namely the European Prison Rules and the CPT's country visit reports.

In the Netherlands since the 1970s, a system of rights of complaint and appeal for prisoners has been developed, the result of which can currently be found in the Penitentiary Principles Act (Penitentaire beginselenwet). This system of legal protection for prisoners is described by Pauline Jacobs and Anton van Kalmthout as unique in the world. In this chapter, the question if, and if so to what extent, the Dutch system of rights of complaint and appeal for prisoners is in line with the European standards is investigated. To this purpose, first the European standards on complaint and appeal procedures for prisoners as developed by the ECtHR and the CPT is explored. Second, the Dutch system of complaint and appeal for prisoners and its historical development is investigated. Finally, the Dutch complaint and appeal procedure for prisoners in the light of these European standards is reviewed.

Lastly, Corentin Durand, Hugues de Suremain and Nicolas Ferran show that the European Convention on Human Rights and the jurisprudence of the European Court of Human Rights have played a key role in the transformation of prison regulations in France. European standards constitute a widely-shared normative horizon, with reference to which national policies are promoted, criticised and measured. This influence has been strengthened and supplemented by litigation in front of the ECtHR, largely led by activist organizations committed to the protection of prisoners' rights. Nevertheless, the transformative potential of European law must be assessed with regards to existing professional and institutional resistances, as shown by the on-going legal struggle about strip-searches. Moreover, the rationalities conveyed by ECtHR jurisprudence and the recommendations of the Council of Europe very often prove to be largely compatible with policies that reduce prisoners' space of autonomy and allow the strengthening of prison officials' discretionary power. Lastly, prison law is proving unable to deal with structural problems such as the material conditions of detention or overpopulation.

2.2 Curve and minor resistance to the European monitoring

The second part focuses on national reactions, such as curve and minor active resistance, to this European control by studying Southern countries deeply affected by the economic crisis and austerity policies such as Greece and Italy and several Nordic states among which are Denmark, Sweden, Finland and Island.

The chapter on Italy drafted by Giuseppe Caputo and Sofia Ciuffoletti provides an analysis of the influence exerted by the European Court of Human Rights on the Italian policies for the protection of prisoners' rights. As a matter of facts, Italy has been targeted, in the last decade, by Strasbourg case law, specifically for its general prison conditions and for the endemic and persistent phenomenon of overcrowding. On the one hand, the poor material conditions of detention (a reality for almost all the penitentiary institutes in Italy) were not tackled by long term measures, on the other hand, no effective judicial remedies existed in order to immediately redress and compensate prisoners detained in conditions deemed in violation of Article 3 of the European Convention of Human Rights. The aim of this chapter on Italy is, therefore, to decode the Italian reaction to the European input, evaluating the Italian strategy on the basis of the principle of effectiveness.

With a view to helping fill a gap in the literature, the contribution from Leonidas Cheliotis and Sappho Xanakis problematizes the role of ECtHR penal and prison litigation and relevant recommendations by the CM and the CPT in the case of a multiply criticized and censured EU member-state: Greece. Although one might expect states occupying a peripheral position in the international arena to be prone to responding positively to pressures from prominent or otherwise powerful actors abroad, the case of Greece illustrates that being a small power may actually be associated with a reduced degree of effectiveness of foreign pressures. Indeed, the paper goes on to argue that foreign pressures may well have unintended, counterproductive effects within such a context, insofar as Greece's ongoing exposure to ECtHR censure and European monitoring has functioned in politically convenient ways for successive Greek governments seeking to manage socio-economic tensions in the country.

For their part, the Nordic countries are characterised by a kind of exceptionalism and strong nationalism in penal and prison matters. In this respect, the control over prisons has been pronouncedly national in character. Lauri Koskenniemi and Tapio Lappi-Seppälä show that each Nordic country has specific legislation on the enforcement of custodial sanctions and prisoners' basic rights as explicitly defined in the law, as well as prisoners' right to an appeal. While prison conditions and practices meet generally well the relevant international standards, the Council of Europe and the European Union have undertaken a monitoring of Nordic prison policies by expressing critical comments, notably both in the reports of CPT and in the rulings of the ECtHR. The ECtHR has also initiated a process of oversight of Danish and Finish prison policies by addressing the issue of long term solitary confinement in Denmark and by condemning Finland for requiring dangerous inmates to wear closed overalls. The article offers an overview of the control of prisons in the Nordic countries and explores those prison conditions and practices detected as problematic by the European monitoring system.

2.3 Strong national resistance to the European oversight and absence of European monitoring

The third part is dedicated to tensions, strong national resistance (such as independence, refusal and avoidance) to this European monitoring and even absence of European oversight due to the existence of important national tradition (which is reflected in particular in a tendency to apply the ECtHR jurisprudence), autonomy and sometimes political distrust towards European institutions in these countries. This last part includes the UK and Spain.

The contribution from Simon Creighton, Nicola Padfield and Rosaria Pirosa focuses on the monitoring of penal and prison policies in England and Wales in the wider context of the uneasy relationship between the European Court of Human Rights and the United Kingdom, with its strong common law traditions and growing Euroscepticism. A brief historical section introduces the Human Rights Act 1998 and its impact on the culture of public decision-making. The chapter also considers the domestic acceptance of the role of the Strasbourg Court in determining the duties and obligations of the state in the areas of parole, prison discipline and in the incorporation of Article 2 case-law into the domestic system for investigating deaths in custody. But the authors argue, by focusing on 'whole life' imprisonment and prisoners' voting rights, that today the relationship with 'Europe' remains as tense as ever. In assessing those controversial policy areas, at a time when the UK government may seek to withdraw from the ECHR as well as the EU, the authors explore the changing relationship between the European Court of Human Rights and domestic courts.

Lastly, Spain is a country not really being monitored by the European Court of Human Rights according to Esther Pascual Rodríguez and Clara Rey Sánchez. The European monitoring of the Spanish prison system is very limited as no ECtHR judgment deals stricto sensu with Spanish prison conditions. The chapter discusses the limited monitoring of penal and prison policies in Spain by European institutions, particularly by the ECtHR, which has not yet ruled on claims against Spain concerning prison conditions or other aspects of life in prisons, like the access of inmates to healthcare services or their prison regime. The ECtHR has, however, delivered a few judgments on Spain and deprivation of liberty, mainly in relation to incommunicado detention. An examination of Spain's reaction to these judgments reveals its reluctance towards the monitoring of its penal policies by European institutions. Rodriguez and Sánchez examine the national supervisory mechanisms for the oversight of Spain's prison system, with the Judge for Prison Supervision as the core figure. The examination focuses on the strengths and weaknesses of the domestic supervisory mechanisms, highlighting the many potential areas for improvement where an alignment with some of the criteria set forth by the ECtHR is needed.

While this book is divided in three parts, each chapter takes a similar approach in order to keep unity and coherence:

- An account of the procedural and other obligations imposed by the ECtHR and the CMin, and the penal and prison system in that country.
- An examination of how national countries react to this European monitoring, particularly to the procedural obligations.
- An assessment of the effectiveness of the legislative, administrative and practical changes and responses to the European monitoring.

- The contribution to the field of prison and penal studies made by this analysis of monitoring as a modernising process.

The book has a concluding chapter that draws together and compares the key contributions that this mapping of monitoring activities across Europe has produced.

Notes

1 See ECtHR, *Loizidou v. Turkey*, 18 December 1996, § 50. This principle makes reference to the realisation in social practices of the rules provided by the law.
2 ECHR, 23 July 1968, case 'Relating to Certain Aspects of the Laws on the Use of Languages in Education in Belgium', Nos. 1474/62, 1677/62, 1691/62, 1769/63, 1994/63, 2126/64; ECtHR *Marckx v. Belgium*, 13 June 1979, No. 6833/74.
3 France passed a Prisons Law on 24 November 2009, Germany passed a Federal Prison Law on 17 June 2008, and Belgium passed a Federal Prison Law on 12 January 2005.
4 Council of Europe, Resolution (2004)3 of the Committee of Ministers on Judgments Revealing an Underlying Systemic Problem, 12 May 2004.
5 ECtHR, *Sulejmanovic v. Italy*, 16 July 2009, No 22635/0; *Stella v. Italy*, 16 September 2014, No 49169/09, 16 September 2014; ECHR, *Torregiani v Italy*, 8 January 2013, No 43517/09.
6 ECtHR, *Bamouhammad v. Belgium*, 17 November 2015, No 47687/13; ECHR, *Vasilescu v. Belgium*, 25 November 2014, No 64682/12.
7 ECtHR, *Torregiani v Italy*, 8 January 2013, No 43517/09.
8 ECtHR, *Greens and MT v. United Kingdom*, 23 November 2010, No 60041 and 60054.
9 See for instance ECtHR, Kalashnikov v. Russia, Kalashnikov v. Russia, 15 July 2002, no. 47095/99; Ilhan v. Turkey, 27 June 2000, no. 22277/93; Mouisel v. France, 14 November 2002, no 67263/01; Keenan v. UK, 18 April 2001, no 27229/95.
10 See www.echr.coe.int/Documents/Priority_policy_ENG.pdf.
11 ECtHR, *Laduna v. Slovakia*, 13 December 2011, no 31827/02, § 59.
12 ECtHR, *László Magyar v. Hungary*, no. 73593/10 46.
13 ECtHR, *M. vs. Germany*, 17 December 2009, No 19359/04.
14 ECtHR, *Murray v. The Netherlands*, 26 April 2016, No 10511/10.
15 See the Recommendation 1743 (2006)1 "Memorandum of understanding between the Council of Europe and the European Union" adopted by the Assembly on 13 April 2006 (14th sitting) and the Assembly debate on 13 April 2006 (14th Sitting), Doc.10892, report of the Political Affairs Committee, rapporteur: Mr Kosachev.
16 See www.venice.coe.int/WebForms/pages/?p=01_Presentation.
17 See European Parliament, Resolution 2011/2897(RSP), B7–0687/2011.
18 OJ C 32, 5.2.1996, p. 102.
19 OJ C 98, 9.4.1999, p. 299. A4–0369/98.
20 Commission Green Paper on the application of EU criminal justice legislation in the field of detention – Strengthening mutual trust in the European judicial area – of 14 June 2011 (COM (2011) 327 final).
21 2011/2897(RSP), B7–0687/2011.
22 European Parliament resolution of 25 November 2009 on the Communication from the Commission. An area of freedom, security and justice serving the citizen – Stockholm Programme. P7 – TA (2009) 090. Stockholm Programme, OJ C 115, 4.4.2010.
23 Written Declaration on infringement of the fundamental rights of detainees, from MEPs – 06/2011, 14.02.2011.
24 European Parlimanet, *resolution* of *2 April 2014* on the mid-term review of the *Stockholm Programme* (2013/2024(INI)).

25 Report A5–00094/2004. Rapporteur: Maurizio Turco.
26 Commission Green Paper, *op. cit.*, p. 1.
27 See www.europarl.europa.eu/committees/en/libe/home.html#menuzone.
28 Visits to Italian prisons by the Delegation of the Committee on Civil Liberties, Justice and Home Affairs, 26–28 March 2014.
29 Report from the Committee on Civil Liberties, Justice and Home Affairs delegation to Italy on the situations of prisons and correction centres, 9 April 2014, European Parliament.
30 ECtHR, *Torreggiani and others v. Italy*, 8 January 2013, 43517/09.
31 EU Commission Green Paper, *op. cit.*, pp. 11–12.
32 Report of 12 June 2006 on alleged secret detentions and unlawful inter-state transfers involving Council of Europe Member States, Parliamentary Assembly, Committee on Legal Affairs and Human Rights, Rapporteur: Dick Marty, PACE doc. 10957, 12 June 2006; Second Report of 11 June 2007 on secret detention and illegal transfers of detainees involving the Council of Europe Member States, Parliamentary Assembly, Committee on Legal Affairs and Human Rights, Rapporteur: Dick Marty, PACE Doc. 11302.
33 Resolution of 6 July 2006 on the alleged use of European countries by the CIA for the transportation and illegal detention of prisoners (2006/2027(INI)), P6_TA (2006)0316) European Parliament; European Parliament, Directorate General for internal policies, Policy Department's citizen rights and constitutional affairs, Justice, Freedom and Security, note on the results of inquiry into the CIA's programme of extraordinary rendition and secret detention in European States in light of the new legal framework following the Lisbon treaty, 2012, PE 462–456; Final Report of 30 January 2007 on the alleged use of European countries by the CIA for the transportation and illegal detention of prisoners (2006/2200 (INI)), doc. A6–0020/2007), European Parliament; European Parliament resolution of 10 October 2013 on alleged transportation and illegal detention of prisoners in European countries by the CIA (2013/2702(RSP)).
34 ECtHR, *Nasr and Ghali v. Italy*, 23 February 2016, No 44883/09.
35 CJEU, Aranyosi-Căldăraru du 5 avril 2016 (C 404/15 et C 659/15 PPU.
36 CoE, White paper paper on prison overcrowding, PC-CP (2015) 6 rév 7; ECtHR, *Torreggiani and others v. Italy*, 8 January 2013, No 43517/09.
37 ECtHR, *Torreggiani and others v. Italy*, 8 January 2013, No 43517/09.
38 ECtHR, *Vasilescu v. Belgium*, 25 November 2014, n° 64682/12.
39 ECtHR, *Torreggiani and others v. Italy*, 8 January 2013, No 43517/09.
40 ECtHR, *Ananyev and others v. Russia*, 10 January 2012, No 42525/07, 60800/08.
41 ECtHR, *Torreggiani and others v. Italy*, 8 January 2013, No 43517/09.
42 ECtHR, *Stella and others v. Italy* (dec), 16 September 2014, No 49169/09 54908/09 55156/09.
43 ECtHR, *Torreggiani and others v. Italy*, 8 January 2013, No 43517/09.
44 ECtHR, *Mursic v. Croatia (GC)*, 20 October 2016, No 7334/13 no. 22635/03.
45 ECtHR, *Ananyev and others v. Russia*, 10 January 2012, No 42525/07, 60800/08, §§ 205–206.
46 ECtHR, *Sulejmanovic v. Italy*, 16 July 2009, application no. 22635/03.
47 ECtHR, *W.D. v. Belgium*, 6 December 2016, no 73548/13; ECtHR, *Bamouhammad v. Belgium*, 17 November 2015, no 47687/13, §§ 115–123; Revised Action Plan submitted by the Belgian State (DH-DD(2016)474 related to L.B. v. Belgium, 2 October 2012, no 22831/08, Claes v. Belgium, 10 January 2013, no 43418/09, Dufoort v. Belgium, 10 January 2013, no 43653/09; Swennen v. Belgium, 10 January 2013, no 53448/10), 7 April 2016; Committee of Ministers, Human Rights Meeting (1259e Meeting), 7–9 June 2016, Strasbourg.
48 ECtHR, Stella and others v. Italy (dec), 16 September 2014, No 49169/09 54908/09 55156/09.

49 ECtHR, *Torreggiani and others v. Italy*, 8 January 2013, nos 43517/09, 46882/09, 55400/09, 57875/09, 61535/09, 35315/10 et 37818/10, § 50; Vasilescu v. Belgium, 25 November 2014, no 64682/12, § 75; *Bamouhammad v. Belgium*, 17 November 2015, no 47687/13, §§ 165–166.

References

Abels, D. (2012). Prisoners of the International Community: The Legal Position of Persons Detained at International Criminal Tribunals. The Hague: Springer Asser-press.

Alkema, E. A. (2000). "The European Convention as a Constitution and its Court as a Constitutional Court". In: P. Mahoney, F. Matscher, H. Petzold and L. Wildhaber, eds, Protecting Human Rights: The European Perspective: Studies in Memory of Rolv Ryssdal. Bonn: Karl Heymanns Verlag, pp. 41-63.

Andenas, M. and Bjorge, E. (2013). "National implementation of ECHR rights." In: A. Follesdal, B. Peters and G. Ulfstein, eds., *Constituting Europe: The European Court of Human Rights in a National, European and Global Context*. Cambridge: Cambridge University Press, pp. 181–262.

Bates, E. (2010). The Evolution of the European Convention on Human Rights: From Its Inception to the Creation of Permanent Court of Human Rights. Oxford: Oxford University Press.

Belda, B. (2010). Les droits de l'homme des personnes privées de liberté : Contribution à l'étude du pouvoir normatif de la Cour européenne des droits de l'homme. Brussels: Bruylant.

Blackburn, R. and Polakiewicz, J. (2001). Fundamental Rights in Europe: The European Convention on Human Rights and Its Member States, 1950–2000. Oxford and New York: Oxford University Press.

Bond, M. (2013). The Council of Europe: Structure, History and Issues in European Politics. New York: Routledge.

Cameron, I. (2013). "The court and the member states: Procedural aspects." In: A. Føllesdal, B. Peters and G. Ulfstein, eds., *Constituting Europe: The European Court of Human Rights in a National, European and Global Context*. Cambridge: Cambridge University Press, pp. 25–61.

Christoffersen, J. (2011). "Individual and constitutional justice." In: J. Christoffersen and M. R. Madsen, eds., *The European Court of Human Rights Between Law and Politics*. Oxford: Oxford University Press, pp. 181–203.

Christoffersen, J. and Madsen, M. R. (2011). *The European Court of Human Rights Between Law and Politics*. Oxford: Oxford University Press.

Cliquennois, G. (2013). "Which penology for decision making in French prisons?" *Punishment & Society*, 15(5), pp. 468–487.

Cliquennois, G. and Champetier, B. (2013). "A new risk management for prisoners in France: The emergence of a death-avoidance approach." *Theoretical Criminology*, 17(3), pp. 397–415.

Feeley, M. and Rubin, E. (1998). Judicial Policy Making and the Modern State: How the Courts Reformed America's Prisons. Cambridge: Cambridge University Press.

Feeley, M. and Van Swearingen, R. (2004). "The prison conditions cases and the bureaucratization of American corrections: Influences, impacts and implications." *Pace Law Review*, 24, pp. 433–475.

Føllesdal, A., Peters, B. and Ulfstein, G. (2013). Constituting Europe: The European Court of Human Rights in a National, European and Global Context. Cambridge: Cambridge University Press.

Foster, S. (2011). *Human Rights and Civil Liberties*. Harlow: Pearson.

Foucault, M. (1975). *Surveiller et Punir*. Paris: Gallimard.

Guetzkow, J. and Schoon, E. (2015). "If you build it, they will fill it: The consequences of prison overcrowding litigation." *Law & Society Review*, 49(2), pp. 401–432.

Herzog-Evans, M. (2012). *Droit pénitentiaire*. Paris: Dalloz.

Keller, H. and Stone Sweet, A. (2008). *A Europe of Rights: The Impact of the ECHR on National Legal Systems*. Oxford: Oxford University Press.

Lambert Abdelgawad, E. (2013). "The Court as part of the Council of Europe: The Parliamentary Assembly and the Committee of Ministers." In: A. Føllesdal, B. Peters and G. Ulfstein, eds., *Constituting Europe: The European Court of Human Rights in a National, European and Global Context*. Cambridge: Cambridge University Press, pp. 263–300.

Popelier, P., Heyning, C. and Nuffels, P. V. (2011). Human Rights Protection in the European Legal Order: The Interaction Between the European and the National Courts. Portland: Intersentia.

Rodley, N. and Pollard, M. (2009). The Treatment of Prisoners under International Law. Oxford: Oxford University Press.

Sadurski, W. (2009). "Partnering with Strasbourg: Constitutionalisation of the European Court of Human Rights, the accession of Central and East European States to the Council of Europe, and the idea of pilot judgments." *Human Rights Law Review*, 9, pp. 397–453.

Schoenfeld, H. (2010). "Mass incarceration and the paradox of prison conditions litigation." *Law & Society Review*, 44(3), pp. 731–768.

Simon, J. (2014). Mass Incarceration on Trial: A Remarkable Court Decision and the Future of Prisons in America. New York: The New Press.

Simon, J. (2011). Editorial: "Mass incarceration on trial." *Punishment and Society*, 13(1), pp. 251–255.

Snacken, S. and Dumortier, E. (2012). Resisting Punitiveness in Europe: Welfare, Human Rights, and Democracy. Abingdon: Routledge.

Spano, R. (2014). "Universality or diversity of Human Rights? Strasbourg in the age of subsidiarity." *Human Rights Law Review*, 14(3), pp. 487–502.

Suremain, H. (2013). *Surpopulation carcérale : les juridictions nationales au pied du mur*, Lettre " Actualités Droits-Libertés " CREDOF [online], 7 February 2013.

Tulkens, F. (2007). "The European Convention on Human Rights between International Law and Constitutional Law." In: European Court of Human Rights (ed.), *Dialogue Between Judges*. Strasbourg: Council of Europe, pp. 8–15.

Van Zyl Smit, D. (2010). "Regulation of prison conditions." *Crime and Justice*, 39(1), pp. 503–563.

Van Zyl Smit, D. and Snacken, S. (2009). *Principles of European Prison Law and Policy: Penology and Human Rights*. Oxford: Oxford University Press.

Part I

Cooperation, acceptance and integration of European monitoring

2 Monitoring prisons in Germany

The role of the European Court of Human Rights

Christine Morgenstern and Frieder Dünkel

Introduction

Monitoring of prisons is a multifaceted issue. On the one hand, it means the internal control of prisons by the prison administration (Ministries of Justice), on the other hand, the external control by independent agencies or – and this is one of the most important and influential forms – the individual complaints procedures of prisoners. One can also differentiate according to the preventive nature of control forms such as the work of the Committee for the Prevention of Torture (CPT) on behalf of the Council of Europe from control forms that aim to redress a violation of international human rights or to review prison decisions that curtail national prisoners' rights.

In order to understand the legal position of prisoners and their possibilities of complaints as the most important form of prison control, we will start with a short look at the present prison legislation and at a historical review. Germany is a federation with 16 states. The competence for legislation until 2006 was at the federal level. Therefore, one uniform Prison Act dating from 1976 (in force since 1 January 1977) was relevant for all 16 federal states (the so-called *Länder*). In September 2006, a major Constitutional Law Reform was enacted that redistributed the legislative competences by transferring the competences to the *Länder*, which meant that the 16 federal states now had to create their own prison legislation. The changes of legislative competences did not touch the penal and criminal procedural law and likewise not the competences for complaints procedures in prison law. So, there is still a uniform Federal Criminal Code (CC), the Criminal Procedure Act (CPA) and that part of the 1977 Prison Act, that deals with complaints procedures for prisoners (§§ 109 ff. PA).

1 The history of judicial control of prisons in Germany – national beginnings and the procedure according to §§ 109 ff. Prison Act

1.1 Historical aspects of complaints procedures in the 1977 Prison Act

In 1972, the Federal Constitutional Court (in its landmark decision BVerfGE 33, 1 ff.) ruled for the first time that prisoners, as any other citizen, have and retain all rights unless they are restricted by statutory law. This decision was a landmark in German prison history as it forced the legislator to pass a statutory Prison Law. It took four more years and a decision of the Constitutional Court setting a further time limit (see BVerfGE 45, 187 ff.) to bring about the enactment of the Prison Act on 1 January1977. The Prison Act regulates rights and duties of prisoners and contains a comprehensive system of complaints procedures and judicial review. This general right for a judicial review against decisions of state authorities is guaranteed by the Constitution, see Art. 19 (4) *Grundgesetz*, Basic Law. The §§ 109 ff. PA thus are a concretisation of this constitutional right in the area of prison law and administration. This includes the possibility of appealing against prison administration decisions to a specialized chamber of the district court (*Strafvollstreckungskammer*, see §§ 462 ff. CPA).[1] Any decision and even simple actions of prison guards such as not knocking at the prisoner's cell door can be made the subject of a formal complaints procedure.[2] The idea behind creating a special chamber in the district court was to establish the jurisprudence of specialized judges who know the situation in the prisons located near to the court.

1.2 The 1977 Prison Act and the complaints procedure for adult prisoners, §§ 109 ff. Prison Act

The 1977 Prison Act (PA) was the first statutory law regulating rights and duties of prisoners. It is applicable to adult sentenced offenders (18 years and older).[3]

Most rights for prisoners depend on the discretionary power of the prison administration, such as the right for prison leave and for regular visits. For example, there is a guarantee for at least one one-hour visit per month,[4] but more visits may be granted according to the discretion of the prison administration. It is important to note that discretion does not mean arbitrariness: The prison administration must base its decision on well-founded arguments, which are subject to judicial review. Often the PA also provides rights that depend on the interpretation of indeterminate law terms. Prison leave, for example, may be granted if there is no "risk of abuse" such as trying to escape or reoffending during the inmate's absence from prison (see § 11 (2) 1977 PA). As the jurisprudence has clarified, the risk level which can be tolerated with regard to public safety depends on the specific circumstances and the nature of the crime for which the inmate was sentenced. The longer the sentence, which a prisoner has served, the less discretion is given to the prison administration to deny prison leave, which is seen as an essential part of the reintegration process and also has the function of countering the negative effects of imprisonment.[5] This also applies to prisoners serving a life or other very long sentence.[6]

Each and every decision or action of the prison administration can be subject to judicial review. The jurisprudence of the courts often relates to questions such as which personal belongings the prisoner may have in his cell (television set, radio, cd-player and other electronic devices); if the denial of prison leave, the transfer to an open prison or other relaxations of the regime are justified; if a disciplinary punishment was just and proportionate, and so on.

The complaints procedure is written, and oral hearings are not obligatory (see § 115 (1) PA), but they can be organized if the judge considers it appropriate. The subject of the complaint is defined by the prisoners' written request, which first goes to the prison director who will present his or her views and the reasons for the decision in a written statement. The prisoner does not have to prove the facts; the inquisitorial principle obliges the judge to investigate the facts. If the prisoner's rights have been violated by the prison administration's decision or action, the court may declare the wrongfulness of the decision and remedy the situation as far as possible. However, if the law gives the prison administration discretionary power, the court regularly cannot overrule the prison governor's decision, but will refer the case back to the prison governor with the attached condition that he must release a new decision under observation of the legal arguments given by the court. In certain circumstances, the court may also definitely accept the prisoner's claim and grant the required prison leave or visit.

The complaints *procedure* is a mixture of elements of civil, administrative and criminal procedural law. The inquisitorial principle stems from criminal procedure. But with regard to prison complaints the judge is not restricted to a certain body of evidence (as in criminal proceedings), and can use any evidence to ascertain the facts. The prisoner can choose a lawyer in any stage of the complaints procedure. The judge will appoint a lawyer at the state's expense if the appellant is indigent and the case is likely to be successful (thus following the rules of civil procedural law, see § 120 (2) PA). The rules on reappraising indefinite legal terms ("unbestimmter Rechtsbegriff")[7] or discretionary decisions follow the administrative procedural law. Although the capacity of a prisoner to have discretionary decisions of the prison administration reviewed is not very strong (the court has only a restricted power to change the decision), courts have often annulled a governor's decision because of arbitrary or not well-founded arguments.

A prisoner can appeal to the High Court of the federal state (*Oberlandesgericht*) if a complaint to the district court is not successful (see § 116 PA). The High Court will only review questions of law, not questions of fact.

If the prisoner claims there has been a violation of constitutional rights, an appeal can be made to the Federal Constitutional Court (FCC, *Bundesverfassungsgericht, abbreviated as BVerfG*), which is the court of last resort on the national level (see Art. 93 Abs. 1 Nr. 4a FC).[8] Having the right to make an individual constitutional complaint puts the prisoner in a rather strong position. Additionally, such cases have set important standards for prison practice as a whole. The most important jurisprudence concerning German Prison Law originates from the FCC, including the principle of social reintegration or rehabilitation (*Resozialisierungsgrundsatz*, see Morgenstern, 2015) as a fundamental constitutional principle based on the constitutional right to protect human dignity (Art. 1 *Grundgesetz*, literally Basic Law, BL) and the constitutional principle of the social welfare state (Art. 20 BL): The FCC obliges the state to develop a prison regime which focuses primarily and effectively on the social reintegration of offenders.[9] Accordingly § 2 (1) of the 1977 PA states that the sole aim of the execution of prison sentences is the reintegration of offenders. The protection of society plays a subordinate role and is best guaranteed by the social reintegration of the offender.[10] While other aims of punishment such as general deterrence and retribution play a certain role in the sentencing stage, they are explicitly excluded from influencing the execution of sentences (including decisions on conditional/early release, see §§ 57, 57a CC).

1.3 Efficiency of individual complaints procedures (the role of the Federal Constitutional Court (FCC) and of the jurisprudence of High Courts

The efficiency of complaints is often characterized as being very modest, as probably less than 5 per cent of the complaints are successful. This does not necessarily mean that the complaints mechanisms are ineffective, but could be because prison administrations base their decisions in most cases on well-founded arguments.[11] One reason for low success rates could be that the PA often gives room for discretion, which limits the possibilities for a judicial review (see above). On the other hand, successful complaints, in particular those decided by the FCC, have had a major impact on general practice, e.g. concerning prison leave and other forms of relaxation of the prison regime. All in all, the complaints procedure mechanisms in Germany can be seen as a success, as every decision or action taken by the prison authorities can be made subject to a judicial review, which has a moderating effect in and of itself since the prison authorities must always explain their actions and decisions by legal arguments to prisoners.

Although court decisions bind prison authorities, there have been reports of cases where the prison administration did not follow the court decision, e.g. continued to deny prison leave or other measures for the reintegration of offenders. In order to cope with defiant or refractory prison administrations, in 2013 an amendment of § 120 (1) PA established the possibility of imposing a financial penalty (*Zwangsgeld*) of up the 10,000 € in order to enforce a court decision, e.g. if the court has set a deadline for a specific measure in favour of the prisoner to be implemented.[12]

2 European monitoring of prisons in Germany

2.1 European convention on human rights

Despite the comprehensive and effective national monitoring framework, European standards and norms have been and remain important for German prison law and prison practice. This is particularly true as regards the European Convention on Human Rights (ECHR) and the jurisprudence of its enforcement mechanism, the European Court of Human Rights (ECtHR).

The ECHR of 1950 entered into force in 1953, and Germany was among the first states to ratify it. The legal status of the Convention in Germany formally is the status of an ordinary statute, and in the legal hierarchy it stands below the German constitution (*Grundgesetz*). Nevertheless, not only scholars but also the FCC grant it a special intermediate position. While the constitution itself has not taken the greatest possible steps in opening itself to international law connections:[13]

> the provisions of the Basic Law are to be interpreted in a manner that is open to international law. At the level of constitutional law, the text of the Convention and the case-law of the European Court of Human Rights function as interpretation aids to determine the contents and scope of fundamental rights and of rule-of-law principles of the Basic Law.[14]

This means – in short – that while national courts and authorities must implement the ECHR in principle, this is not necessarily the case when duties resulting from the Convention are (or seem to be) in conflict with those resulting from the German Basic law. This also means that in cases of dissent between the FCC and the ECtHR the latter claims to have the final say, or in the FCC's own, somewhat euphemistic words, there is no need to enforce ECtHR judgments in a "schematic" way.[15] This insistence on sovereignty, in particular in questions of penal law, can also be seen in relation to the European Union.[16] Since there is a high degree of congruence between the rights enshrined in the ECHR and those in the Basic Law, this stance usually does not lead to great difficulties. It did, however, in a specific question concerning the penal system – and divergent decisions on preventive detention by the two Courts will be considered below.

The Convention's safeguards are regularly applied by German courts, including in prison cases – for example, by the German Supreme Court, which argued that the covert surveillance of talks between spouses during a visit in remand detention violated Art. 6 (1) ECHR (fair trial).[17] Most prison cases, however, are solved within the German system of prisoner rights as described above. Notwithstanding, the traditional German assumption that these standards are higher than the European standards has been shattered at least to a certain extent, for example by a series of judgments by the ECtHR concerning excessive periods of remand detention or because of restrictions on the possibility of offenders appealing against their detention and accessing files (Morgenstern, 2013).

In two prison cases (yet), the ECtHR even found violations of Art. 3 ECHR by German authorities:[18] The appellant had been complaining about his prison conditions and fought with prison staff. He was then taken to a security cell, where he was strip-searched and apparently left naked for seven days. Even if placement for several days in the security cell might have been justified initially because of the danger to himself or others, depriving him of his clothes during his entire stay there constituted inhuman and degrading treatment.

More recently, the Court stated that Art. 3 ECHR includes an obligation on prison authorities to seek independent medical advice on the appropriate treatment for a drug-addicted prisoner – the German authorities failed to do so in the case of *Wenner*,[19] this failure constituted a violation of Art. 3 ECHR. Concerning medical issues, currently also a violation of Art. 8 ECHR, the right to privacy, is examined by the Court. The appellant, who was detained for several months and suffered severe medical problems, argues that the authorities' and later the domestic courts' refusal to provide him with a copy of his entire prison medical records violated his right to private life.[20]

2.2 CPT

The second pillar of the protection of prisoner's interests and to prevent violations of Art. 3 ECHR in Europe is the *European Convention for the Prevention of Torture and Inhuman or Degrading Treatment or Punishment*, adopted in 1989, with its control organ, the *European Committee for the Prevention of Torture* (in short: CPT). Its influence in Germany can be described as discreet but noticeable, at least in some areas (Cernko, 2014). Germany ratified the Convention in 1990 and has received visits from the CPT eight times.[21] Two of the visits have been so-called "ad-hoc" visits, connected to reports of maltreatment of foreigners awaiting deportation at Frankfurt/Airport and to problematic conditions for prisoners in preventive detention (see the case study below for more details).

The decentralised organisation of prisons on the state (*Länder*) level is reflected in the agenda of the CPT. In 2015, the CPT visited 15 places of deprivation of liberty in six different *Länder*. As regards prisons, the areas of concern have only partly changed between 1991 and 2016. A comprehensive analysis of the first five visits of the CPT (including that of 2005) shows that most of the standard issues raised during CPT visits (as reflected, for example, in the CPT-standards, last updated 2015) can be found in Germany as well, with the noticeable exception of practices like slopping-out, multi-occupancy dormitory-style cells or the need for individual beds and blankets (Cernko, 2014: 318 et sequ.). On the other hand, typical problems reported from many other European and Non-European countries are, in contrast to the perception of the German system as being of a particularly high standards, also found repeatedly – the lack of suitable out of cell activities being just one example (for example CPT, 2012: 28).

At the time of the first visits overcrowding and infrastructural problems, and, in Eastern Germany, staff training and attitudes came under scrutiny (CPT, 1993, 1997 for example with regard to Waldheim Prison, Saxony; Bützow Prison, Mecklenburg-Vorpommern but also in Western Germany Hamburg Remand Prison). That these problems have been overcome largely because of refurbishment programmes, a better single-occupancy policy and ultimately because of a sharp decline in prisoner numbers is acknowledged by the Committee in later reports (for example CPT, 2012: 27 et sequ.).

In addition to the still unsolved problem of insufficient activities in many prisons, the lack of suitable information provided after arrest is a recurring theme in the CPT reports. This relates to information concerning access to a lawyer and the right to notify relatives, in particular with regard to foreigners. Another point of concern is certain coercive measures used in prisons and psychiatric institutions. The possibility of withholding the right of all access to outdoor exercise is criticised sharply by the committee, despite its very rare use. The same is true for the use of corporal restraints. In particular the practice of "fixations" (immobilisation of agitated prisoners that pose a risk for others or themselves), led to so-called immediate observations by the committee during the visits in 2000 and 2005 (CPT, 2003: 13; CPT, 2007: 13) and these were followed-up during the visits in 2010 and 2012 (CPT, 2012: 9 and 2014: 19). The CPT acknowledged that there had been some improvement insofar as these measures are now used rarely and controlled better, but it remained concerned about their use and the lack of sufficient and adequate record-keeping related to such incidents.

3 Impact, implementation and mutual effects

3.1 Preventive detention as a case study

3.1.1 The landmark decision of M vs Germany (Dec. 2009)

By far the most significant impact on German law and practice in prison matters concerns preventive detention. The relevant jurisprudence and policy for this sanction therefore can serve as a case study for the interplay between national and European control mechanisms.

German sanction law has adopted a dual track approach; the Penal Code provides not only for penal sentences, but also for "measures of correction and prevention". The use of such measures permits those who pose a long-term danger to society to be securely detained and thus removed from society while being treated. Prominent amongst these measures is preventive detention (*Sicherungsverwahrung*) for long or even indefinite periods after the completion of an initial sentence. In German legal doctrine such preventive detention is not regarded as punishment, or a "penalty", in the sense the term is used in the Art. 7 ECHR. It is therefore not subject to the same constraints of sentence proportionality and the prohibition of retrospective imposition as are penalties imposed for criminal offences.

The potential threat posed by the use of preventive detention to fundamental liberties was recognised, but for a long time such measures were used relatively rarely. However, as in several other European countries (see Drenkhahn and Morgenstern, 2016; Drenkhahn, Morgenstern and van Zyl Smit, 2012), a reaction to some serious sexual offences resulted in a tightening of the criminal law in the late 1990s: The 1998 reform of the Penal Code not only saw less restrictions placed on the use of preventive detention, but also the absolute limit of ten years on the length of the first term of preventive detention was replaced by a provision that allowed for its indefinite extension. This could even happen retrospectively. Several aspects of these changes were brought before the Federal Constitutional Court (FCC), but it took the view that because preventive detention was not a punishment but a "measure", the strict prohibition of retroactivity set out in the German Basic Law was not applicable.[22] One of the appellants in that case sought a remedy before the ECtHR. In a series of about a dozen cases, including the (leading) case of *M v Germany* (ECtHR, 17 December 2009, App. No. 19359/04) and the latest (and probably concluding) case of *Bergmann v Germany* (7 January 2016,

App. No. 23279/14), the ECtHR has tried to clarify the prerequisites of preventive detention in conformity with the human rights standards of the Convention.[23]

The relevant provisions are Art. 5 ECHR (Right to liberty) and Art. 7 ECHR (No punishment without law). Art. 5 ECHR guarantees the right to liberty, but includes a closed list of exceptions to this right. Preventive detention – just as any other deprivation of liberty ordered by state institutions – therefore needs to be justified on the basis of one of the exceptions set out in that list. Art. 5 (1) (a) ECHR allows for deprivation of liberty following a conviction by a competent court and this is in principle accepted by the ECtHR as a legitimate basis for most cases of preventive detention.[24] This is, on the contrary, not the case for Art. 5 (1) (c) ECHR: This permits the arrest or detention of persons for preventive reasons, but only in situations where a concrete and specific potential offence can be identified and the aim of the arrest or preliminary detention is to bring the detained person before a judge for trial (typically at the pre-trial stage). Whether preventive detention can be justified under a third provision, Art. 5 (1) (e) ECHR, is a matter of dispute, depending on whether the person affected can be considered to be "of unsound mind".

Since the applicant in *M.* was affected by the above-mentioned criminal law reform, the ECtHR had to decide whether the connection between the original conviction in which preventive detention had been ordered and the prolonged preventive detention based on the new law was strong enough – that is, whether it had a "sufficient causal link" in the sense of Art. 5 (1) (a) ECHR. This, according to the court, was not the case: the new retroactive legislation was a new element between the initial decision and the ongoing detention. Therefore, preventive detention of more than ten years was not covered by Art. 5 (1) (a) ECHR in these cases which predated the reform (M. v Germany, 17 December 2009, App. No. 19359/04, § 96 ff.; Drenkhahn, Morgenstern and van Zyl Smit, 2012: 170–173).

A second problem became obvious when the ECtHR had to decide on the conformity of the German practice of preventive detention with Art. 7 ECHR. The ECtHR interprets the concept of 'penalty' autonomously and independently, and is thus not bound by the domestic concept and doctrine concerning penalties. When assessing the legal character of the sanction, it placed great emphasis on the empirical reality of how preventive detention was implemented in Germany. In 2009, it noted that persons who were subject to it were held in prison, albeit in separate wings. The Court stated that

> minor alterations to the detention regime compared to that of an ordinary prisoner serving his sentence, including privileges such as detainees' right to wear their own clothes and to further equip their more comfortable prison cells, cannot mask the fact that there is no substantial difference between the execution of a prison sentence and that of a preventive detention order.
>
> (M. v Germany, 17 December 2009, App. No. 19359/04, § 127)

According to the ECtHR (and supported by many German scholars and practicioners (cf. for example Dünkel and van Zyl Smit, 2004 with an account in

English language, Drenkhahn and Morgenstern, 2016) this was also true for the psychological care and support. In making this assessment, the ECtHR relied on findings of the Council of Europe's Commissioner for Human Rights and the CPT to hold that there was very limited treatment, additional to that offered to prisoners serving long prison sentences, available to those in preventive detention (see above).

The ECtHR accordingly found violations of Art. 5 (1) (a) and Art. 7 ECHR. As a result, German legislation and practice changed drastically (as will be described below), even if – from a doctrinal point of view – there still is a disagreement between the German FCC and the ECtHR. Despite these considerable reforms, the European Court in 2016 confirmed its stance, this time concluding that

> the more preventive nature and purpose of the revised form of preventive detention do not suffice to eclipse the fact that the measure, which entails a deprivation of liberty without a maximum duration, was imposed following conviction for a criminal offense and it is still determined by courts belonging to the criminal justice system.
>
> (Bergmann v Germany, 7 January 2016, App. No. 23279/14, § 181)

3.1.2 German Reception of this decision in preventive detention and beyond

The decision in the case of M. had a tremendous effect. Because of the visible disagreement between the German FCC and the ECtHR, the German courts were unsure how to react. Some ruled that persons in the situation of M. should be freed immediately (for details Drenkhahn, Morgenstern and van Zyl Smit, 2012); others opposed this view and denied the "most serious cases" automatic release. The legislator sought to clarify the situation with a transitional act, but in May 2011, the German FCC declared all provisions dealing with preventive detention unconstitutional.[25] However, the Court held on to the two-track system which it considered to be deeply rooted in German penal culture, and did not nullify the existing provisions, but gave the legislator two years to produce amendments to the law. These developments on the level of European human rights law and German constitutional law thus ultimately required a whole new concept of preventive detention. In the leading judgment of May 2011,[26] the FCC emphasised that the constitution (and, implicitly, the ECHR) contains an "Abstandsgebot", literally a requirement of interspace (or difference) that should be maintained between the two forms of deprivation of liberty for dangerous offenders – imprisonment and preventive detention. As a "measure of correction and prevention" (and thus something different from a punishment), it only qualifies if there is a visible difference between the way the measure and a prison sentence are enforced.

The resulting seven requirements by the FCC concern the court order, the regime (consequently orientated towards rehabilitation and treatment) and the judicial review. According to the ultima ratio principle, preventive detention must only be used as a last resort and subject to strict limitations, and during the execution of the preceding prison sentence measures should be taken to reduce the dangerousness of the offender to a degree that means that further detention is not required. Taking a multidisciplinary approach, all therapeutic possibilities should be exhausted and even new individualized treatment should be developed if standardized therapies are shown to be ineffective. High costs and intensive efforts may not be used as arguments to deny treatment – here, the FCC is in line with the European Prison Rules and requests by the CPT (van Zyl Smit and Snacken, 2009). Another principle calls for separation of persons in preventive detention from the general prison population with regard to both accommodation and regime activities. A further "minimization requirement" means that it has to be borne in mind at all times that preventive detention should be oriented towards ultimately enabling freedom. The regime should be relaxed in various ways, by allowing furloughs or other forms of temporary release from detention wherever possible.

The Court considered both Federal and State legislation against this background. Both fulfilled their obligations in time as a result of an amendment to the Penal Code (s. 66c), provisions for specialized judicial review and various State Acts on the execution of preventive detention. Still, the whole construct is not entirely consistent because every single one of these requirements is also a principle of German *prison* law with the overall purpose of social reintegration (Drenkhahn, 2013: 320; Morgenstern and Drenkhahn, 2016: para. 35). It remains to be seen whether a discernible difference between preventive detention and imprisonment as a punishment is established by withdrawing resources from normal prisoners and allotting them to those in preventive detention. The somewhat surprising new enthusiasm for therapeutic approaches towards offending shown by the Federal Constitutional Court has in any case already leveraged the principles of appropriate treatment and brought an allocation of resources for these purposes (Morgenstern and Drenkhahn, 2016: para. 32; Suhling and Wischka, 2013: 48 f.).

As mentioned above, the ECtHR, in contrast, still considers preventive detention to be a punishment ("penalty"), because it is imposed and enforced within the Criminal Justice System. The Court only makes an exception when the detainee is of "unsound mind" and thus falls under Art. 5 (1) (e) ECHR. According to the Court, however, the term "unsound mind" "does not lend itself to precise definition since its meaning is continually evolving as research in psychiatry progresses".[27] Therefore, it only points to three basic criteria as minimum conditions and grants a certain discretion to national authorities in determining when a person is of unsound mind (Winterwerp v Netherlands, 24 October 1979, App. No. 6301/73, § 39). First, it has to be established that the detainee has a true mental disorder by a competent authority on the basis of objective medical expertise, second, the mental disorder must be of a nature which warrants compulsory confinement, and third, the validity of continued confinement depends upon the persistence of such a disorder.

As regards the German situation, it is of particular importance that detaining a person as a mental-health patient is only "lawful" for the purposes of subparagraph (e) of Article 5 § 1 of the ECHR if it is effected in a hospital, clinic or other appropriate institution (Bergmann v Germany, 7 January 2016, App. No. 23279/14, § 99 with further references). When these conditions are fulfilled, the Court is ready to accept preventive detention, even in cases where it was prolonged retroactively. It did so in the *Bergmann* case, which is similar to that of M.

In particular, the Court regarded the newly constructed preventive detention centre, a separate building on the premises of a prison (several of which now exist in Germany), as a suitable institution to treat mental disorders properly, because psychiatric, psychotherapeutic or socio-therapeutic treatment are provided to reduce the risk the detainees pose to the public. In general, the Court welcomes "the extensive measures which have been taken in [Germany] on judicial, legislative and executive levels with a view to adapting preventive detention to the requirements, in particular, of the fundamental right to liberty" (Bergmann v Germany, 7 January 2016, App. No. 23279/14, § 123). In the case under review, it therefore accepted the legitimacy of the detention under Art. 5 (1) (e) ECHR.

In our opinion (see also Drenkhahn and Morgenstern, 2016), this decision blurs the line between psychiatric institutional treatment (such as in mental health clinics under s. 63 of the German Penal Code) and preventive detention centers that still are part of the prison system. It does so by accepting the "trick" of the Federal Constitutional Court that persons who were considered as still dangerous were relabelled from being "bad criminals" into being "mad patients" that need therapy in a closed setting (see also Drenkhahn, 2013). On the other hand, it pacifies the heated discussions on how to solve the problem of retroactive preventive detention and bridges the gap between the different stances of the two courts.

3.2 Further European monitoring activities and their influence

Apart from the remarkable development in the field of preventive detention, European influences are less visible, but nonetheless traceable. In particular, the Federal Constitutional Court regularly uses international and European Human Rights standards at least as auxiliary arguments. It obviously does so when using the guarantees of the ECHR. However, it also takes into account the so-called "soft law" regulations, namely the European Prison Rules updated in 2006, and other recommendations in that field.

As early as 1965 the Federal Constitutional Court[28] drew on the relevant recommendation of the Council of Europe, when it had to decide upon the constitutionality of provisions regulating remand detention (that is, of their compatibility with the human rights as enshrined in the German Basic Law). The crucial point was the question of proportionality. To account for what it called "state-of-the art legal development", the FCC consulted the (now obsolete) Resolution (65) 11 of the Committee of Ministers on "Remand in Custody".

Some thirty years later, the FCC seems increasingly inclined to draw on the Council of Europe's soft law when needed. It has argued in a decision on juvenile prison legislation that it "may hint at a practice that does not comply with requirements of the German constitution" when "standards and requirements of international law referring to human rights as can be found in the guidelines and recommendations of the Council of Europe are not considered or are not met".[29] It is remarkable how the court swung the moral hammer by criticizing German practice as not conforming to European standards that typically (in Germany as elsewhere) are thought to be lower than national standards.

Another decision of the FCC referred to the conditions of remand detention, where various standards set by the CPT as well as the current recommendation on remand in custody[30] were used to show that certain practices (in this case locking-up remand prisoners most of the day in their cells while sentenced prisoners were allowed to move relatively freely within the prison or certain areas) were incompatible with Human Rights in the German Basic Law.[31] In yet another decision, CPT standards for prison cell size were used to show that in the case under consideration the human dignity of the prisoner was not violated (even if the cell only measured 6 m^2).[32]

Apart from their use in jurisprudence, CPT-standards as well as criticism from the CPT reports, but also the European Prisons Rules and other relevant recommendations, are sometimes used during the legislative reform process, for example as regards the Remand Prison Acts and the Juvenile Prison Acts of the Länder (Morgenstern, 2013; Dünkel, 2011a with regard to ERJOSSM; Kühl, 2012; Faber, 2014).

3.3 Mutual influences and problems

Finally, it should be mentioned that the "Europeanisation" works in two directions: In its landmark decision on "irreducible" life sentences in 2013,[33] the ECtHR relied heavily on the relevant decision of the German Constitutional Court.[34] This decision outlawed such sentences in 1977, stating that there must be a right to hope and to a chance of being reintegrated into society for all offenders. Another example is the influence of the German Prison Act (see above) on the development of the 2006 revised version of the European Prison Rules (van Zyl Smit and Snacken, 2009).

While the many layers of Human Rights based instruments found at the national, international and European level certainly have strengthened the normative basis of prisoner's rights immensely, the multitude of different instruments and controlling mechanisms also has its problems: So far, the CPT, the Mechanisms under OPCAT, the Working Group on Arbitrary Detention and additionally (and not even yet mentioned) the European Commissioner on Human Rights[35] have never complained officially that German authorities have not collaborated fully. It also seems that all reports required from them have been delivered duly (even if sometimes somewhat delayed). For the authorities involved, however, the frequency of visits, the many different monitoring institutions and the additional workload related to such visits may lead to an indifferent, if not skeptical, stance towards these mechanisms (Cernko, 2014).

Conclusion

Judicial control over German prisons has been dominated by national jurisprudence under the guidance of the FCC. Consequently, for many years European influences, and in particular the jurisprudence of the European Court of Human Rights, have been of minor importance. This changed considerably in 2009 with the case of "M. vs. Germany", which has been discussed as special case study in this article. It had enormous impact on legislation and practice concerning preventive detention in Germany. The Federal Constitutional Court in recent years also not only sought to incorporate the jurisprudence of the European Court of Human Rights in its judgments concerning prison matters but also "soft law" recommendations by the Council of Europe, mainly the European Prison Rules.

Even if high court case law has an indirect preventive effect by setting precedents and shaping the overall prison culture, other preventive mechanisms that function in addition to the retrospective review of potential violations of prisoners' rights have influenced prison law and practice in Germany more recently. This is primarily the case for the work of the CPT, which is generally acknowledged by the German authorities and has impacted at least discreetly on new prison legislation. With a slight reservation concerning the multitude of different institutions and instruments that may lead to a certain fatigue by the prison administrations and staff, we therefore conclude that the monitoring of prisoners' rights generally works sufficiently well in Germany.

Notes

1 The competence of this chamber apart from decisions on complaints according to §§ 109 ff. Prison Act is the decision on conditional early release according to §§ 57, 57a Criminal Code. It is a constitutional obligation that a judge or court has to decide on conditional release, see Art. 104 (2) of the Federal Constitution (*Grundgesetz* = Basic Law). Parole boards with other members than judges therefore are not allowed in German legislation.

2 See BVerfG NStZ 1996, 511; and BVerfG, decision of 4 July 2006–2 BvR 460/01.

3 In most cases older than 24, as youth prisons regularly deal with 14- to 24-year-old offenders, see Dünkel, 2011).

4 The one hour (and further visits) can be split if appropriate. The new legislation of some federal states provides 4 hours per month, and additional visits by children, husbands or relevant relatives, see for a summary Thiele, 2016.

5 See e.g. BVerfG, decision of 23 May 2013–2 BvR 2129/11; BVerfG, decision of 19 January 2016–2 BvR 3030/14).

6 See BVerfGE 45, 187 ff., 238; 64, 261 ff., 277; 98, 169 ff., 200; 109, 133 ff., 150 f.

7 For example, prisoners are only allowed to have personal belongings in their cell room to an "adequate amount" ("angemessener Umfang"). This is considered to be an indefinite legal term.

8 As a very last resort a complaint to the European Court on Human Rights (ECtHR) is possible, see Art. 34 ECHR.

9 See e.g. BVerfGE 116, 69, 85 f. with further references.

10 See e.g. BVerfGE 109, 133; 116, 69.

11 See Laubenthal/Nestler/Neubacher/Verrel-Bachmann 2015, P, § 109 note 18 with further references.

12 See Laubenthal/Nestler/Neubacher/Verrel-Bachmann 2015, P, § 109 note 129, 130. So far, however, no relevant case law has been published, which may be seen as an indicator for the preventive effectiveness of this rule.

13 Decision of October 14, 2004, reg. nr. 2 BvR 1481/04 (so-called Görgülü-decision), www.bverfg.de/entscheidungen/rs20041014_2bvr148104e.html; in print: BVerfGE

111, 307 et seq. All published decisions of the German Federal Constitutional Court (from 1998 onwards), are available on the Court´s website: www.bverfg.de.

14 Decision of the FCC (official collection) BVerfGE 128, 326 (headnote 2a) citing earlier decisions as established case-law.

15 BVerfGE 128, 326, §§ 35, 46 et seq.

16 For example in the recent judgment of the FCC, 15.12.2015–2 BvR 2735/14 on an Italian European Arrest Warrant, and in the so-called Lisbon-decision, FCC, 22.9.2009–2 BvR 2136/09.

17 Bundesgerichtshof (German Supreme Court), Neue Juristische Wochenschrift 2009, 2463.

18 Hellig v. Germany – 20999/05, Judgment 7.7.2011 [Section V].

19 Wenner v. Germany – 62303/13; Judgment of 1 September 2016. The domestic authorities had not examined the necessity of drug substitution treatment with regard to the criteria set by the relevant domestic legislation and medical guidelines, nor accessed the help of expert medical advice. Despite the applicant's previous medical treatment with drug substitution therapy for seventeen years, no follow-up had been given to the opinions expressed by external doctors on the necessity to consider providing the applicant with that treatment again.

20 Sokolow v. Germany, 11642/11, lodged on 17 February 2011.

21 All visits but the last are fully documented on the website of the CPT (www.cpt.coe.int/en/states/deu.htm), including press releases, the CPT reports, the government's responses and translation into German. The last visit took place only in November 2015, the report will be published in due time.

22 BVerfGE 109, 133, 167, 5 February 2004, App. No. 2 BvR 2029/01; BVerfGE 128, 326, 364 f., 4 May 2011, App. No. 2 BvR 2365/09 et al. Art. 104 (2) GG reads: An act may be punished only if it was defined by a law as a criminal offence before the act was committed.

23 All decisions can be found in the databank of the ECtHR (http://hudoc.echr.coe.int), some German cases in matters of preventive detention are still pending.

24 ECtHR, 24 June 1982, App. No. 7906/77, van Droogenbroeck *v* Belgium; Weeks *v* United Kingdom (1988) 10 E.H.R.R. 293; Stafford *v* United Kingdom (2002) 35 E.H.R.R. 32; M. *v* Germany, 17 December 2009, App. No. 19359/04; Grosskopf *v* Germany, 21 October 2010, App. No. 24478/03; Kallweit *v* Germany, 13 January 2011, App. No. 17792/07.

25 BVerfGE 128, 326, 4 May 2011, App. No. 2 BvR 2333/08 and others.

26 This was already spelled out seven years earlier (FCC 5 February 2004, App. No. 2 BvR 2029/01, cf. Dünkel and van Zyl Smit, 2004) but not adequately implemented.

27 Bergmann v Germany, 7 January 2016, App. No. 23279/14, § 96 ff.

28 BVerfGE 19, 342 (345).

29 The first was a decision of the Federal Constitutional Court relating to Juvenile Justice in 2006, BVerfGE 116, 69 (90). See also FCC, 13.11.2007–2 BvR 939/07; and the Constitutional Court of Berlin, VerfGH Berlin, Beschl. v. 03.11.2009–184/07. Other courts, however, have not adopted this view, namely the Constitutional Court of Bavaria VerfGH Bayern Vf. 3-VI-09, Vf. 3 VI/09.

30 Recommendation (2006) 13 of the Committee of Ministers to Member States on the use of remand in custody, the conditions in which it takes place and the provision of safeguards against abuse.

31 FCC, 17.10.2012–2 BvR 736/11 (= published in Strafverteidiger 2013, p. 521 et seq.).

32 FCC, 7. 11. 2012–2 BvR 1567/11.

33 Vinter et al v. United Kingdom – 66069/09, 130/10 and 3896, Judgment 9.7.2013 [Grand Chamber]. This judgment has been weakened by the decision of the Grand Chamber in the case of Hutchinson v. United Kingdom – 57592/08 (referred in July 2015).

34 FCC in the official collection BVerfGE 45, 187.

35 He has visiting rights comparable to that of the CPT, during his visit 2006 his priority was to see prisons where preventive detention was executed, *Commissioner of Human Rights 2007.*

References

Cernko, D. (2014). Die Umsetzung der CPT-Empfehlungen im deutschen Strafvollzug. Berlin: Duncker & Humblodt.CPT (1993). Report to the German Government on the Visit to Germany carried out by the CPT from 9 to 20 December 1991. CPT/Inf (1993) 13.

CPT (1997). Report to the German Government on the Visit to Germany carried out by the CPT from 14 to 26 April 1996. CPT/Inf (1997) 9.

CPT (2003). Report to the German Government on the Visit to Germany carried out by the CPT from 3 to 15 December 2000. CPT/Inf (2007) 20.

CPT (2007). Report to the German Government on the Visit to Germany Carried out by the CPT from 20 November to 2 December 2005. CPT (2006) 36/CPT/Inf (2007) 18.

CPT (2003). Report to the German Government on the Visit to Germany carried out by the CPT from 3 to 15 December 2000. CPT/Inf (2007) 20.

CPT (2012). Report to the German Government on the Visit to Germany carried out by the CPT from 25 November to 7 December 2010. CPT/Inf (2007) 6.CPT. (2014). Report to the German Government on the Visit to Germany carried out by the CPT from 25 November to 2 December 2013. CPT/Inf (2007) 23;

Drenkhahn, K. (2013). "Secure preventive detention in Germany: Incapacitation or treatment intervention?" *Behavioral Sciences and the Law*, 31, pp. 312–327.

Drenkhahn, K. and Morgenstern, C. (2017). "Preventive detention in Germany and Europe." In: A. Felthous and H. Sass (eds.), *International Handbook on Psychopathic Disorders*. Hoboken: John Wiley & Sons (in publication).

Drenkhahn, K., Morgenstern, C. and van Zyl Smit, D. (2012). "What is in a name? Preventive detention in Germany in the shadow of European Human Rights Law." *Criminal Law Review*, 3, pp. 167–187.

Dünkel, F. (2016). *Youth Justice in Germany*. Oxford: Oxford Handbook on Juvenile Justice. DOI: 10.1093/oxfordhb/9780199935383.013.68

Dünkel, F. (2011a). "Die Europäischen Grundsätze für die von Sanktionen oder Maßnahmen betroffenen jugendlichen Straftäter und Straftäterinnen (European Rules for Juvenile Offenders Subject to Sanctions or Measures ERJOSSM)." *Zeitschrift für Jugendkriminalrecht und Jugendhilfe*, 22, pp. 140–154.

Dünkel, F. (2011b). "Germany." In: F. Dünkel, J. Grzywa, P. Horsfield and I. Pruin (eds.), *Juvenile Justice Systems in Europe: Current Situation and Reform Developments*, Vol. 2, 2nd Ed. Mönchengladbach: Forum Verlag Godesberg, pp. 547–622.

Dünkel, F. (1996). *Empirische Forschung im Strafvollzug – Bestandsaufnahme und Perspektiven*. Bonn-Bad Godesberg: Forum-Verlag.

Dünkel, F. and van Zyl Smit, D. (2004). "Preventive detention of dangerous offenders reexamined: A comment on two decisions of the German Federal Constitutional Court." *German Law Journal*, 5, pp. 619–637.

Faber, M. (2014). Länderspezifische Unterschiede bezüglich Disziplinarmaßnahmen und der Aufrechterhaltung von Sicherheit und Ordnung im Jugendstrafvollzug. Mönchengladbach: Forum Verlag Godesberg.

Kühl, J. (2012). Die gesetzliche Reform des Jugendstrafvollzugs in Deutschland im Licht der European Rules for Juvenile Offenders Subject to Sanctions or Measures (ERJOSSM). Mönchengladbach: Forum Verlag Godesberg.

Laubenthal, K., Nestler, N., Neubacher, F. and Verrel, T. (2015). *Strafvollzugsgesetze*. 12th Ed. München: C. H. Beck.

Morgenstern, C. (2015). "'Der Resozialisierungsgrundsatz' – Social Reintegration as the dominant narrative for community punishment in Germany?" In: G. Robinson and F. McNeill (eds.), *Community Punishment: A European Perspective*. London, Routledge, pp. 72–94.

Morgenstern, C. (2013). "Remand detention in Europe: Comparative and Pan-European aspects as elements of a wider European penology." In: T. Daems, S. Snacken and D. van Zyl Smit (eds.), *Europan Penology?* Oxford: Hart Publishing, pp. 185–207.

Morgenstern, C. and Drenkhahn, K. (2016). "§ 66c." In: W. Joecks and K. Miebach (eds.), *Münchener Kommentar zum StGB*, W., Vol. 2, 3rd Ed. München: C.H. Beck, pp. 1087-1125.

Suhling, S. and Wischka, B. (2013). "Behandlung in der Sicherungsverwahrung." *Kriminalpädagogische Praxis*, 41, pp. 47–61.

Thiele, C. W. (2016). Ehe- und Familienschutz im Strafvollzug. Strafvollzugsrechtliche und – praktische Maßnahmen und rahmenbedingungen zur Aufrechterhaltung familiärer Beziehungen von Strafgefangenen. Mönchengladbach: Forum Verlag Godesberg.

van Zyl Smit, D. and Snacken, S. (2009). *Principles of European Prison Law and Policy: Penology and Human Rights*. Oxford and New York: Oxford University Press.

Wirth, W. (2006). "Arbeitslose Haftentlassene: Multiple problemlagen und vernetzte Wiedereingliederungshilfen." *Bewährungshilfe*, 53, pp. 137–152.

3 The European oversight of France

Corentin Durand, Nicolas Ferran and Hugues de Suremain

Introduction

In many aspects, the French example has the characteristics of a laboratory with regard to the legal protection of the rights of prisoners. First of all, the highest courts (one of which is judicial: the Court of Cassation; and the other administrative: the Council of State) display a certain amount of respect with regard to the European Court of Human Rights (ECtHR), the main actor in change as regards the law for prisoners (Van Zyl Smit and Snacken, 2009; Belda, 2010). Eminent members regularly assert that the Council of State recognizes *de facto* the *erga omnes* principle of the jurisprudence of the ECtHR (Sauvé, 2010). The Court of Cassation has taken a more formal position on this matter, declaring in its most formal plenary session that "*States which are party to this Convention are held to respect the decisions of the European Court of Human Rights, without waiting to be challenged before the European Court of Human Rights nor having to modify their legislation*".[1]

Against the backdrop of an increasing pressure on the part of transnational institutions, the law applicable to prisons presents the singularity of having undergone a dual process of development: in legislation, where it has been largely consensual and rapid in terms of the law for the enforcement of sentences (concerning the "external" legal status of the prisoner); and in jurisprudence, where it has been conflictual and incremental with regards to the recognition of rights behind the prison walls (concerning the "internal" legal status of the prisoner).

Moreover, the country benefits from a well-structured network of activist organizations committed to prison issues and active in legal procedures for the protection of the rights of prisoners. One of these, the French section of the International Prisons Observatory (OIP-SF), plays a pivotal role and, at least to a certain extent, is in position to orient legal cases along the most strategic lines, by drawing on the resources of European law.

Yet, in spite of a context which is in principle favourable, the French prison system suffers from structural problems, leading to reports of violations of the European Convention on Human Rights (ECHR). In particular, prison overcrowding is endemic. On 1 March 2017, the number of detainees held in establishments for prisoners serving sentences of less than two years (*maisons d'arrêt*) was 47,554, which is 14,231 detainees over their operational capacity (Direction de l'administration pénitentiaire, 2017).

In this context, the present study aims to account for the processes by which the influence of the ECHR is taken into account by the national legislator, administrative and judicial courts, as well as prison authorities. To what extent does this influence allow for the extension of emancipation spaces for the prison population and for increased discretionary power for prison authorities?

This contribution considers the possible conditions for structural change through increased litigation. We will first consider the influence of the ECHR and the jurisprudence of the ECtHR in the transformation of regulatory prison provisions (1), before analysing what the limits of its potential transformative power are (2). We will conclude by looking at the possible conditions and foreseeable consequences of increasing prison litigation (3).

1 The ECHR, the horizon and lever for regulatory change

Even prior to the involvement of the ECtHR, the Convention and the corpus of jurisprudence from the Court constitute a focal point for discussions and reforms concerning the prison policies in France. They form a largely shared regulatory horizon (1.1), on which inclinations to reform have been based since the beginning of the new millennium (1.2). This influence has been strengthened and supplemented by ECtHR litigation activity (1.3).

1.1 A (nearly) shared regulatory horizon

The ECHR and the jurisprudence of the ECtHR have played a wide role in the transformation of the "structure of political conflicts" on criminal detention since the end of the twentieth century (Bérard, 2014: 449). The ECtHR, along with the Committee for the Prevention of Torture (CPT) and the Council of Europe, form an "institutional triad which puts forward proposals whose very existence partially changes the terms of the public discussion" (Chantraine and Kaminski, 2007: 15; see also Snacken, 2014). In particular, ECtHR judgments against France play a crucial part in the framing of the public problem of prisons in terms of the rights of detainees. Arising from and spread by national and international institutions whose actions contribute to structuring the field of prisons in France, and in particular associations that are considered as privileged partners, the debate about rights has therefore been advocated as much by the institutional actors as by activists and detainees themselves.

Although claims for rights were already present in the prison revolts of the 1970s, reference to the ECtHR has gradually become established as central in associated arguments since the 1990s, as much in litigation cases as in advocacy (Bérard, 2014). This is particularly true for the articles guaranteeing the right to life (Article 2), the right not to suffer inhuman and degrading treatment (Article 3), the right to a fair trial (Article 6), the right to respect of private life (Article 8) and the right to an effective remedy (Article 13).

The dissemination in the public debate of legal arguments, as well as media coverage of the State being sentenced by administrative courts and by the ECtHR have facilitated a certain ownership of the debate about rights with detainees themselves. In 2006, a consultation carried out by several organizations, among those OIP-SF, with all people being detained in France showed the significance of references to the jurisprudence of the ECtHR (OIP, 2007). In addition, a study of the petitions sent by detainees to the Controller general of prisons shows that a quarter of the legal references that they contain refer to supra-legal sources, and in particular the ECHR. Moreover, the concepts of inhumanity and degradation, concerning Article 3 of the Convention, are frequently cited (Durand, 2014a).

On its part, the administration also asserted the adoption of a policy for rights as a lever "to develop the prison system",[2] and from there, as an instrument of legitimization. Moreover, in 2007 it stated that it intended to transform the European Prison Rules into "an ethical framework and an action charter" (Direction de administration pénitentaire, 2007), established on the basis of 8 of the 108 European prison rules. The repeated references to the ECtHR in the recent circulars is equally the sign of this "ownership process".

European standards therefore constitute if not a largely shared regulatory horizon, at least a resource that is regularly resorted to, not without ambivalence, and against which national prison policies are promoted, criticised and measured.

1.2 A regulatory lever for reform

The weakness of the legal status of prisoners emerged in the public discussion as a political problem at the turn of this century, even before any judgments against France by the Court of Strasbourg. Putting prison reform on the agenda was done with the ECHR and the recommendations of the Council of Europe as a focal point.

In June 1999, following a campaign by OIP-SF, the highest-ranking judicial magistrate in France was commissioned by the Government to issue a report on the independent control of prisons (Canivet, 2000). Setting the terms of the debate for the ten following years, it recommended a system of public control, combining local voluntary delegates and professional controllers. Above all, it established as a precondition the complete reshaping of the applicable regulatory framework, breaking from the broad discretionary power of prison personnel and to the hands-off doctrine upheld by administrative courts. Instead, it demanded the legal definition of a legal status of "detained citizen", specifying the restrictions on fundamental rights that were to be allowed. To provide grounds for this demand, the report referred widely to European law, while at the same time jurisprudential dynamics for a category of protection for prisoners had not yet been initiated by the Court of Strasbourg. Moreover, it made European jurisprudence relative to the "quality of the law" – implying accessibility and predictability of standards – a strategic argument. Two parliamentary inquiry reports followed (Mermaz and Floch, 2000; Hyest and Cabanel, 2000). Although that of the Senate paid little attention to the rights of prisoners, that of the National Assembly backed many recommendations by Guy Canivet, putting them on the legislative agenda. A draft law had been prepared on this basis, but because of the upcoming Presidential election in 2002, which was dominated by the issue of insecurity, the government backtracked. During the preparatory work for the prison law of 24 November 2009 all reference to the Canivet Report were jettisoned (Bérard and Chantraine, 2013).

This attention to the Convention was then also significant in the criminal law field. The law of 15 June 2000 known as the "presumption of innocence law", which was the fruit of a broad consensus, profoundly modified the procedure with the aim to better respect the European requirements as regards a fair trial and provisional detention. This inspiration arises very clearly from both the explanatory statement for the governmental project and the parliamentary debates. The text sets out the grounds for the measure with the objective of making this measure exceptional and of a maximum duration.

Until the early 2000s, European law was able to function as a relatively consensual regulatory support in putting on the agenda reforms aimed at the reduction of prison overcrowding as a *sine qua non* condition for the implementation prisoners' rights. However, the fall in the prison population, which started in 1996, was halted abruptly by the beginning of the presidential campaign in the summer of 2001 which was marked by a particularly repressive vision of criminal law. This turning point on security marks the limits of the *soft power* of the ECHR, and points to the importance of litigation in the development of French prison law for the last twenty years.

1.3 Development of French prison law through the courts

The impact of the jurisprudence of the ECtHR on the changes in French prison law has been undeniable (Belda, 2010). In particular, the development of the jurisdictional control of the acts and actions of the prison authorities has led to a corpus of jurisprudence which to a certain extent defines the reach of the rights of prisoners.

Being classified as "internal measures of", the decisions taken by the prison administration were regarded by jurisprudence as not being open to appeal. In anticipation,[3] with regard to judgments rendered against other countries, an administrative judge admitted for the first time a verification of the legality of a disciplinary cell punishment in 1995,[4] then subsequently that of a solitary confinement measure in 2003.[5] But it was necessary to wait for the *Boussouar*, *Payet* and *Planchenault* Council of State rulings of 14 December 2007[6] to see the scope of the courts' control of the prison authorities extend substantially (Guyomar, 2009) and, as a corollary, the sphere of influence of European case-law. According to the Vice-President of the Council of State, it has been "*strongly inspired*" by European solutions, "*in an implicit constant dialogue with European judges*" (Sauvé, 2008).

In parallel, the judge widened the responsibility of the State by determining the events of suicide,[7] accidental death in a fire in a cell,[8] or damage to personal effects[9] as "simple" negligence (and not gross negligence). Whereas the European Court disputed the effectiveness of the remedy available in the event of a breach of the integrity or the dignity of prisoners because of the length of the process,[10] the use of summary procedures made it possible “to apprehend, in a broad sense, the issue of the legal status of prison authority actions in a completely new way” (Guyomar, 2014). In particular, in adapting the positive-obligations approach from European jurisprudence, national judges can order, in an extreme emergency, protection measures in the event of a violation of Articles 2 or 3 of the ECHR, in the event of detention conditions which are dangerous or not in accordance with the respect of human dignity, for instance in the form of injunctions to provide material improvements.

As far as prison authorities are concerned, the European influence was felt down to the most sensitive dimensions of its action. In addition to the question of strip searches, examined on p. 68, European jurisprudence has undoubtedly curbed the highly security-based orientation of prison policy since 2003. For example, certain courts censured measures of prolonged solitary confinement (a measure intended to prevent internal disorder or escapes) which targeted high-risk prisoners. Similarly, guided by jurisprudence from Strasbourg, the Council of State censured the secret measure of “security rotation” (repeated transfers of prisoners likely to escape). More recently, the measure of occasionally switching the lights on during the night in a cell holding a prisoner convicted for a terrorist attack was stopped.[11]

However, French prison law still bears the marks of the conditions of its emergence, namely a patchwork progression, lacking in structured ambition. In particular, the law has freed itself from Guy Canivet’s initial plan to establish, in the emancipatory term of citizenship, a framework determining the relationship between the public power and detainees. Moreover, European jurisprudence leaves room for a case-based approach of structural problems, with a set of largely unspecified standards, such as the use of the concept of the “inherent constraints of detention”.[12]

2 The reception of ECtHR jurisprudence in France: an ambivalent dynamic

Although the jurisprudence of the ECtHR has widely contributed to the changes in the French prison authorities, its potential for a transformation must be viewed through the prism of professional and institutional resistances (2.1). It is also questioned by the relative convergence of European law with the modernising rationalities of the prison authorities (2.2), as well as by its difficulty in taking into account structural prison problems (2.3). We aim at assessing various compliance patterns from correctional institutions, by taking into account the ways court orders are translated into social policy by policymakers and administrators.

2.1 A potential for transformation in the face of professional and institutional resistance: the example of strip-searching

The legal conditions for body searches affect the visible expression of the exercise of power in prison and have been considered as such by the prison control bodies and by prison trade-union organizations. The provisional assessment of a ten-year legal and political battle reveals that internal social dialogue has so far prevailed over the European regulatory requirements.

French law has for a long time been very permissive in the area of body searches. The regulatory provisions that provided that "*prisoners must be searched regularly and as often as the head of the establishment deems necessary*" were abrogated in 2010. The methods practised were endorsed by the Council of State in 2000[13] and remained in force until 2011. The use of this intrusive and humiliating measure was therefore massive, to the point of being classed as a "*penitentiary reflex*" by the senatorial board of inquiry in 2000 (Hyest and Cabanel, 2000). It became the subject of a growing number of criticisms (for instance CNCDH, 2004; CPT, 2007), which founded backing in recent jurisprudence from the ECtHR,[14] soon to be joined by national courts.[15] According to the European and French courts, full body searches only comply with Article 3 of the Convention on the condition of being both strictly necessary in terms of security, and conducted according to adequate conditions and procedures. In 2007 and 2009, France was condemned in Strasbourg for not having respected these requirements.[16]

It is under the influence of this jurisprudence that the prison law of 24 November 2009 came to provide a framework for the use of body searches as an exceptional measure. A few months later, a representative from France assured a United Nations body that "*pursuant to the decisions of the Court of Strasbourg, the systematic nature [of strip searches] from now on is forbidden and they take place only in the event of a necessity suggested by serious suspicions*" (Mattéi, 2010).

The reality was however quite different, according to Controller general's (CGLPL, 2011: 231–256) or the Public Defender of Rights' (Défenseur des droits, 2011: 131) reports stating that the administration continued to make very frequent, even systematic, use of body searches, under pressure in particular from prison guards trade unions. In a report on the application of the prison law of July 2012, Senators Lecerf and Borvo stressed that the wording of the decrees[17] taken pursuant to the law had been written in ambiguous terms which "*essentially, made it possible for the establishments to maintain their former practices*" (Lecerf and Borvo Cohen-Seat, 2012).

For its part, the OIP-SF launched a litigation campaign which resulted, between 2011 and 2013, with the courts calling into question the system of systematic full body searches in about fifteen establishments.[18]

Being forced to react, the Minister of Justice overhauled practices in this area by sending to prison officers a simple memo.[19] Although it confirms the "*ban on systematic searches*", and the necessary respect of the principles of necessity and proportionality, this memorandum also underlines that the temporary application of an "*extra-ordinary system of full body searches*" of a detainee "*identified as presenting risks*" is possible after having been recognised in jurisprudence.[20] It provides moreover that decisions to conduct a search do not have to be notified to the people concerned, depriving them of the concrete possibility to engage an effective remedy. As it could be feared, this memo has not put an end to illegal practices, as was recently and worriedly noted by the Controller general of prisons, who stated about one particular prison that "body searches is a local practice that violates the rights of detainees and do not comply with the law", and that integral body searches are still systematic in certain divisions (CGLPL, 2016).

Moreover, a recent reform of the law[21] ignores the principle of individualizing searches, authorizing full body searches "*in places and for a period of time determined independently of the nature of the detainee*" when there exists "*serious reasons to suspect the introduction into the prison of banned objects or substances or such as which pose a threat to the safety of people or property*". It signals the probable return of systematic full body searches. To date, the courts have not had the opportunity to rule on this new practice.

As a long-term test of strength whose outcome is still uncertain, the case of searches raises the wider question of the capacity of the law, and in particular of European law, to put an effective end to practices which are clearly intrusive and humiliating, within a reasonable time. This question arises with all the more acuteness in light of the shock wave from the attacks of 2015, which threatens the corpus of jurisprudence developed in the preceding decade. A significant example is the decision taken concerning permanent video surveillance in a cell holding a prisoner accused in connection with the Paris attacks, in which the Council of State cast aside the arguments of excessive breach of the right to private life of the interested party, judging that this measure was justified by the context of the terrorist attacks in France and the presumption that the applicant enjoys the support of an international terrorist organization.[22]

2.2 *A potential of transformation limited by the relative convergence of rationalities*

The institutional and professional resistance witnessed with regard to strip searches are nevertheless an exception. With regard to several topics, on the contrary, a kind of convergence can be observed between the rationalities of European law and those implemented by the prison authorities, including in the implementation of measures that lead to undermining the protection of the fundamental rights of detainees. This convergence is based on correctional standards, in particular those issued by the Council of Europe (Snacken, 2014).

This is particularly true in the differentiation of the modes of detention, which was one of the principal sources of division in prison debates in the 2000s. The promotion of risk management by prison services comprising different levels of constraint was therefore at the heart of the attempt at the modernization of the prison system, after the failure of the "liberal" reform spell of 1999–2002 (Cliquennois, 2013). These measures were initially deployed in an experimental manner, with the common feature of varying the freedom of movement permitted to detainees according to their ability to conform to internal rules. The prison law of November 2009 provided a legal base to this system. Objections to the breach introduced, in legal terms, by this measure, are rather well summarized by the position of the Socialist Party in Parliament: "*The introduction of such a measure would amount to abolishing any reference to a general and impersonal standard which the detainee could claim a right to. And all this just to set up a moving, fluctuating, system in response only to the requirements of the prison authorities*"[23]. To this, the government retorted by invoking the European Prison Rules, which recommend that each prisoner is assessed in order to determine the risk they would pose to the community in the event of escape and, consequently, be subjected "*to a security measure corresponding to the level of risk identified*", with the necessary level having to be "*regularly reassessed*"[24]. The case-law shows the acceptance by the ECtHR of such a differentiation of detention regimes, while controlling the measures they imply.[25] The Council of State accepted that such decisions be monitored but rejected that they be subjected to the obligation of providing the grounds for them,[26] which significantly reduces the practical interest of an appeal, and which appears to violate the right to a fair trial.[27]

The role of jurisprudence in these processes, which stiffen social relations in prisons as a result of handling risk, in particular on the basis of Article 2 of the ECHR (protection of the right to life), has been widely documented. In particular, G. Cliquennois and B. Champetier have shown that the "prevention of death" constitutes "*the institutional response and the concomitant adaptation to the pressure of jurisprudence . . . and the criticisms of the families of prisoners and activist associations who demand the application of the right to the life by publicising cases of suicide*" (Cliquennois and Champetier, 2013). Jurisprudence itself reflects this dual predictive and restraining logic in the management expected in prisons. The Council of State has thus ruled that it is incumbent on prison officials to take the life protection measures required by the nature of detainees, with respect to the profile of the occupants of the cells.[28] Another Order criticises a medical service for not having controlled antidepressant treatment, using toxicology tests, for a prisoner who ended up committing suicide.[29] The European Court upheld a violation of Article 2 of the ECHR on the grounds of the notable absence of "*an effective system for immediately transmitting information on the risks generated by the state of health of prisoners between the various parties within the establishment*" and of the absence of body searches which would have made it possible for the administration to seize the belt with which the prisoner had hung himself.[30]

One sees here the necessity to prevent risks to threats to life appearing among the justifications for a reduction of the space of autonomy accorded to prisoners (by the use of restraining measures such as special monitoring, "naked cells", paper pyjamas or tear-proof sheets), and a return to discretionary powers (through decisions which assign detainees to restraining measures in varying degrees). In this respect, the prison law of 2009 manages to turn around the requirement of a reduction of arbitrariness to obtain "a change of paradigm and absolute decisional power" (Herzog-Evans, 2010).

Due to a lack of adequate developments on the ground in the right to autonomy and, more broadly, respect to private life, European jurisprudence seems to lack the resources to counter other very recent changes in prisons, which results in undermining fundamental rights of prisoners. Furthermore, the criteria used by the European Court of Human Rights contribute to a large extent to this logic of surveillance and risk management (Cliquennois and Champetier, 2013).

An exit door could result from an increase in litigation, under conditions which force the courts to examine the actual consequences, with regards to fundamental rights, of these policies on the material conditions for detention.

2.3 *The difficulty for European law to take into account structural problems*

The intervention of administrative courts with regard to the material conditions of detention has drawn much attention. Yet, the interest of these procedures remains considerably limited by a restrictive approach to the scope of the injunctions likely to be ordered. The Council of State stated that the measures ordered "*must come into effect at the very earliest opportunity*",[31] implying that judges cannot order measures of a magnitude which would require a thorough examination of their feasibility, and which would aim at solving a complex and/or structural problem. Only in one case has the judge ordered the closure of an unsanitary disciplinary block, after seven years of proceedings. However, this decision has not been implemented yet. It is thus primarily on the grounds of liability, that is to say damages claims, that the question of the poor conditions in prisons related to overcrowding has been dealt with.

The limited capacities of the judge for summary procedures (*juge des référés)* and the requirement prohibiting him/her from interfering with the course of judicial proceedings explain why the remedies on this particular issue do not seem to have had any significant effects on criminal law policies. The Court of Cassation, the judicial Supreme Court, has drastically limited the opportunities for detainees to put forward the inhumane conditions they experienced in support of requests for release, by requiring the demonstration of a health risk. This ground for appeal is consequently considered to be ineffective by the Court of Strasbourg.[32] In this regard, the clarification of European requirements concerning conditions of detention in overcrowded establishments, provided by the GC judgment Mursic v. Croatia, is seemingly not capable of altering the position of national courts, which reflects a desire to sit on the sidelines of criminal policy orientations and of a certain understanding of the security and material constraints that prison authorities face.[33]

Whereas the hopes raised by the reductionist tendencies of the Conference for Consensus on the prevention of reoffending in 2013 fizzled out, a proportion of the actors are relying on the ECtHR to bring about a reorientation of criminal policy by means of a pilot judgment (or at least a quasi-pilot judgment[34]) in which the Court of Strasbourg would recognize the structural nature of the problem of prison overcrowding.[35] To date, about thirty appeals from detainees in several French prisons have thus been lodged before the European Court in the context of a campaign initiated by OIP-SF and communicated to the French government.[36]

Nevertheless, the prospect of an increase in such litigation campaigns cannot but lead us to question the relative weakness of the stakeholders in these legal proceedings, namely the non-profit sector, legal professionals, and detainees themselves.

3 The challenge of increased litigation to obtain structural changes

The challenge of increased litigation nevertheless faces several structural obstacles. On the one hand, the association sector and activist legal professionals are few in number and have limited resources (3.1). On the other, detainees are, due to their history and their situation, particularly vulnerable citizens (3.2). Lastly, the objective of increased litigation carries with it the risk of a bureaucratization of the handling of cases (3.3).

3.1 The weakness of the association sector and criminal law 'cause lawyers'

In the line with the judicialisation of action by the association sector on foreigners rights (Israël, 2003), several organizations for the defence of the rights of detainees have, since the turn of the year 2000, integrated appeals to the courts in their repertory of action.

A pioneer and leader of this activist involvement in the law, the OIP-SF association, founded in 1996, is at the origin of around a hundred rulings returned by domestic courts, and several rulings condemning France before the European Court of Human Rights (Ferran, 2014; Suremain, 2014). Litigation activity has also been undertaken by other associations, which include former prisoners, such as *Robin des lois*[37] or *Ban public*,[38] as well as, from time to time, by trade associations[39] or general associations.[40]

Despite a better established and more diversified presence than in certain neighbouring countries, the association sector suffers from a structural weakness in view of the multiplicity of litigation areas and the resources deployed by the ministry for justice. As such, OIP-SF legal action is based on the expertise of a single paid lawyer, assisted by one or two trainee lawyers. The relationships with detainees, as well as a network of lawyers and academics are thus crucial to the prospect of increased litigation.

The mobilization of lawyers nevertheless runs up against the weak structuring of the profession as regards prison law. Although there is today some specialized training, all the lawyers we questioned indicated that they did not encounter prison law during their initial training.[41] Moreover, diffusion channels for favourable jurisprudence solutions are scarce and there are great regional disparities in the capacity of local lawyers to take on complex prison law cases.

Indeed, the engagement of lawyers in prison law remains today largely dependent on the activity of a certain number of "cause lawyers", that is legal professionals who engage in strategic litigation in order to achieve an outcome besides individual cases (Sarat and Scheingold, 1998). More recently, a network of lawyers was created in May 2015, and one year later had brought together nearly 70 members, primarily young professionals. The network creates, in particular through digital tools, a collective knowledge at the national level in the field of prison law (A3D, 2016). Yet, a major obstacle to this development is of a financial nature, as legal aid is not sufficient to mitigate the low financial resources of prisoners and certain procedures – in particular the compulsory preliminary administrative appeal in disciplinary matters – do not open up the right to legal aid. In particular, several of the lawyers questioned underlined the inadequacy of the remuneration compared to the workload necessary to provide effective legal representation, in particular in cases concerning enforcing sentences. Under these conditions, many lawyers refuse to take legal aid cases.

3.2 Detainees as weakened citizens

Control of the prison authorities by the courts can only occur when they are applied to. For this reason, the first people involved in litigation are the detainees themselves. People who have been handed very lengthy sentences and who are particularly likely to be subject to security measures, have largely initiated litigation action in France, most often with the assistance of advocacy groups (Suremain and Bérard, 2009). There are nevertheless many obstacles to engage in legal action as a prisoner, in particular the availability and the understanding of legal resources, the fear of reprisals from staff, and the disconnect of certain procedures from the situations which they claim to solve.

The sociology of law in prisons has highlighted the material constraints weighing on access and understanding of legal resources by socially weakened persons. The legal texts are seldom available. Even there, interviews carried out with detainees underline the difficulty of grasping the complexity of legal statements.[42] Thus, although general references to rights have developed in prisons (Salle and Chantraine, 2009; Durand, 2014a), knowledge of precise legal provisions remains the exception, and the complexity of the procedures is a major barrier to a remedy in the courts.

In addition, studies all point to prisoners' fear of reprisals, either formal or informal (CPT, 2009). The Controller general for prisons has described various types of retaliation: "direct opposition to procedures, in the form of failing to send the complaint to the public prosecutor"; "pressure for a complaint to be withdrawn"; "punishments in prison" (CGLPL, 2013). The cultural figure of "litigators" (*procéduriers*) unsettles the fragile equilibrium of social relations in prisons and crystallises the illegitimate use of the law in prisons (Durand, 2014b).

Lastly, a number of the detainees questioned underline the inadequacy of the remedy in the courts in changing their situation. These reserves point in particular to the lengthy duration of legal procedures. Indeed, the nature of the penitentiary field is particularly significant in these problems, as shown by the example of the control of disciplinary proceedings. Compulsory administrative appeals do not lead to the suspension of contested sanctions. Except for in exceptional emergency procedure, detainees will thus have already served the entirety of their sanction by the time of a decision. One lawyer questioned specified that the rare clients who wished to enter an appeal do so as a matter "of principle", with no illusions as to the consequences on their sanction. Risky and uncertain, seeking remedy in the courts generally only offers the possibility of symbolic victories, which are important as such, but disconnected from the daily prison life of those who engage in legal action.

Although increased litigation would be likely for a time to invert this radically asymmetrical power relationship, it would be advisable to anticipate, as an assumption, the risk of a bureaucratization of the handling of these legal cases which, far from increasing their effect, would do nothing but deteriorate the quality of them.

3.3 The risk of bureaucratization the handling of legal cases

Litigation cases concerning the rights of foreign nationals show, taking into account the experience gained since the 1970s, the risk of bureaucratization to which prison litigation is exposed, resulting in requests being dealt with according to expeditious and derogatory rules. Due to a lack of power to control the upstream for disputed decisions, the administrative justice has endeavoured to control flows downstream, by creating procedures which allow for quicker and simpler treatment of this litigation. This process was also documented in the case of prison litigation in the US (Feeley and Swearingen, 2004).

Although litigation in the rights of prisoners in France has not reached the levels of that for litigation for foreign nationals, far from it, one finds comparable characteristics therein. As such, despite the normalization sought by the legislator in this field, the law for enforcing sentences is characterized, in judicial practice, by attenuated, or even essentially formal, safeguards, if compared to common law. The Court of Cassation's jurisprudence still has only weak references to European law for the most common measures relating to reducing sentences, permission for temporary leave, or withdrawal of a reduced sentence.[43]

The same strategies are apparent on the administrative court side, where litigation however seems to be very limited. Through a fear of fanning the flames, jurisprudence curbs the effectiveness of remedies by limiting the chances of obtaining a decision from a judge in good time, especially with regard to disciplinary matters. This despite the repeated violations of the right to an effective remedy established with regard to France in the subject matter of the urgent consideration of grievances.[44]

Therefore, the risk of a weakening of the procedural safeguards in the processing of cases is serious and documented and should be taken into account by strategies to increase prison litigation.

Conclusion

Through its normative influence and the litigation that it has enabled, the ECtHR has broadly contributed to transforming in the last twenty years the backdrop against which prison policies are drafted and implemented. In particular, the development of jurisdictional oversight of prison authorities has enabled the specification of the scope of the rights of detainee. Inside prisons, the reference to the law, and in particular to the law of the ECHR and to the sentences of the ECtHR, represents a new resource which transforms, without upending them, the power relations within the prison.

However, the extent of these transformations remains ambiguous. The dialogue among the legislator, prison authorities, national courts and European institutions supposes a series of adaptation and translation operations (Daems, 2017). The case of strip searches, which has been at the centre of a legal battle for a decade, points to the possibility of forms of professional and institutional resistance while meeting the European normative requirements. Nonetheless, such resistance remains an exception, and the analysis of the dialogue between European and French institutions cannot be content with the alternative between compliance and non-compliance. On the contrary, the limits should be placed within the complexity of the respective institutional commitments.

In order to dispel the myth of a European law that is necessarily emancipatory, it is crucial to stress the partial convergence of the rationalities conveyed by the case law of the ECtHR with the decrease of the autonomous space recognized to detainees and the return of discretionary power. As in the case of the protection of the right to life, the valorisation of procedural standards, derived in particular from the recommendations of the Council of Europe, is failing to stem, or even reinforcing, the reduction of the autonomy of detainees and the development of new forms of arbitrariness in prisons.

Furthermore, the dialogue between European and national institutions remains incapable of tackling structural problems such as material conditions of detention or overcrowding. In particular, the reluctance of the ECtHR to intervene in the field of criminal policy, both at the level of the decision as well as with regard to the remission of sentences, deprives it of the means to deliver solutions that are worthy of the structural problems that directly undermine the fundamental rights of detainees. Nowadays some stakeholders in the field of prisons bet on a possible pilot judgment in order to effect a reorientation of criminal policy.

If on the one hand it seems useful from an emancipatory perspective, the development of prison litigation runs nevertheless into several structural obstacles, first and foremost the lack of effectiveness of the existing remedies, to which detainees and many of their defence counsels point, in delivering solutions to the problems linked to imprisonment within acceptable terms. In particular, the principle of subsidiarity, which is at the very centre of the dialogue between national and European courts, urgently requires the implementation in national law of an effective remedy, adapted in its timescale and its competence to the reality of daily prison life. Due to its own procedural requirements, the ECtHR cannot compensate in the long term for this absence, and would gain from working toward the establishment of such an internal jurisdictional control

As an indispensable regulatory reference and essential lever for the transformation of the operation of detention establishments, European law is but an ambiguous resource for the rationalities which it conveys, likely to reinforce the liberties of the prison population as much as the discretionary scope of the prison authorities, and is dependent on the social forces which interpret it, resist it or feed it. These reflections are apparently necessary prerequisites for the development of a "rights policy" in the correctional domain. While breaking with an idealized vision of social change through the law, the goal is to integrate legal action into the complex system of power relations and replace it with complementary modes of political action.

Notes

1 Council of State, Plenary Session (*Ass. Plén.*), 15 April 2011, No. 10–17.049.
2 CircularDAP, 14 January 2009 on the implementation of the European Prison Rules in prisons.
3 The public conclusions pronounced in the cases cited in this paragraph are proof of such attention to the case law of other States. The ECtHR thus condemned the absence of effective remedy against solitary confinement decisions (Ramirez-Sanchez C. France, 4 July 2006, req. No. 59450/00).
4 CE [Conseil d'Etat], 17 February 2015, *Marie*, No.97754.
5 CE, 30 July 2003, *Remli*, No. 252712.
6 No. 290730, No. 306432 and No. 290420.
7 CE, May 23, 2003, Chabba, No. 244663.
8 CE, 17 December 2008, *Zaouiya*, No. 305594.
9 CE, 9 July 2008, Minister of Justice, versus Boussouar, No. 306666.
10 ECtHR, 5e Sect. 10 November 2011, *Plathey versus France*, Req. No. 48337/09.
11 Administrative Court (TA) Limoges, 30 June 2016, No. 1400680.
12 For a refusal of the right to assembly on these grounds, see CE, ord., 27 May 2005, No. 280866.
13 CE, 8 December 2000, No. 176389.
14 ECtHR, 24 July. 2001, Valasinas versus Lithuania, No. 44558/98; 4 February 2003, Van DER Venn versus Netherlands, No. 50901/99.
15 EC, 14/11/2008, No.315622.
16 ECtHR 12 June 2007, Frérot versus France, req. No. 70204/01; 9 July 2009 Khider versus France, No 39364/05. See for a later judgment: ECtHR, 20 January 2011, El Shenawy versus France, No.51246/08.
17 Order No. 2010–1634 of 23 December 2010; Circular of 14/04/2011 relating to the methods for checks on detainees.
18 For instance, CE, 06/06/2013, *OIP-SF*, No. 368816.
19 Memorandum of 15 November 2013 relating to the methods for checks on detainees.
20 CE, 6 June 2013, *M. E*, No. 368875.
21 Law No. 2016–731 of 3 June 2016 reinforcing the fight against organized crime, terrorism and their financing.
22 CE, ord., 28/07/2016, No. 401800.
23 Speech by Jean-Jacques Urvoas (MP) in the September 15, 2009 plenary session of the Assemblée nationale.
24 Recommendation Rec(2006)2 of the Committee of Ministers of the Council of Europe to member states on the European Prison Rules (Adopted on 11 January 2006).
25 See the last rulings delivered by the Strasbourg Court on 12 January 2016 against la Poland in the Karykowski (no. 653/12), Prus (no. 5136/11) and Romaniuk (no. 59285/12) cases.
26 CoE, 28 March 2011, No. 316977.
27 See Stegarescu and Bahrin v. Portugal, 06/04/2010, No.46194/06.
28 CE, 17 December 2008, No.305594.
29 Administrative Court of Appeal (CAA), Douai, 22 September 2015, No. 14DA00602.
30 Ketreb C. France, 19 July 2012, No. 38447/09.
31 CE, 13 August 2013, No.370902.
32 Yengo C. France, 21/05/2015, No.50494/12.

33 See, establishing the administrative case law in this matter : CE, 13 janvier 2017, n°389711.
34 As in the case Vasilescu v. Belgium, 2 April 2013, No 4743/12 68495/12 54052/12.
35 As happened in the US Supreme Court's decision – Brown v. Plata, 23 May 2011-, which orders that radical measures be implemented aimed at putting an end to overcrowding in Californian prisons.
36 ECtHR, 5th Section, Décisions de communication of 11 February 2016, *J.M.B. v. France and 9 other applications*, No. 9671/15 et seq.; *F.R. v. France and 3 other applications*, No. 12792/15 et seq.
37 See, for example, CE, 29 March 2010, *OIP-SF and Korber*, No. 319043. The association is directed by François Korber, a former prisoner who was at the origin of several appeals during his time in prison (see, for example, CE, 4 November 1994, No.157435; CE, 30 July. 2003, No. 249563; CE, 15 July 2004, No.265594).
38 See, for example, CE, 24 September 2014, No. 362472.
39 See, for example, CE, 21 October 1988, Trade union of French lawyers (Syndicat des avocats de France), No. 70066.
40 See, for example, CE, 11 April 2014, League of human rights (Ligue des droits de l'homme), OIP-SF and others, No.352473.
41 Semi-structured interview conducted between 2014 and 2015 with six lawyers working in prison law in the Paris area and in the regions.
42 Semi-structured interviews cconducted between 2014 and 2015 with 23 detainees in two detention facilities.
43 Ruling of 15 April 2013. See, on the contrary, about the revocation of a release on parole, Crim. 15 April 2015 No.1804.
44 See for instance, Payet, 20 janvier 2011, n° 19606/08; Plathey, 10 novembre 2011 no 48337/09 , Cocaign, 3 novembre 2011, n°32010/07.

Bibliography

Avocats pour la défense des droits des détenus – A3D. (2016). *Rapport d'activité*, Grenoble: A3D.

Belda, B. (2010). Les droits de l'homme des personnes privées de liberté: Contribution à l'étude du pouvoir normatif de la Cour européenne des droits de l'homme. Brussels: Bruylant, p. 760.

Bérard, J. (2014). "Genèse et structure des conflits politiques sur les droits des détenus dans la France contemporaine." *Déviance et Société*, 38(4), pp. 449–458.

Bérard, J. and Chantraine, G. (2013). *Bastille Nation (2000–2010): French Penal Politics and the Punitive Turn*. Ottawa: Red Quill Books, p. 204.

Canivet, G. (2000). Amélioration du contrôle extérieur des établissements pénitentiaires: rapport au ministre de la justice. Paris: La Documentation française, p. 229.

CGLPL. (2016). Recommandations en urgence relatives à la maison d'arrêt des hommes du centre pénitentiaire de Fresnes. Paris: CGLPL.

CGLPL. (2013). *Rapport d'activité*. Paris: Dalloz.

CGLPL. (2011). *Rapport d'activité*. Paris: Dalloz.

Chantraine, G. and Kaminski, D. (2007). "La politique des droits en prison." *Champ pénal/Penal Field*, [Online], uploaded on September 27, 2007. URL : http://champpenal.revues.org/document2581.htm

Cliquennois, G. (2013). "Which penology for decision making in French prisons?" *Punishment and Society*, 15, pp. 468–487.

Cliquennois, G. and Champetier, B. (2013). "A new risk management for prisoners in France: The emergence of a death-avoidance approach." *Theoretical Criminology*, 17, pp. 397–415.

Comité de prévention de la torture. (2009). 20 ans de lutte contre la torture: 19e rapport général du Comité européen pour la prévention de la torture. Strasbourg: Council of Europe Editions.

Comité de prévention de la torture. (2007). Rapport au Gouvernement de la République française relatif à la visite effectuée en France. Strasbourg: Conseil de l'Europe CPT.

Commission nationale consultative des droits de l'homme. (2004). *Etude sur les droits de l'Homme dans la prison*. Paris: La Documentation française.

Daems, T. (2017). "Slaves and statues: Torture prevention in contemporary Europe." *British Journal of Criminology*, 57, pp. 627–643.

Défenseur des droits. (2011). *Rapport d'activité*. Paris: Défenseur des droits.

Direction de l'administration pénitentiaire. (2007). Les règles pénitentiaires européennes : une charte d'action pour l'AP. Paris: Ministère de la Justice.

Direction de l'administration pénitentiaire. (2017). Statistique mensuelle des personnes écrouées et détenues en France. Paris: Ministère de la Justice.

Durand, C. (2014a). "Construire sa légitimité à énoncer le droit: Étude de doléances de prisonniers." *Droit et société*, 87(2), pp. 329-348.

Durand, C. (2014b). "La figure du détenu procédurier, cristallisation des usages illégitimes du droit." In: N. Ferran and S. Slama (eds.), *Défendre en justice la cause des personnes détenues*. Paris: La Documentation française, pp. 65–70.

Feeley, M. and Swearingen, V. (2004). "The prison conditions cases and the bureaucratization of American corrections: Influences, impacts and implications." *Pace Law Review*, 24, pp. 433-475.

Ferran, N. (2014). "La personne détenue encore à la recherche de son juge en France." *Déviance et Société*, 38(4), pp. 476-478.

Guyomar, M. (2014). "Les perspectives d'évolution de la jurisprudence du Conseil d'Etat." In: N. Ferran and S. Slama (eds.), *Défendre en justice la cause des personnes détenues*. Paris: La Documentation française, pp. 241–246.

Guyomar, M. (2009). "La justiciabilité des mesures pénitentiaires devant le juge administratif." *Actualité juridique: Edition droit administratif*, 8, pp. 413–415.

Herzog-Evans, M. (2010). "Loi pénitentiaire n° 2009–1436 du 24 novembre 2009: changement de paradigme pénologique et toute puissance administrative." *Recueil Dalloz*, 1, pp. 31–38.

Hyest, J.-J. and Cabanel, G.-P. (2000). Prisons: une humiliation pour la République: Rapport de commission d'enquête. Paris: Sénat.

Israël, L. (2003). "Faire émerger le droit des étrangers en le contestant, ou l'histoire paradoxale des premières années du GISTI." *Politix*, 62(16), pp. 115-143.

Lecerf, J.-R. and Borvo Cohen-Seat, N. (2012). Loi pénitentiaire de la loi à la réalité de la vie carcérale: Rapport d'information fait au nom de la commission des lois du Sénat. Paris: Sénat.

Mattéi, J.-B. (2010). Audition de la France par le Comité contre la torture des Nations unies." Hearing at the United Nations Office, Geneva, April 27.

Mermaz, L. and Floch, J. (2000). La France face à ses prisons: Rapport fait au nom de la commission d'enquête. Paris: Assemblée nationale.

OIP. (2007). "Les États généraux de la condition pénitentiaire: l'engagement sur parole." *Dedans-Dehors*, pp. 58–59.

Salle, G. and Chantraine, G. (2009). "Le droit emprisonné ?" *Politix*, 87(3), pp. 93-117.

Sarat, A. and Scheingold, S. (1998). Cause Lawyering: Political Commitments and Professional Responsibilities. Oxford: Oxford University Press.

Sauvé, J.-M. (2010). "Le principe de subsidiarité et la protection européenne des droits de l'homme.". Paper presented at In: the Conférences du Conseil d'État, Paris, April 19.

Sauvé, J.-M. (2008). "Le contrôle de l'administration pénitentiaire par le juge administratif." Paper presented at the In: Institut d'études judiciaires de l'Université de Lille II,. Paris, February 24.

Snacken, S. (2014). "Les structures européennes de contrôle des administrations pénitentiaires." *Déviance et Société*, 38(4), pp. 405–423.

Suremain (de), H. (2014). "Genèse de la naissance de la 'guérilla juridique' de l'OIP-SF et premiers combats contentieux." In: N. Ferran and S. Slama (eds.), *Défendre en justice la cause des personnes détenues*. Paris: La Documentation française, pp. 47–52.

Suremain (de), H. and Bérard, J. (2009). "La gestion des longues peines au révélateur des luttes juridiques." *Champ pénal/Penal Field*, [Online], 6 uploaded on December 31, 2009. URL : http://champpenal.revues.org/7698 ; DOI : 10.4000/champpenal.7698

Van Zyl Smit, D. and Snacken, S. (2009). *Principles of European Prison Law and Policy: Penology and Human Rights*. Oxford: Oxford University Press.

4 The Dutch complaint and appeal procedure for prisoners in the light of European standards

Pauline Jacobs and Anton Van Kalmthout

Introduction

For a long time, the Netherlands has served as an example with regard to treatment of prisoners and prison conditions.[1] The Second World War resulted in an increasing awareness that people who are deprived of their liberty should be treated humanely has, *inter alia*, led to the creation of a system of rights of complaint and appeal for prisoners. This system is firmly rooted in the Penitentiary Principles Act (*Penitentaire beginselenwet*).[2] This system of legal protection for prisoners is unique in the world.

In this chapter, we will investigate the European standards for domestic complaints procedures set up by the European Court of Human Rights (ECtHR) and the European Committee for the Prevention of Torture and Inhuman or Degrading Treatment or Punishment (CPT). We will assess if, and if so to what extent, the Dutch system of rights of complaint and appeal for prisoners is in line with these European standards. First, we will investigate the standards for national complaint and appeal procedure for prisoners as formulated by the ECtHR. Second, we will scrutinise the standards as formulated by the CPT. Third, we will elaborate on the Dutch system of complaint and appeal for prisoners and its historical development. Finally, we will review the Dutch complaint and appeal procedure for prisoners in the light of the European standards.

1 ECtHR standards for complaint and appeal procedures for prisoners

Within the Council of Europe, traditionally much attention has been paid to issues relating to deprivation of liberty. This is reflected in the many recommendations on this point, most notably the European Prison Rules, lastly revised in 2006.[3] These rules very clearly outline the material rights of prisoners. Although these rules are not legally binding, they possess strong moral authority. In the European Prison Rules, much value is attached to an effective system of complaint and appeal procedures for prisoners in securing the protection of prisoners against ill-treatment, to which Rule 70 is dedicated. Rule 70.1 determines as a general rule that prisoners, individually or as a group, shall have ample opportunity to make requests or complaints to the director of the prison or to any other competent authority. If mediation seems appropriate this should be tried first (Rule 70.2). Rule 70.3 adds that if a request is denied or a complaint is rejected, reasons shall be provided to the prisoner and the prisoner shall have the right to appeal to an independent authority. Prisoners shall not be punished because of having made a request or having lodged a complaint (Rule 70.4). According to Rule 70.7 prisoners are also entitled to seek legal advice about complaints and appeals procedures and to legal assistance when the interests of justice require.

Although the ECHR does not contain articles that were written specifically for prisoners, the ECtHR in its case law has developed a system that affords protection to those deprived of their liberty. Article 3 ECHR has played an important role in guaranteeing protection against ill-treatment, containing the negative obligation for States to refrain from torture and from inhuman or degrading treatment or punishment. Article 3 ECHR is absolute and permits no derogation.[4] It has played a crucial role in cases where prisoners complained about their detention conditions or their treatment in prison. Nowadays, most complaints under Article 3 ECHR are brought to the ECtHR by prisoners.

Standards for national complaint and appeal procedure for prisoners have been formulated by the ECtHR within the framework of Article 13 ECHR. This article guarantees the right to an effective remedy by determining that "Everyone whose rights and freedoms as set forth in this Convention are violated shall have an effective remedy before a national authority notwithstanding that the violation has been committed by persons acting in an official capacity". Before lodging a complaint with the ECtHR as a rule all national remedies must be exhausted according to Article 35 ECHR. This rule is based on the assumption – reflected in Article 13 ECHR – that there is an effective remedy available to deal with the substance of an "arguable complaint" under the ECHR on the national level to grant appropriate relief. Article 35 ECHR, however, does not require that recourse should be added to remedies that are inadequate or ineffective.[5]

In the 1983 case of *Silver and others against the United Kingdom*, the ECtHR has developed general criteria for domestic remedies for prisoners to be qualified as "effective" in the sense of Article 13 ECHR:

> (a) where an individual has an arguable claim to be the victim of a violation of the rights set forth in the Convention, he should have a remedy before a national authority in order both to have his claim decided and, if appropriate, to obtain redress;
>
> (b) the authority referred to in Article 13 may not necessarily be a judicial authority but, if it is not, its powers and the guarantees which it affords are relevant in determining whether the remedy before it is effective;
>
> (c) although no single remedy may itself entirely satisfy the requirements of Article 13, the aggregate of remedies provided for under domestic law may do so;
>
> (d) neither Article 13 nor the Convention in general lays down for the Contracting States any given manner for ensuring within their internal law the

> effective implementation of any of the provisions of the Convention – for example, by incorporating the Convention into domestic law."[6]

These criteria were upheld and refined in later case law. In recent years, the ECtHR has identified concrete and specific elements that are relevant in determining whether domestic complaint and appeal procedures for prisoners can be qualified as "effective" in the sense of Article 13 ECHR. The following points were identified by the ECtHR in its case law.

First, the authority which deals with the grievances should have the mandate to monitor the violations of prisoners' rights and should be independent from the penitentiary system's bodies.[7] Within the domestic procedure there should also be a possibility to hear the complainant or to ensure his or her effective participation in the proceedings. In this way, the ECtHR requires the procedure to be adversarial. The ECtHR has acknowledged, in line with Rule 70.7 of the European Prison Rules, that to use available legal remedies the complainant should have the possibility to have access to legal assistance.[8] Besides, the supervisory authority must have the right to render binding and enforceable decisions within a reasonably short time limit.[9] A further requirement for a remedy to be "effective", is that it must be available not only in theory but also in practice. That a remedy is available in practice must be demonstrated by the government with examples of case-law of the relevant domestic courts or decisions of the administrative authorities.[10] The ECtHR, in this respect, has reiterated that Article 35 ECHR provides for a distribution of the burden of proof. When the state claims non-exhaustion of national remedies, it is incumbent on the state to satisfy the ECtHR that the remedy was an effective one available in theory and practice at the relevant time, i.e. that it was accessible, was capable of providing redress in respect of the applicant's complaints and offered reasonable prospects of success.[11]

The ECtHR has acknowledged that an efficient system of detainees' complaints is an important safeguard for the prevention of violations of Article 3 ECHR on the domestic level. According to the ECtHR, "[t]o be efficient, the system must ensure a prompt and diligent handling of prisoners' complaints, secure their effective participation in the examination of grievances, and provide a wide range of legal tools for the purpose of eradicating the identified breach of Convention requirements".[12] In the area of complaints about inhuman or degrading conditions of detention under Article 3 ECHR, the ECtHR observed in the case of *Varga and other against Hungary* that two types of relief are possible: an improvement in the material conditions of detention and compensation for the damage or loss sustained on account of such conditions.[13] With this, the ECtHR requires both a preventive and compensatory remedy. The preventive remedy entails that if the applicant is held under inhuman or degrading conditions of detention there must be a domestic remedy in place to put an end to the ongoing violation. The compensatory remedy entails that when the applicant is released after having endured these inadequate condition, he should have an enforceable right to compensation for the violation that has occurred.[14] In cases concerning Article 3 ECHR, the preventive and compensatory remedies have to be complementary in order to be considered effective. Compensatory remedy alone is in the view of the ECtHR not enough, since "the prospect of future compensation would legitimate particularly severe suffering in breach of this core provision of the Convention and unacceptably weaken the legal obligation on the State to bring its standards of detention into line with the Convention requirements".[15] A combination of both remedies is thus required, not only to compensate the prisoner for the grievance he has suffered, but also to urge Member States to make sure that practices are amended in line with Article 3 ECHR and future violations are prevented.

2 CPT standards for complaint and appeal procedures for prisoners

The importance of Article 3 ECHR inspired the drafting of the 1987 European Convention for the Prevention of Torture and Inhuman or Degrading Treatment or Punishment. Article 1 of this Convention established the CPT. The aim of the CPT is to prevent torture and inhuman or degrading treatment or punishment (together referred to as ill-treatment) and it places a non-judicial preventive mechanism alongside the judicial reactive mechanism of the ECtHR. The CPT exercises its preventive task through its periodic follow-up and ad-hoc visits to places where people are deprived of their liberty, such as police stations, prisons, holding centres for immigration detainees, psychiatric hospitals and so on. During these visits, the CPT has the power to move around without restriction, to talk to prisoners in private and to access any information necessary to investigate whether there is a risk of ill-treatment. The CPT has developed Standards for some of the substantive issues which it pursues when carrying out visits. The CPT reports that are drawn up after its visits, complemented by the general reports (which are drawn up every year) and the CPT Standards, provide detailed information on how persons deprived of their liberty should be treated. In this way, the CPT seeks to provide States with clear guidelines on how persons who are deprived of their liberty ought to be treated and, more generally, to stimulate discussion on such matters.[16] Even though the CPT Standards and reports are not binding on States, the CPT has developed its own standards and safeguards for prisons and other places of detention in a more detailed manner than any other European instrument in order to be able to monitor conditions in prisons and other places of detention more objectively (Morgan, 2001, 717; Murdoch, 2006, 45). Over the years, the CPT has become a "fact finder" for the ECtHR. In addition to this fact-finding task, the CPT has increasingly become a creator in new penal law and policy (Morgan, 2001), as CPT norms are more often applied in individual cases before the ECtHR,[17] especially in cases in which the ECtHR is confronted with aspects of detention regarding which the ECtHR has not previously ruled (Van Zyl Smit and Snacken, 2009).

Like the ECtHR, the CPT considers effective grievance and inspection procedures as fundamental safeguards against ill-treatment and other types of abuse of authority in prisons. This means that "prisoners should have avenues of complaint open to them both within and outside the context of the prison system, including the possibility to have confidential access to an appropriate authority".[18] This is not only in the interest of the prisoners themselves, because a well-functioning complaints system can also "serve as a valuable source of information for prison management about potential problems in the establishments as well as allaying tension among prisoners by ensuring that their concerns are treated seriously and, where appropriate, that suitable remedies are proposed".[19] The daily practice is, however, that in many countries the complaints and appeal systems are not functioning as a real safeguard for persons deprived of their liberty. In many of its visits reports the CPT has repeatedly commented on shortcomings in the existing domestic complaints and appeal procedures. The recommendations intended to solve these shortcomings refer sometimes to the standards as set by the ECtHR and the European Prison Rules but also contain a long list of additional criteria for reliable and effective domestic systems of complaint and appeal procedures. As for the ECtHR, a vital issue for the CPT is whether a complaint may result in an improvement in the prisoner's situation or a form of compensation for the grievance suffered.

According to the CPT a reliable and effective complaints procedure, however, must also offer the prisoner at least the following guarantees.

1) All prisoners should be provided with precise written information on the avenues of complaint available to them, as well as with confidential access to the bodies authorised to receive complaints. They should be given a standard complaints form covering all categories of complaints. These forms should be freely available and not be subject to a specific application to the Governor. In case of indigent prisoners, the prison authorities should make arrangements for the provision of free-of-charge writing paper, envelopes and stamps.[20]
2) The complaints procedure should offer appropriate guarantees of confidentiality, independence, impartiality and thoroughness.[21]
3) Prisoners should be able to place the complaints in a locked complaints box (to be opened only by specially designated persons), located in each accommodation unit. Serious misgivings have been expressed by the CPT about the practice in some countries that the lodging of a complaint with an outside authority is systematically brought to the management of the establishment where the prisoner concerned is held, because this "is almost certainly not conductive to prisoners developing a sense of trust in complaints procedures".[22]
4) Expeditious investigation is of key importance to the effective functioning of the complaints system. Therefore, in all cases, the investigation should be carried out expeditiously (with any delays justified) and prisoners should be informed within clearly defined time periods of the action taken to address their concern or of the reasons for considering the complaint not justified.[23]
5) The existence of an internal complaints procedure may never prohibit a prisoner to lodge a complaint to an external, independent body.[24]
6) All written complaints should be registered centrally within a prison before being allocated to a particular service for consideration. In all cases, internal complaints should be processed expeditiously (with any delays duly justified in writing) and prisoners should be informed in writing, within clearly

defined time periods, of the action taken to address their concerns or of the reasons for considering the complaint not justified. In addition, statistics on the types of internal complaints made should be kept as an indicator to the management of areas of discontent within the prison.[25]

7) Prisoners may never be deterred from making a complaint by the fear of counter disciplinary action and complaints lodged at internal level may never result in some form of punishment of the prisoner concerned. The necessary steps should be taken to ensure that any information suggesting that a prisoner has been subjected to threats and/or reprisals for having exercised his/her right to lodge applications or complaints is investigated properly and, if confirmed, that this results in appropriate sanctions.[26]
8) It is also in the interests of both prisoners and prison staff that clear disciplinary procedures be both formally established and applied in practice; any grey zones in this area involve the risk of seeing unofficial (and uncontrolled) systems developing. Disciplinary procedures should provide prisoners with a right to be heard on the subject of the offences it is alleged they have committed, and to appeal to a higher authority against any sanctions imposed.[27]
9) Juveniles should have avenues for complaint open to them within the establishments' administrative system and should be entitled to address complaints – on a confidential basis – to an independent authority. Complaints procedures should be simple, effective and child-friendly, particularly regarding the language used. Juveniles (as well as their parents or legal representatives) should be entitled to seek legal advice about complaints and to benefit from free legal assistance when the interests of justice so require.[28]

In these standards, several of the ECtHR's standards can be recognised, such as the importance attached to ensure a prompt and diligent handling of prisoners' complaints and the independency of the body dealing with the complaints. Some of these CPT standards also correspond with the standards on requests and complaints of art. 70.1–70.7 of the European Prison Rules. At the same time, the CPT standards focus more on specific and practical aspects, such as confidential access to the complaints authority. They provide guidance in a more detailed manner on how to arrange for a reliable and effective complaints procedure. In this way, the standards as formulated by the CPT form an addition to the more general standards of the ECtHR and the European Prison Rules.

3 The Dutch system of complaint and appeal for prisoners

3.1 A short history of the right to complaint and appeal for prisoners

As stated in the introduction, the Second World War resulted in an increasing awareness of the need for improvements in the Dutch prison system. This development was inspired by the fact that many people of the Dutch resistance against the German dictatorship had personally experienced the tough circumstances in prison during the war. This awareness led to major reforms in prison legislation, despite the limited amount of resources available in these years.

In 1947, the Fick Committee presented a report that formed the basis for the new 1953 Penal System (Framework) Act (*Beginselenwet Gevangeniswezen*). This new law introduced an external supervision system for prisons, prescribing that each penitentiary institution had to be supervised by an independent Supervisory Committee (*Commissie van Toezicht*), consisting of 6–15 members of the general public. Amongst the Supervisory Committee, there must at least be a member of the judiciary, a lawyer, a medical practitioner and a social work expert. Originally the main tasks of the Supervisory Committee were to oversee the enforcement of custodial sentences, to take cognizance of any grievances lodged by prisoners, to maintain regular and personal contact with prisoners and to advise the Minister of Justice, the prison governor and the Central Board for the Administration of Justice (transformed since 1998 into the Council for the Administration of Criminal Justice and Protection of Juveniles, *Raad voor Strafrechtstoepassing en Jeugdbescherming*). This provided the Supervisory Committee with the possibility to counterbalance the powerful role of the prison governor in decisions regarding daily life in prison and the treatment of prisoners. Despite growing awareness in the 1960s and 1970s that deprivation of liberty only involves a loss of the right to physical liberty and no more than that (and that, as a result, prisoners should be limited in their rights no more than strictly necessary for the deprivation itself), it took until the revision of the Penal System (Framework) Act in 1977 before prisoners were entitled to lodge complaints with an external, independent body about decisions taken against them in the penitentiary institution. Until then, prisoners could only informally bring complaints under the attention of the Supervisory Committee. To keep the complaint procedure smart, quick and accessible for the prisoner, the law assigned the handling of these complaints to a special committee of the Supervisory Committee, attached to every penitentiary institution. This Complaints Committee (*beklagcommissie*) is composed of three members of the Supervisory Committee, the chairman preferably being a member of the judiciary. The Complaints Committee can take binding decisions. The governor and the complainant may appeal against the Complaints Committee's decision by taking their case to the Appeals Committee comprised of the Council for the Administration of Criminal Justice and Protection of Juveniles.

In 1998, the Penal System (Framework) Act was replaced with the Penitentiary Principles Act (PPA, *Penitentiaire beginselenwet*) and the Penitentiary Order (*Penitentiaire Maatregel*). Except for some minor changes, this new Act, which is still in force today, upheld the basis and structure of the justice system for prisoners, including the right to lodge a complaint and to appeal the decisions of the Complaints Committee. The procedure to file a complaint and to make an appeal carries a strong administrative-law character.[29]

The most significant decisions of the Complaints Committee are published online,[30] as well as all the jurisprudence of the Appeals Committee of the Council for the Administration of Criminal Justice and Protection of Juveniles. The most important decisions are published and annotated in the journal *Sancties*. The many decisions by the Appeals Committee are an important and rich source of information on the legal position of prisoners and many different aspects of prison life, not only for legal scholars, but also for, e.g., legal practitioners, prisoners and prison governors.

3.2 The current system of complaint and appeal for prisoners

3.2.1 Complaints (Articles 60–68 PPA)

On the basis of Article 56 PPA, every prisoner should be informed about his rights, including his right to file a complaint and appeal upon arrival in the prison. This information should be in writing, in a language he understands. In practice, this is mostly done by handing the prisoner a copy of the house rules, which is available in different languages. According to Article 60 PPA each prisoner may file a complaint with the Complaints Committee concerning a decision taken by or on behalf of the governor. Complaints can also be lodged on the grounds of delayed or the absence of decision making. The taking of a decision shall be deemed omitted or refused if a decision is not taken within the statutory term or – when such term is not defined – is not taken within a reasonable time. The restriction "decisions taken by or on behalf of the governor" means that no complaints are possible against purely factual behaviour of the staff that cannot be seen as belonging to their executive duty. Complaints on general rules or regulations that are applicable to all prisoners are also excluded. The only way to challenge general rules is to institute interim relief proceedings (*kort geding*) at the civil court. When a prisoner wants to make a complaint, he must file his complaint with the Complaints Committee of the penitentiary institution where the decision was taken. This must be done no later than seven days after the day of which the prisoner is notified of the decision. A complaint filed after the end of this period shall nevertheless be admissible if, in reason, it cannot be concluded that the prisoner is in default. The written complaint must mention as accurately as possible the decision to which the complaint relates and the reasons for the complaint. The complaint must be written in Dutch, but – if needed – may be written in another language (Article 61 PPA).

To guarantee a confidential procedure, prisoners can make use of standard complaints forms that can posted in special post boxes. Only members of the Supervisory Committee have access to these boxes. After having received a copy of the complaint by the secretary of the Complaints Committee the governor must provide the Committee with his written comments and opinion on the prisoner's complaint. The complainant also receives a copy of this reply. To avoid a formal hearing and to try to deal with the complaint in a more informal way the secretary of the Complaints Committee may hand over the complaint to a member of the Supervisory Committee – who is not member of the Complaints Committee – with the request to try to mediate between the detainee and the governor (Article 63 PPA). After a successful mediation the case will be dropped. Otherwise, the complaint is reviewed by the Complaints Committee, consisting of three members of the Supervisory Committee, unless the chairman of the Complaints Committee regards the complaint as simple or as manifestly inadmissible or manifestly unfounded. If that is the case, he can review the complaint on his own (Article 62 PPA). If the case is dealt with by the entire Complaints Committee, the applicant as well as the governor are invited to a non-public hearing[31] during which both parties are heard and can ask each other questions and react to each other's statements. The Complaints Committee may also obtain written and oral information from other persons. The complainant is entitled to be assisted free of charge by a lawyer and – if needed- an interpreter (Article 65 PPA). An important safeguard for the complainant is that pending the outcome of the complaint review, the chairman of the Appeals Committee may at the complainant's request, and after hearing the governor, suspend all or part of the implementation of the decision to which the complaint relates (Article 66 PPA). After the oral hearing, the Complaints Committee must deliver a decision on the complaint within four – in exceptional circumstances eight – weeks counting from the date on which the complaint was received (Article 67, paragraph 1 PPA). This decision must, in principle, be in writing, although the law allows the chairman of the Complaints Committee to communicate the decision orally to the parties. However, if one of the parties decides to lodge an appeal, a written report still has to be made. The decision must be reasoned and dated and must contain a report of the hearing. It has also to mention the possibility for both parties of appealing to the Appeals Committee (Article 67 PPA). If the complainant has insufficient command of the Dutch language, a translation in a language he understands will be provided free of charge (Article 67 PPA).

In its decision, the Complaints Committee declares the complaint as wholly or partly a) inadmissible, b) unfounded or c) founded. A complaint must be declared founded if the Complaints Committee concludes that the decision to which the complaint relates 1) is contrary to a statutory regulation in force in the prison or a provision binding upon all parties of a treaty in force in the Netherlands; or 2) is unreasonable or unjust, if all interests in the case are weighed up. If a complaint is declared fully or partly well-founded the Complaints Committee has the following options: It may 1) instruct the governor to take a new decision in conformity with the decision of the Complaints Committee, 2) annul the decision of the governor by replacing it with its own decision, 3) limit itself to an annulment in whole or in part. When the annulment concerns a decision of the governor that has already been implemented and cannot be reversed, the Complaints Committee can determine that the complainant will be compensated. This compensation may be given in kind, such as extra visit(s) or telephone calls, but also financial compensation is possible. To this end the Appeals Committee has formulated certain compensation tariffs to harmonize the compensation amounts that are applied by the Complaints Committees.[32] These amounts have a symbolic rather than a real compensatory character (Article 68 PPA).

3.2.2 Appeal (Articles 69–71 PPA)

Both the claimant and the governor may lodge an appeal against the decision of the Complaints Committee within seven days after having received the decision. They may file their appeal to the Appeals Committee *(Beroepscommissie*) of the

Council for the Administration of Criminal Justice and Protection of Juveniles. This Council, with its 75 members, appointed by the Crown, has two separate sections: the Section Advice and the Section for the Administration of Justice. The Appeals Committee operates in varying composition of three members from the Section for the Administration of Justice, assisted by a secretary of the Council. The Appeals Committee deals not only with appeals concerning all penitentiary institutions, but is also the appeal instance for juveniles in juvenile institutions and persons with a hospital order who stay in a forensic hospital.

Generally, the appeal procedure and the competences of the Appeals Committee are the same as described for the Complaints Committee. There are, however, some differences: in appeal mediation is excluded, the appeal review is always done by three members, the judgment should always be in writing and the law prescribes only that the decision in appeal has to be delivered as soon as possible, without determining a time limit. Furthermore, the Appeals Committee may determine that a) the governor and the complainant are given the opportunity to clarify the notice of appeal only in writing; b) the oral comments can be made before a member of the Appeals Committee and c) in case oral information is obtained from another person, the governor and the complainant are exclusively given the opportunity to submit in writing the questions they wish to ask that person (Article 69 PPA).

The Appeals Committee can decide

a) to declare the appeal as wholly or partially inadmissible; or
b) to wholly or partly confirm the resolution of the Complaints Committee, either with adoption or with improvement of the grounds; or
c) wholly or partly annul the Complaints Committee's resolution. If that is the case, the Appeals Committee will do what the Complaints Committee should have done (Article 71 PPA).

The appeal procedure does not suspend the implementation of the decision of the Complaints Committee, except when this decision also allows a compensation to the complainant. However, pending the outcome of the appeal review, the chairman of the Appeals Committee may, at the request of the person who lodged the appeal, and after hearing the other persons involved, suspend all or part of the implementation of the decision of the Complaints Committee (Article 70 PPA).

3.2.3 Special procedures (Articles 72–74 PPA)

The complaints and appeal system as described in the previous paragraphs is applicable to adult detainees in all types of prisons and, except few differences, also to juveniles in youth detention centres and detainees in forensic psychiatric institutions. The respective provisions are laid down in Articles 65–78 of the Young Offenders Institutions (Framework) Act *(Beginselenwet justitiële jeugdinrichtingen*) and Articles 56–70 of the Hospital Orders (Framework) Act (*Beginselenwet verpleging ter beschikkinggestelden*). In all three laws, the right to complain is restricted to decisions taken by or on behalf of the governor. This means that the decisions taken by an authority other than the governor are beyond the reach of the complaint provisions. This is especially the case with respect to the decisions of the penitentiary consultant (Article 15 PPA) and decisions on medical intervention by or on behalf of the physician of the institution.

The penitentiary consultant (*selectiefunctionaris*) is an external public servant who decides where a prisoner should be placed. Prisoners who disagree with his committal to the selected penitentiary institution, or his transfer to another institution may submit a reasoned objection that is dealt with by the same penitentiary consultant (Article 17 PPA). If the prisoner is not satisfied with the decision about his objection, he can lodge an appeal with the Appeals Committee that will deal with the case as described before. Also, the decisions of the medical staff are not decisions taken by or on behalf of the governor. A prisoner who wants to object to a decision taken against him by a member of the medical staff has first to make a written request to the Medical Adviser of the Ministry of Safety and Justice to mediate in the dispute. If mediation is not possible, the prisoner can still lodge an appeal with the Appeal Committee of the Council for the Administration of Criminal Justice and Protection of Juveniles. In this case, the composition of the Appeals Committee that is dealing with medical issues must consist of a legal expert and two physicians. The provisions with respect to these medical appeals, as laid down in Articles 28–34 of the Penitentiary Order, are not different from the provisions for ordinary appeals. Noteworthy is that the rights conferred to the prisoner with respect the appeal procedure may also be carried out by a) the trustee if the prisoner has been placed under legal restraint; b) the mentor if a mentorship has been established for the benefit of the prisoner and c) the parents or guardian in case the prisoner is a minor. However, the Medical adviser or the Appeals Committee may veto this right in case they consider this not being in the interest of the prisoner (Article 34 Penitentiary Order).

4 Current use of the complaint and appeal procedure in the Netherlands

In 2015, the number of complaints taken to the Complaints Committees of 24 prisons which accommodated in that year about 40.000 prisoners was 15 065. Due to this high number – in some prisons the annual number of complaints was between 1500 and 2500 – the Complaints Committees in many cases needed more weeks for reviewing the complaints than the prescribed four. Also because of the high number of complaints, in many cases the Complaints Committee deals with cases not in a bench sitting with three members, but complaints are dealt with by only one member, assisted by the Secretary of the Committee.

The list of grievances which gave cause to lodge a complaint concerned issues that are of high importance in the day to day life of prisoners: labour and activity programmes, outdoor exercise, treatment, contact with the outside world, disciplinary sanctions and security measures, regime, medical care, information, personal belongings, prison leaves and financial items. With respect to 14 477 complaints the case could be settled. In 15 per cent the complaint was withdrawn after mediation, 18 per cent were declared not admissible and 25 per cent not founded.

Only 8 per cent were considered well-founded by the Complaints Committee and 1.5 per cent partly founded. The remaining 10 per cent concerned mainly complaints that were transferred to and dealt with by another institution.[33]

Also, the Appeals Committee of the Council for the Administration of Criminal Justice and Protection of Juveniles is confronted with a high caseload every year. In 2015, the total number of new cases amounted to 4 454. Together with the remaining cases from the previous year the caseload in 2016 was 5 262. Of these cases 1 133 concerned requests for suspending decisions of the governor or the Complaints Committee. Most appeal cases (2 768) were appeals against decisions of the Complaints Committee of the prisons. Of these cases 42 per cent were dealt with after an oral hearing, the remaining 58 per cent were settled in writing. The number of appeals against decisions of the Complaints Committees of forensic psychiatric hospitals amounted to 671 of which 62 per cent were settled after an oral hearing. From the 83 appeals against decisions of the Complaints Committees for juvenile institutions 62 per cent were settled by the Appeals Committee after an oral hearing. The 75 appeals concerning medical interventions were almost all dealt with by an oral hearing. The Appeals Committee needed 92 sessions for all the oral hearings. Although the Appeals Committee strives to handle an appeal case within four months it realised this target norm only in 44 per cent of the cases.[34]

Judging by the number of complaints and appeals that are being dealt with by the Complaints and Appeals Committees on a yearly basis, one could say that the right to complain and appeal has become an important and indispensable "touchstone for the lawfulness and quality of the police of prisons", as intended by the legislator in 1977.[35] However, the high number of complaints puts pressure on the current complaint and appeal procedure. In many cases, complaints cannot be dealt with within the prescribed four weeks and the different Complaints Committees and Appeals Committee suffer from a huge caseload. Still, the complaint and appeal procedure remains to have an important function in the Dutch prison system, as it not only provides relief for prisoners who claim to have been the victim of unlawful treatment in prison, but it has also created a normative framework for the assessment of treatment in prison, which has a strong preventive function. Besides, as noted by the Council for the Administration of Criminal Justice and Protection of Juveniles in 2011, it works as an effective vent for feelings of unrest in prisoners by extracting the pressure of the boiler.[36]

Conclusion

The existence of effective grievance procedures is one of the most important fundamental safeguards against ill-treatment and other types of abuse of authority in places where persons are deprived of their liberty. Across Europe, a wide range of different complaint and appeal mechanisms can be found. However, the mere existence of such mechanism does not mean that it also forms an effective safeguard against ill-treatment. To be effective such a system has to comply with certain criteria, as formulated by the European Prison Rules, the ECtHR and the CPT. Over the years, the CPT has concluded that in many countries of the Council of Europe adequate complaint and appeal procedures for prisoners are lacking or inadequate. For this reason, the CPT has decided to pay specific attention to this topic in its 2017 General Report.

The Netherlands belongs to the few countries where the complaint and appeal system has gotten a high approval rating by the ECtHR and the CPT.[37] Except the fact that not all complaints and appeals can be settled within the prescribed time limits, one can conclude that the Dutch system reflects the main criteria as set by the ECtHR, the European Prison Rules and the CPT: the procedure is smart, easily accessible and based on confidentiality (Hagens 2011). It provides a preventive and compensatory remedy because the grievances are dealt with by an external, independent body that has the competence to issue binding and enforceable decisions and the power to redress complainant's situation or – if that is not possible anymore – to provide financial or other forms of compensation. It is also an effective remedy because of the effective participation of the prisoner in the complaint and appeal procedure and because of his entitlement to assistance of a lawyer.

Notes

1 In this contribution, the term 'prisoner' not only refers to persons who are deprived of their liberty in connection with a suspected or proven criminal offence but also to irregular migrants who are detained in detention centres for migrants and who are subject to the same penitentiary laws as criminal suspects or sentenced prisoners.

2 See for more details: P. Jacobs, 'The Development of *Rechtsburgerschap* of Prisoners: A National and European Perspective', in: F. de Jong (ed.), *Overarching Views of Crime and Deviancy: Rethinking the Legacy of the Utrecht School*, The Hague: Eleven International Publishing 2015, pp. 385–399.

3 Recommendation (2006) 2 of the Committee of Ministers on the European Prison Rules.

4 This has been emphasized in the case law of the ECtHR, see *inter alia* ECtHR 1 June 2010, *Gäfgen v. Germany* (Grand Chamber), app.no. 22978/05, par. 123–124.

5 ECtHR 21 December 2000, *Egmez v. Cyprus*, app.no. 30873/96, par. 65.

6 ECtHR 25 March 1983, *Silver and others v. the UK*, app.nos. 5947/72, 6205/73, 7052/75, 7061/75, 7107/75, 7113/75 and 7136/75, par. 113.

7 ECtHR 10 January 2012, *Ananyev and others v. Russia*, app.nos. 42525/07 and 60800/08, par. 215.

8 ECtHR 6 September 2016, *Alimov v. Turkey*, app.no. 14344/13, par. 66.

9 ECtHR 10 January 2012, *Ananyev and others v. Russia*, app.nos. 42525/07 and 60800/08, par. 104, 106 and 216.

10 ECtHR 10 March 2015, *Varga and others v. Hungary*, app.nos. 14097/12, 45135/12, 73712/12, 34001/13, 44055/13 and 64586/13, par. 50 and ECtHR 10 January 2012, *Ananyev and others v. Russia*, app.nos. 42525/07 and 60800/08, par. 110 and ECtHR 6 September 2016, *Alimov v. Turkey*, app.no. 14344/13, par. 66.

11 See, e.g. ECtHR 14 June 2016, *Pugžlys v. Poland*, app.no. 446/10, par. 43.

12 ECtHR 10 January 2012, *Ananyev and others v. Russia*, app.nos. 42525/07 and 60800/08, par. 214.

13 ECtHR 10 March 2015, *Varga and others v. Hungary*, app.nos. 14097/12, 45135/12, 73712/12, 34001/13, 44055/13 and 64586/13, par. 48.

14 ECtHR 10 March 2015, *Varga and others v. Hungary*, app.nos. 14097/12, 45135/12, 73712/12, 34001/13, 44055/13 and 64586/13, par. 48.

15 ECtHR 10 March 2015, *Varga and others v. Hungary*, app.nos. 14097/12, 45135/12, 73712/12, 34001/13, 44055/13 and 64586/13, par. 49.

16 The full text of the CPT Standards, as well as all published reports on CPT visits to States Parties, together with the responses of the authorities concerned, can be accessed on the CPT's website: <www.cpt.coe.int/en/> (last accessed on 2 January 2017).
17 See chapter 1 in this book.
18 Denmark: Visit 2002/par. 63.
19 Czech Republic: Visit 2010/par. 21.
20 Estonia: Visit 2012/par. 102, Moldova: Visit 2015/par. 144, Sweden: Visit 2015/par.101, Gibraltar: Visit 2004/par.58.
21 FYROM: Visit 2007/par. 50.
22 Visit 2015/par. 110, Bulgaria: Visit 2010/par. 149.
23 Ireland: Visit 2014/par. 83.
24 Bulgaria: Visit 2010/par.149, Ireland: Visit 2010/par. 103.
25 Georgia: Visit 2014/par. 126, Greece: Visit 2015/ par.95, Finland: Visit: 2014/par. 90, Denmark: Visit 2014/ par.73.
26 United Kingdom: Visit 1990/par. 182, Bosnia/Herzegovina: Visit 2015/par. 119.
27 CPT 12th General report 2002/par. 55.
28 CPT/Inf/C (2002) [rev.2015] Section: 77/86, 21/01/2015.
29 C. Kelk (edited by M. Boone), *Nederlands detentierecht*, Deventer: Kluwer 2015, p. 8.
30 On www.commissievantoezicht.nl/uitspraken-zoeken/ (last accessed on 2 January 2017).
31 According to Article 62, paragraph 4 PPA a public hearing is only prescribed in case "the Complaints Committee is of the opinion that a non-public review is incompatible with any stipulation binding upon all parties of a treaty in force in the Netherlands".
32 These compensation tariffs are published on <www.rsj.nl/Rechtspraak/Rechtspraak procedure/> (last accessed on 2 January 2017).
33 These numbers are based on the annual reports of the Prison Supervisory Committees and published on <http://dji.nl/over-dji/organisatiestructuur/commissie-van-toezicht/index.aspx> (last accessed on 2 January 2017).
34 These numbers are taken from the annual report 2016 of the Council for the Administration of Justice and Youth Protection, pp. 45–56. See <www.rsj.nl/Over-de-Raad/Jaarverslagen/> (last accessed on 2 January 2017).
35 See: Explanatory Notes to the Penitentiary Principles Act, in: Handboek rechtspositie gedetineerden, SDU Den Haag 2001, p. 147.
36 Raad voor Strafrechtstoepassing en Jeugdbescherming, Reactie op het rapport 'Toenemend appel', een verkennend onderzoek van de Erasmus Universiteit Rotterdam naar de toename van het aantal beroepszaken ex artikel 69 van de Penitentiaire beginselenwet, Den Haag 2011, p. 22.
37 See: ECtHR 10 January 2012, *Ananyev and others v. Russia*, app.nos. 42525/07 and 60800/08, par. 215 and CPT Report to the Netherlands 1992, par. 144, Report to the Netherlands 2007, par. 49, Report to the Netherlands 2013, par. 49–50 and Report to the Netherlands 2017, par.79.

References

Books and articles

Author unknown. (2001). *Handboek rechtspositie gedetineerden*. Netherlands: SDU Den Haag.

de Lange, J. (2008). *Detentie Genormeerd: Een onderzoek naar de betekenis van het CPT voor de inrichting van vrijheidsbeneming in Nederland*. Nijmegen: Wolf Legal Publishers.

Hagens, M. (2011). Toezicht op menswaardige behandeling van gedetineerden in Europa: Een onderzoek naar de verhouding tussen het EHRM en het CPT bij de effectuering van het folterverbod. Nijmegen: Wolf Legal Publishers.

Jacobs, P. (2015). "The development of 'Rechtsburgerschap' of prisoners: A national and European perspective." In: F. de Jong (ed.), *Overarching Views of Crime and Deviancy: Rethinking the Legacy of the Utrecht School*. The Hague: Eleven International Publishing, pp. 385–399.

Kelk, C. (2015). *Nederlands Detentierecht*. Deventer: Kluwer.

Morgan, R. (2001). "The European Committee for the prevention of torture and inhuman or degrading punishment or treatment." In: D. Van Zyl Smit and F. Dünkel (eds.), *Imprisonment Today and Tomorrow: International Perspectives on Prisoners' Rights and Prison Conditions*. The Hague: Kluwer Law International, p. 717.

Murdoch, J. (2006). *The Treatment of Prisoners: European Standards*. Strasbourg: Council of Europe Publishing.

Van Zyl Smit, D. and Snacken, S. (2009). *Principles of European Prison Law and Policy: Penology and Human Rights*. Oxford: Oxford University Press.

Legislation, documents and reports

Recommendation (2006) 2 of the Committee of Ministers on the European Prison Rules.

Denmark: Visit 2002.

Czech Republic: Visit 2010.

Estonia: Visit 2012.

Moldova: Visit 2015.

Sweden: Visit 2015.

Gibraltar: Visit 2004.

FYROM: Visit 2007.

Armenia: Visit 2015.

Bulgaria: Visit 2010.

Ireland: Visit 2014.

Bulgaria: Visit 2010.

Ireland: Visit 2010.

Georgia: Visit 2014.

Greece: Visit 2015.

Finland: Visit: 2014.

Denmark: Visit 2014.

United Kingdom: Visit 1990.

Bosnia/Herzegovina: Visit 2015.

The Netherlands: Visit 1992.

The Netherlands: Visits 1992, 2007, 2013 and 2017.

CPT 12th General report 2002.

CPT/Inf/C (2002) [rev.2015].

Raad voor Strafrechtstoepassing en Jeugdbescherming, Reactie op het rapport 'Toenemend appel', een verkennend onderzoek van de Erasmus Universiteit Rotterdam naar de toename van het aantal beroepszaken ex artikel 69 van de Penitentiaire beginselenwet, Den Haag 2011.

Cases

European Court of Human Rights

ECtHR 1 June 2010, *Gäfgen v. Germany* (Grand Chamber), app.no. 22978/05.

ECtHR 21 December 2000, *Egmez v. Cyprus,* app.no. 30873/96.

ECtHR 25 March 1983, *Silver and others v. the UK*, app.nos. 5947/72, 6205/73, 7052/75, 7061/75, 7107/75, 7113/75 and 7136/75.
ECtHR 10 January 2012, *Ananyev and others v. Russia*, app.nos. 42525/07 and 60800/08.
ECtHR 6 September 2016, *Alimov v. Turkey*, app.no. 14344/13.
ECtHR 10 March 2015, *Varga and others v. Hungary*, app.nos. 14097/12, 45135/12, 73712/12, 34001/13, 44055/13 and 64586/13.
ECtHR 6 September 2016, *Alimov v. Turkey*, app.no. 14344/13.
ECtHR 14 June 2016, *Pugžlys v. Poland*, app.no. 446/10.

Part II

Curve and minor resistance to European monitoring

5 Marriage Italian style

A decryption of Italy and ECtHR's relationship concerning prisoners' rights

Giuseppe Caputo and Sofia Ciuffoletti[1]

Introduction

Concerning prison policies, Italy has gone from being the bad student of Europe to being among the teacher's pets within a five year time frame. This was due to the prompt answer that the Italian government provided as a redress after the finding of a violation of Article 3 of the Convention in two subsequent and highly publicized cases concerning inhuman and degrading prison conditions: *Sulejmanovic* and *Torreggiani*.

Both at the ECtHR and at the Committee of Ministers level, Italy convinced Europe that its strategy, a combination of compensatory and preventive remedies, along with other minor measures, was a successful one in order to achieve the goal of decreasing the endemic phenomenon of overcrowding and providing decent conditions of detention, respectful of the human rights enshrined in the 1950 European Convention. This article aims at deconstructing this idyllic version, investigating the whole Italian model of compliance with the European stimulus through the lens of the effectiveness of the protection of rights offered both at a European and domestic level.

We will use the principle of effectiveness (Arnull, 2011) extending the notion from its interpretative roots to a wider semantic area. As an interpretative tool, the principle of effectiveness is part of the judicial activist methods (along with the evolutive interpretation or living instrument doctrine and the doctrine of autonomous concepts[2]) and linked with the idea of the judicial creativity.[3] The essence of the doctrine of effectiveness is that States' compliance with the Convention cannot be limited to prohibiting conducts that contravene the Convention, they need to put in place positive actions. The Court, by using this approach, has elaborated a case law imposing positive obligations on contracting States. Following this theoretical perspective, we propose to evaluate the efforts made by Member States in order to conform to ECtHR's judgments on the basis of an empirical analysis of these actions, testing their suitability for the purpose of reducing the overcrowding rate in a long term perspective and of increasing prison conditions for each inmate (Schoenfeld, 2010; Simon, 2014), protecting their rights by making them justiciable (Francioni, 2007).

Our analysis relies on the EU-funded Prison Litigation Network project[4] and on the critical analysis of the Italian prison and penological system (Santoro, 2004 and 2015, Melossi and Pavarini, 1981) from a legal sociological standpoint, as well as on the literature on the European system of rights as a new *forum* for the protection of minorities and marginalities within our societies (Van Zyl Smit and Snacken, 2009). The fieldwork conducted across Italian prisons allowed us to measure the impact of the new system of remedies on the everyday life of prisoners and to assess the effective protection of their rights. Certainly, Europe has become a relevant context for the substantive justice of Italian prisoners and it can undoubtedly be affirmed that "there is a judge in Strasbourg" for Italian prisoners. Nevertheless, our study seeks to decode and evaluate the direct consequences of the measures implemented at a domestic level on the quality of life of prisoners in Italy, as well as the improvements in the protection of their rights.

1 Crime and punishment

1.1 The Europeanization of the Italian penitentiary system

During the last decade, the European Court has developed a consistent case law aiming at interpreting Article 3 of the Convention as to include a right for prisoners to be held in decent detention conditions (Van Zyl Smit and Snacken, 2009; Snacken, 2011). Italy has, since the beginning, became one of the most relevant context for the analysis of the Strasbourg Court's case law on the issue of prison conditions and overcrowding.

The first step taken by the Court in order to challenge the domestic prison condition in Italy is the Grand Chamber judgment *Sulejmanovic v. Italy*.[5] The judgment constitutes the first serious intervention of the European Court of Human Rights in the field of prison overcrowding and prison conditions in Italy, requiring a reflection over the domestic prison policy and legislation and demanding a revision of the persistent paradigm of systemic violation of some of the more basic prisoners' human rights.

This is a pivotal moment for Italy since it represents the very first time the inhuman and degrading condition of the Italian prison system becomes an open topic in the public debates. This confirms a trend toward the interpretation of the case law of international courts, and the Strasbourg court particularly, as the arena in which new conflicts arise and get solved, shaping the new grammar and the new semantic of rights in our contemporary societies (Stone Sweet, 2009; Keller and Stone Sweet, 2008). In this regard, the Sulejmanovic judgment has shown the potential impact of the European Court in a topical matter and has been received with great interest by the Italian media, prison professionals and scholars.[6]

The *Sulejmanovic* judgment was final in 2009 and a first set of deflationary measures was presented by the Italian Government in an action plan of 29 June 2012. These measures included changes to the law, with the introduction of a new form of house detention[7] and a program to build new prisons (so called *Piano Carceri*[8]). The measures entailed a decrease in the number of the Italian prison population. According to the data provided by the Italian Ministry of Justice, from 68.258 prisoners at the date of 30 of June 2010 the prison population decreased to 66.487 prisoners at the date of 31 of May 2012.

One very important issue remained nonetheless dramatically unsolved. The internal way of complaining to a judicial authority about the material conditions of detention in Italy showed a lack of effectiveness due to the generic nature of the measure itself. As stated by the Constitutional Court in judgment n. 26 of 1999, the Surveillance Court (*Tribunale di Sorveglianza*) is the judicial authority appointed to protect and guarantee the human rights of prisoners against any detrimental acts or decisions of the prison administration according to the principles and procedures set out in Articles 35 and 69 of the Italian Penitentiary Law. This principle was subsequently confirmed in the Constitutional Court decision n. 266 of 2009 but lacked a proper implementation in terms of a shared normative ideology from the part of the Surveillance Judges (Santoro, 2015) and due to the practical ineffectiveness of an eventual judgment establishing a violation. The dearth of a defined judicial procedure in this domain only increased the difficult access to a substantial protection for prisoners in the event of an administrative violation of their fundamental rights.

The situation was acknowledged as such in the further *Torreggiani* judgment, where a Pilot Judgment Procedure was enacted by the Court. The Court decided to apply this procedure in view of the growing number of persons potentially concerned in Italy and of the judgments finding a violation liable to result from the applications in question.

The Court concluded that the State must have put in place, within a year from the date in which the judgment became final, a set of effective domestic remedies combining a preventive and a compensatory function.

Contrary to the first pilot judgment on overcrowding and prison conditions, *Ananyev v Russia*,[9] the Court decided to adjourn the examination of applications dealing solely with overcrowding in Italian prisons during one year, pending the adoption of measures at national level. Comparing this provision with the *Ananyev* case, there seems to be a sort of "double standard" concerning the adjournment of similar cases in Pilot Judgment Procedures. In the *Ananyev* case, the Court, after having reminded that adjournment is a possibility rather than an obligation, as clearly shown by the inclusion of the words "as appropriate" in the text of Rule 61 § 6 and the variety of approaches used in the previous pilot judgments[10], evaluates that due to the "fundamental nature of the right protected by Article 3 of the Convention and the importance and urgency of complaints about inhuman or degrading treatment, does not consider it appropriate to adjourn the examination of similar cases".[11] On the contrary, the Court observes that "continuing to process all conditions-of-detention cases in a diligent manner will remind the respondent State on a regular basis of its obligations under the Convention and in particular those resulting from this judgment".[12] This safeguard seems no more operative in the *Torreggiani* case where, on the contrary, the Court chooses to adopt a more deferential approach and to adjourn all similar cases. We could argue that the Court had expectations of the diligent compliance of Italy, even if the scope and potential reach of a Pilot Judgment Procedure against a Member State also depends from decision. We shall see whether and how these expectations have been met.

1.2 Redemption: the Stella judgment and the execution procedure in front of the committee of ministers of the council of Europe

The decision in *Stella v. Italy*[13] offered a positive evaluation of the system of remedies put in place by the Italian government, considering that no evidence enabled the Court to find that those same remedies did not offer, "in principle", prospects of appropriate relief for the complaints submitted under Article 3 (prohibition of inhuman or degrading treatment) of the Convention.

Interestingly enough, the applications in the present case had been lodged before the entry into force of the new legislative provisions, thus allowing the Court to examine the situation at a time in which no remedy was available for the applicants. Nevertheless, respectfully asserting the crucial importance of its subsidiary role, the Court considered that there were grounds in the *Stella* case for departing from the general principle that the exhaustion requirement should be assessed with reference to the time at which the application was lodged and that this exception could apply to all similar cases pending before it.[14] Those exceptions seem to include specifically situations in which, after a Pilot Judgment Procedure, the State enacts a number of measures aimed at resolving the structural problem at a national level.[15] In order to solve the issue, the Italian law gave a six month time limit, starting from the date of the enactment of the law itself (June 2014) to prisoners who had already lodged an application to the ECtHR. The time frame between the *Stella* case (September 2014) and the end of the six month limit (December 2014) left almost no time for prisoners to learn about the deadline and to file an application in front of the domestic judiciary on time.

The analysis of the *Stella* judgment shows how the relevance conferred to the effectiveness of the remedies, stressed once and again in the reasoning of the judgment, conflicts with the idea that the "remedies did not offer, *in principle*,[16] prospects of appropriate relief".[17] Indeed, the principle of effectiveness at a European level can have multiple dimensions (Rietiker, 2010) and the *Stella* case clearly implies a more formalistic approach to effectiveness, tested according to specific data that presents a *prima facie* version of effectiveness, as we will try to prove *infra*.

Significantly, though, the Court underlines that the positive evaluation in *Stella* does not undermine an eventual future re-assessment of the effectiveness of the remedies, "notably considering the ability of domestic Courts to provide a uniform case-law that is compatible with the requirements of the Convention".[18]

The decision in *Stella* seemed a clear endorsement of the Italian way of dealing with overcrowding and inhuman and degrading prison conditions. Nevertheless, the real *imprimatur* of the Italian reforms was referred to the execution procedure in front of the Committee of Ministers. The Italian government submitted an action plan and various updated information, while communications were submitted by the NGO Radicali Italiani[19] and by the NGO l'Altro diritto.[20]

The Committee of Ministers with the Resolution CM/ResDH(2016)28,[21] "welcoming the response given by the Italian authorities to the *Torreggiani and Others* pilot judgment through the adoption of major reforms aimed at solving the problem of prison overcrowding and the significant results achieved to date in this area" decided to close the case.

This decision was a further and final *placet* towards the policies enacted by the Italian government in order to face the Pilot Judgment Procedure. Nevertheless, it is interesting to assess the level of consideration that the Committee of Ministers devotes to the effectiveness of the execution in cases of "enhanced supervision" (Lambert-Abdelgawad, 2010 and Shany, 2014). We can argue that in light of the shifting from an individual justice to a constitutional justice in the Strasbourg system (Greer and Wildhaber, 2012), the execution procedure has become less political and more transparent and rigorous (Shany, 2014), also due to the latest rules and working documents adopted by the Committee of Ministers.[22] We shall try to assess the level of attention devoted to the principle of effectiveness of compliance by using Italy as a case study.

1.3 Italy strikes back: the building of the Italian model

As a matter of facts, since the *Stella* judgment and the end of the Pilot Judgment Procedure ratified by the Committee of Ministers, the ECtHR has started to refer to the Italian way as a sort of positive paradigm for the compliance with this kind of Pilot Judgment Procedure. Significantly, the European Court refers to the Italian model of compliance in two subsequent Pilot Judgment Procedures in the *Neshkov and Others v. Bulgaria*[23] and *Varga and Others v. Hungary* cases.[24]

The Court in Neshkov assessed the effectiveness of the Italian preventive measure (art. 35 bis, Law 354/1975), proposing the Italian model to Bulgaria, underlining the judicial nature of the authority supervising prisons, monitoring violations of prisoners' rights and capable or rendering binding and enforceable decisions, indicating appropriate redress.[25]

Discussing possible models of compensatory remedies to be introduced in Bulgaria, the Court also evaluate Italy positively as a paradigmatic experience for tackling the issue of prison conditions and violations of Article 3. In order for the Bulgarian State to comply with the need for a general remedy allowing protection at the domestic level of the rights and freedoms enshrined in the Convention, in this case, the right not to be subjected to inhuman or degrading treatment.

"Another option is to put in place special rules laying down in detail the manner in which claims concerning conditions of detention are to be examined and determined, as was recently done in Italy" (see *Stella and Others*, cited above, §§ 19–20 and 56–63).[26]

In the *Varga* judgment, the Court makes an even more general statement, ratifying the favor for the Italian experience, by saying that:

"The recent example of Italy shows that such measures, implemented in the context of a pilot procedure, can contribute to solving the problem of overcrowding" (see *Stella and Others v. Italy* (dec.), nos. 49169/09, 16 September 2014).[27]

This positive evaluation of the Italian context will, in a recent future, need to take into account the real effectiveness of the interpretation and application of the new remedies by the Surveillance Judge (see *infra*), an issue that has so far shown a reluctant attitude and a restrictive legal reasoning that are potentially undermining the real reach of the so called "Italian model".

2 The Italian reaction

2.1 The Italian system of remedies ante Torreggiani

As a matter of facts, the system existing in Italy prior to the pilot judgment in Torregiani was judged ineffective by the ECtHR. Indeed, the Italian Penitentiary law (P.l.) provided few ad hoc remedies for the protection of prisoners' rights. Existing literature has often underlined that the affirmation of the constitutional rule of law and the recognition of human rights have never really affected the Italian penitentiary system (Bricola, 1977). The fascist penitentiary regulation survived 27 years to the Democratic Constitution of 1948, since the Italian Penitentiary law was adopted only in 1975. Also the adoption of the penitentiary law never led to a general recognition of prisoners' rights along with the introduction of effective remedies. Following the influence of the UN Standard minimum rules of 1955, the 1975 reform introduced a correctional normative model that still considers the prisoners as a sick individual, necessarily affected by physical or mental illnesses (Art. 13 of P.l.). This paternalistic approach implied the lack of a specific prisoners' rights list, rather these rights are an indirect consequence of the rules concerning the prison administration.

Consequently, the judicial system of prisoners' rights protection was very limited. The judicial authority competent for the protection of prisoners' rights in Italy was a special body, namely the Surveillance Court. This body, introduced for the first time with the fascist reform of the penitentiary system in 1931, was competent in the following subjects: supervise the organization of prisons, approve the prisoners' treatment programs, supervise the respect of prisoner's rights with special regard to disciplinary sanctions and prison labour, apply both alternative measures to imprisonment and security measures for "socially dangerous" offenders (e.g. internment in criminal asylum).

According to this system, a prisoner could apply to the Surveillance Court against a prison authority's decision in only two cases, namely violations of the norms concerning the disciplinary sanctions and the prison labour. In these cases, according to Article 14 ter of the Penitentiary law, the procedure was as follows: the prisoner could apply personally within 10 days from the violation and the Court had to decide within the following 10 days. Both the prisoner and the prison authority were only allowed to send written pleadings, while the procedure only allowed the participation of the prisoner's attorney and of the prosecutor in the chamber hearing.

In all other cases, a proper legal application against a prison authority's decision or behavior that infringed upon a prisoner's rights was not provided for by the law. Inmates could merely send non-judicial claims to the Court since Article 35 of the Penitentiary law stated that prisoners were able to communicate with the Judge with an oral or written "complaint" contained "in a sealed envelope".

The original paternalistic conception of the Penitentiary law has been partially outdated by the national jurisprudence that has developed judicial proceedings for the protection of prisoner's rights (a similar process occurs in other contexts such as in the US, see Jacobs, 1977). Firstly, the Italian judiciary gradually expanded the scope of the judicial appeal (Article 14. T P.1.) to all violations of prisoners' rights, going beyond the ones concerning disciplinary power and prison labour's rules.[28]

Secondly, it recognizes the judicial nature of the remedy provided by the Penitentiary law in Article 35. For a long time the Surveillance Courts' case law in the field of prisoners' rights was based on the principle that the Courts' decisions or orders were not binding on prison authorities, they were considered merely discretionary. This interpretation of powers frustrated the potential effectiveness of the Surveillance Courts' decisions and discouraged prisoners from applying against violations of their rights. Only in 2009 a Constitutional Court's judgment (n. 266 of 2009) made clear that the decisions of the Surveillance Courts are binding and that prison authorities have the duty to implement them. However, this decision did not solve the issue once and for all, since Surveillance Courts still lacked proper tools to enforce their orders.

Lastly, a Constitutional Court decision (no. 341 of 2006) ruled the unconstitutionality of Article 69 and affirmed the jurisdiction of the Ordinary Courts in the field of prison labour.

2.2 *First reaction to the ECtHR decision: the introduction of a preventive remedy*

The first reaction from the Italian Government to the requirements of the *Torreggiani*'s decision was the Law-Decree No. 146/2013 of December 2013. The law contained a wide range of norms, in order to reform the system for prisoners' rights protection (i.e. the provision of a national ombudsman and a new judicial procedural remedy to apply to Surveillance Courts) and to face overcrowding (e.g. the reform of the Italian law on drug in order to decrease sanctions and inhibit pre-trial custody for minor offences and a temporary expansion of day release benefit for most crimes).

The new preventive remedy provided for by Article 35 bis p.l. solves most of the problems of the previous system of judicial protection of prisoners' rights, even if it holds serious problems affecting its effectiveness.

According to the new remedy a prisoner can appeal directly, at every time and without any term, to the competent Surveillance Court by claiming a violation of the Penitentiary law by the prison authorities. The only substantial admissibility condition required by the norm is that the damage deriving from the violation has to be "ongoing" at the time of the claim. In case of violation of norms ruling on the application of disciplinary sanctions, the prisoner has to apply within 10 days from the communication of the disciplinary sanction.

The reform reaffirms the competence of the Surveillance Judge for the protection of prisoners' rights, specifically to the Surveillance Court in its monocratic composition. The remedy provided for by Article 35 bis can be used by all prisoners, including prisoners on remand and mentally ill interned, since the norm generically refers to "prisoners". The Law now finally requires the application of the general proceeding rules, regarding litigation and participation to the audition, instead of the special rules previously provided for by the Penitentiary law (Article 14 ter). The procedure to be applied is the one established for the criminal execution and provided for by Articles 666 and 678 of the Italian criminal procedure code. According to the general norms, the prisoner has to be assisted by an attorney who needs to be present, together with the Prosecutor, to the chamber audition. The prisoner can take part in the debate, while the prison administration can now participate in the debate and/or send written pleadings. The decision of the judge can be appealed to the Surveillance Court in its collegial composition (Surveillance Court) within 15 days, the decision of the Court can also appealed in front of the Supreme Court (Corte di Cassazione) within 15 days.

The reform has finally solved the problem of the unclear definition of the powers of the Surveillance Court. Now when the Surveillance Court finds a violation of a norm concerning the system of disciplinary sanctions, it can annul the prison authority's decision. In all other cases, the norm does not explicitly give to the Surveillance Court the power to annul any administrative decision, but it nonetheless states that the judge, "once verified the existence of an ongoing damage, orders the administration to amend it within a certain time frame". Article 35 also provides relevant tools to implement the Judge's decisions. Indeed, when the prison authorities do not enforce the order, the Surveillance Judge has the power to:

a) Schedule a detailed action plan addressed to the prison authority in order to remedy the violation;
b) Annul any decisions of the prison authority that violates the Court's decision;
c) Assign an *ad acta* Commissioner.

The application of the general rules regarding the access to the court and the definition of the powers of the court do not solve all the problems of inadequacy of the system in providing an effective protection to prisoners' rights violations. Indeed, three major concerns still remain. The first regards the term for the decision, since the proceeding does not guarantee a prompt judicial answer. The remedy does not provide any peremptory term for the Judge's decision, (it only implies terms in order to appeal). But the Surveillance Judge's decision is usually taken from three to six months after the prisoner's claim, while the appeal decision may arrive one year or more after the claim. The law does not provide any interim measures to be adopted in urgent cases (an imminent risk of irreparable harm), similar to the ones provided by Article 39 of ECtHR rules.

The second concern regards the complexity of the proceeding in order to appoint the ad acta commissioner, when the prison administration does not enforce the Judge's decision motu proprio. The compliance proceeding can be started only when the Judge's decision is no longer subject to appeal. Whenever the prison administration appeals against the Court's decision in front of the Supreme Court (which is almost always the case, as a traditional defensive strategy), the procedure may take one year or more from the appeal.

Another concern is the lack of rules regarding the burden of proof and the protection of prisoners from the risk of retaliation. Surveillance judges used to apply the judge-made principle affirmanti incumbit probatio, according to which the burden of proof is on the claimant. But the norm does not provide any specific tool facilitating prisoners in accessing any kind of documentation in order to support and substantiate her/his claim. Moreover, the prison administration seems to be under no obligation to provide any better proof than a simple standard report affirming its version of the events. The result is that whenever the word of the prisoners is set against the word of the prison administration, the latter prevails, completely reversing the principle constantly stated by the ECtHR case law on this aspect.

2.3 Second reaction to the ECtHR decision: the introduction of a compensatory remedy

Within the execution procedure, a decision of the Committee of Ministers of the Council of Europe[29]– that appreciated the new preventive remedies (Art. 35bis) but had also asked the Italian Government to carry forward the reform's process – led the Government to enact a new bill[30]introducing a compensatory remedy (Article 35 ter) to be used in cases of violation of Article 3 of the European Convention.

The new Article 35 ter explicitly defines the categories of prisoners covered by the protection of the compensatory remedy, namely all prisoners, including those convicted and on remand. The law breaks up with the tradition, adding a new competent judicial body for prisoner's rights, along with the Surveillance Court. Ordinary civil courts are competent for all the claims coming from prisoners on remand and former prisoners, while the Surveillance Judge (monocratic) is competent for all the claims coming from convicted prisoners.

As for the procedure in front of the Surveillance Court, a prisoner can apply directly in front of the competent Surveillance Judge, claiming a violation of Article 3 of the Convention. According to the new law, the Judge can compensate every time a violation of a right is so serious as to constitute a violation of Article 3 of the Convention. To guide the domestic judge in the interpretation of Article 3, the norm explicitly refers to the ECtHR case law that is binding on national courts.[31]

For the first time, in a civil law system, such as Italy, the Italian legislator urges the Judiciary to consider precedents as a binding source of law, i.e. the ECtHR case law, in order to assess a violation of Article 3 of the Convention.

The procedure in front of the Surveillance Judge is accessible and easy, no legal assistance is necessary in order to draft and send the application (in the following hearing, an attorney must be appointed by the Court) and no legal costs are due[32]. On the contrary, the procedure in front of the Civil Court is an ordinary procedure. Legal assistance is mandatory for the drafting and filing of the application and general legal costs, such as registration fees, are due.

According to Article 35 ter of the Penitentiary Law, the Surveillance Judge, in addition to the usual measures to be adopted in case of violation of a prisoner's rights, has the power to grant a compensation for serious breach of the national law and of the European Convention. The norm has a compensatory ratio as well as a deflationary one, since it aims to reduce the rate of prison overcrowding. Pending the prison execution and when the violation has lasted more than 15 days, a mitigation of the sentence in the measure of 1 day every 10 days spent in the condition that violates Article 3 of the Convention must be granted. When the 10 per cent of day release compensation cannot be applied (e.g. prisoners on remand, former prisoners, violations prolonging for less than 15 days), the norm provides a monetary compensation of 8.00 euros for every day spent in breach of Article 3 of the Convention. The compensatory nature of the remedy is consistent with the ECtHR case law, but it has to be noted that the monetary compensation is three of four times less than the amount generally recognized by the European Court in similar cases, such as in the Torreggiani case.

The compensatory remedy has been variously applied and interpreted by the Italian doctrine and case law. The general reluctance of most of the Italian judges to accept the innovations introduced by the reform has led to a restrictive interpretation and application of the norm and, finally, to its substantial infectiveness. An important role in this sort of judicial ostracism is definitely played by the misinterpretation of the ECtHR's case law.

The first attempt to nullify the application of the remedy came from a technical advice of the Consiglio Superiore della Magistratura (CSM), that suggested the requirement of an "ongoing violation" in order to apply for the compensatory remedy (a condition explicitly and correctly requested only for the preventive remedy[33]). As a result, the compensatory remedy could not be activated in cases of past violations of Article 3 of the Convention, thus frustrating the scope of the same compensatory protection. This kind of interpretation has been widely accepted by most of the Surveillance Judges in the first months from the entry into force of the new remedy, when thousands of prisoners applied to the Surveillance Courts claiming the violation of Article 3 for overcrowding and prison conditions.

A portion of the legal doctrine and a minority of the judiciary is rejecting this interpretative position, arguing that it is based on a wrong textual interpretation of the norm and that it nullifies the intent of the legislator to provide the effective remedies requested by the ECtHR in the Torregiani's case (Santoro, 2015; Della Bella, 2014). The norm introducing the compensatory remedy was not clearly drafted, but it could easily be interpreted in order to enforce the ratio of the law, i.e. the compensation to prisoners after a detention in conditions of overcrowding (Santoro, 2015).

The resistance of the Italian judiciary in granting the remedy may be explained with different arguments among which include cultural resistance to this change. Surveillance Judges have traditionally interpreted their role as judges of the execution of the sentence, specifically competent for alternative measures to detention and penitentiary benefits. They have developed collaborative relationships with prison administration and all other institutional actors involved in the execution phase. This role seems to clash with the new one assigned by the law, consisting in monitoring and controlling the acts of the same administration.

The reluctance of the Italian judiciary may also be explained with pragmatic arguments. The extremely huge number of claims, applied in the first months after the law, has pushed the Courts to develop standardized solutions in order to contain the involvement of their offices in a situation of hugely increased workload. The solution proposed by the above mentioned technical advice of the CSM seemed a good way to cut the number of triable applications without the need for an in-depth investigations. From the entry into force of the remedy until October 2015, about 23.600 claims were filed: only 6.1 per cent have been accepted, while 7.35 per cent have been rejected, 5.2 per cent were found "non suitable" and 77 per cent "inadmissible" mostly because the violation was not ongoing at the time of the decision (Caputo and Ciuffoletti, 2016).

Furthermore, the necessity of a standardized framework to decide on overcrowding cases has led to a limited and superficial interpretation of the ECtHR case law in the field of Article 3, which traditionally takes into account other factors – beyond the amount of personal space – in order to assess the inhuman and degrading conditions of detention. A comprehensive and deep assessment of all the factors affecting the quality of life in prison would require an in depth investigation, especially in cases where prisoners have between 3 and 4 square metres of available living space. Nevertheless the Italian Judiciary has limited its attention only to the living space factor, certainly the easiest to assess if compared to others. Notwithstanding the major attention devoted by the Italian case law on the available living space, the existing case law presents contradictory solutions even on the measuring criterion. It took two years for the Italian judiciary to solve the most controversial issues of all, namely the inclusion or not of the bedding in the measure of the available living space. Only a recent decision from the Corte di Cassazione finally established that the bed cannot be considered "a living space", as the Italian Surveillance Judges had repeatedly proclaimed.

The reluctance of the Italian Surveillance Courts to play their new role as prisoners' rights defender is evident also from the way they have applied (or simply misregarded) the ECtHR's principles in the field of the burden of proof. After an initial period[34] in which Surveillance Judges passively awaited for the prison administration to provide the requested documentation in order to assess the violation, a line of interpretation arose expressly applying the civil procedural principle of the "non-rebuttal" (i.e. whenever an allegation by the applicant is not explicitly rebutted by the part, it is to be considered as proven). Unfortunately this line of reasoning is not gaining a uniform approval and the Italian Surveillance Judges case law shows that it is more likely for the judge to await the prison administration without any term. In any case, Courts are satisfied with a standardized statement by the prison administration about the living space available for prisoners and, eventually, the prison conditions, without any individualization of the information and no material evidence in order to prove the content of the statement.

Conclusion

As we have highlighted, the Italian government's reaction to the various European inputs, seemed clearly compliant, from a political and a cultural point of view. Actually, the Italian government, both after the Sulejmanovic case and even more so after the Torreggiani pilot judgment, implemented a twofold strategy, aiming, on the external front, at answering to the European requests in a very prompt way. On the internal front, instead, the government justified the prison reforms aiming at improving prison conditions, as an irrefutable "European" request[35] (sometimes minimizing the scope of the provisions, for example by stressing their temporary dimension, e.g. the temporary increasing of early release).

In this context, the answers of the government were inadequate to produce a real improvement of prison conditions (Feeley, and Swearingen, 2004). Overcrowding was only faced through deflating and temporary measures, not pursuing decarceration and decriminalization policies, as recommended, inter alia, by the CoE (European committee, 2015).[36] Consequently, overcrowding in Italian prisons has never been totally solved[37] and, as a result, prison population has started increasing again.[38] This is due to the fact that one of the most relevant deflating measure adopted, the increased early release, has not been extended by the government[39] after the positive evaluation of the execution procedure in the Torreggiani case.

At the same time, the relevant reforms in the field of prison litigation found the strong resistance of the Italian judiciary. As we have seen, this fact has played a major role in the reductive implementation of the reforms and nullified the scope of both the preventitive and compensatory remedy.

Lastly, the impact of this context on Italian penitentiary policies deserves to be mentioned. The political and judicial attention on the penitentiary system has pushed prison administration to adopt an adjustment strategy and a new bureaucratic approach to prison management.[40] No real pragmatic strategies and investments have been employed to improve the prisoners' quality of life. Nothing has been done to solve the structural and endemic problems of Italian prisons. Prison administration has only developed an electronic system in order to monitor the level of overcrowding in the prisons[41] and introduced a semi-open regime that allows prisoners to spend from 6 to 8 hours out of the cells, in the corridors of the prison or, rarely, in common rooms. This has partially decreased the detrimental effect of the previous restrictive regime, but it has not improved prison life, since corridors and common spaces are not usually equipped for any kind of social and educational activities. While before the Torreggiani case prisoners were forced to idle inside the cell, now they are forced to idle in the corridors. The reason for this change was to comply with the ECtHR's case law which views the time spent out of the cell as a mitigating factor of the phenomenon of overcrowding.

This scenario has been positively ratified by the Committee of Ministers in the execution procedure against Italy, without any further considerations concerning the effectiveness of the Italian model. This shows the limits of the execution procedure of the ECtHR's judgments, infringing upon the whole idea of the European Court as the new Constitutional arena for human rights at an international level (Greer, 2017).

Expanding the angle of perspective, Italy and the ECtHR seems engaged in a marriage of convenience. While Italy behaves diligently, complying to the requirements of the Pilot Judgment Procedure, the ECtHR is showing a rather lenient attitude towards Italy (see the adjournment of all pending cases in the Torreggiani decision or the departure from the general principle that the exhaustion requirement should be assessed with reference to the time at which the application was lodged in the Stella case). As a result, on one hand, Italy passed the European test with the positive definition of the execution procedure in Torreggiani and the ratification of its system of remedies with the validation of the Italian model. On the other hand, the ECtHR, received an important imprimatur on a Pilot Judgment Procedure by a compliant Member State, after the exposure of the ineffectiveness of the execution procedure against the UK in the prisoners' voting right saga (see infra, Creighton, Padfield and Pirosa).

The Italian model can therefore be seen as formally exemplary, but concretely ineffective for the purpose of reducing overcrowding on a structural basis and turning inhuman and degrading prison conditions into a human rights and dignity based detention.

Notes

1 The authors worked together in an integrated way to the development and discussion of methodology, fieldwork and results, and of all the theories that belong to this work. Giuseppe Caputo developed in particular the Introduction and paragraph 3, Sofia Ciuffoletti paragraph 1 and the conclusion.

2 For a review of all these principles, see G. Letsas, *A Theory of Interpretation of the European Convention on Human Rights*, Oxford: Oxford University Press 2007.

3 See A. Mowbray, *The Creativity of the European Court of Human Rights*, (2005) 5 Human Rights Law Review 57.

4 See www.prisonlitigationnetwork.eu.

5 *Sulejmanovic v. Italy*, application no. 22635/03, 16 July, 2009. The Court, in the *Sulejmanovic* judgment found a violation of Article 3 (prohibition of inhuman or degrading treatment) of the European Convention on Human Rights regarding the applicant's conditions of detention. The *Sulejmanovic* judgment appears to consolidate the previous Strasbourg jurisprudence concerning prison overcrowding, prison conditions and the scope of Article 3 of the Convention. At the same time it provides a practical approach and a set of clear principles and procedural obligations for Member States, consolidating a jurisprudential trend that presumes a violation of Article 3 when the personal space available to prisoners is inferior to 3 m^2 and assuming that when the available space in the cell falls between 3 m^2 and 4 m^2 the violation can be assessed in

the presence of other relevant factors such as such as the possibility of using the toilet in private, availability of ventilation, access to natural light or air, adequacy of heating arrangements, and compliance with basic sanitary requirements. In any other case the Court should rely on elements such as the duration of detention in particular conditions, the possibilities for outdoor exercise, the physical and mental condition of the detainee, and so on.

6 See, inter alia Di Perna, A. (2009), p. 117 and:
https://antonellamascia.wordpress.com/2009/08/07/nel-caso-sulejmanovic-c-italia-la-cedu-accerta-per-la-prima-volta-la-violazione-dell%E2%80%99articolo-3-della-convenzione-per-eccessivo-sovraffollamento-carcerale/
http://camerepenali.it/public/file/Documenti/Documenti%20osservatorio%20carcere/Passione%20-%20commento%20Torregiani%20e%20altri.pdf
www.duitbase.it/database-cedu/sulejmanovic-c-italia
www.sidi-isil.org/wp-content/uploads/2010/02/Di-Perna-SIDI.pdf

7 Law n. 199/2010.

8 www.pianocarceri.it.

9 *Ananyev and Others v. Russia*, applications no. 42525/07, 60800/08, 10/01/2012.

10 *Ivi*, § 235.

11 *Ivi*, §236.

12 *Ibidem*.

13 *Stella and Others v. Italy*, applications no. 49169/09, 54908/09, 55156/09, 16 September 2014.

14 §45.

15 §41.

16 Emphasis added.

17 See *Stella*, cit., § 63.

18 §63.

19 See, inter alia:
https://rm.coe.int/CoERMPublicCommonSearchServices/DisplayDCTMContent?documentId=09000016804a91a6#search=radicali%20italiani%20torreggiani.

20 See: https://rm.coe.int/CoERMPublicCommonSearchServices/DisplayDCTMContent?documentId=09000016804aa9a9#search=altrodiritto.

21 Available at: https://search.coe.int/cm/Pages/result_details.aspx?ObjectID=09000016805c1a5b.

22 Rules of the Committee of Ministers for the supervision of the execution of judgments and of the terms of friendly settlements (adopted by the Committee of Ministers on 10 May 2006 at its 964th Session), Appendix 4, item 4.4 and DGHL-Exec/Inf (2010)1, 18 May 2010 Entry into force of Protocol No. 14: consequences for the supervision of the execution of judgments of the European Court by the Committee of Ministers. All documents available at: www.coe.int/en/web/execution/rules-and-working-methods.

23 *Neshkov and Others v. Bulgaria*, applications nos. 36925/10, 21487/12, 72893/12, 73196/12, 77718/12 and 9717/13, 27 January 2015.

24 *Varga and Others v. Hungary*, applications nos. 14097/12, 45135/12, 73712/12, 34001/13, 44055/13, and 64586/13, 10 March 2010.

25 See, *Neshkov*, cited, §282.

26 *Ivi*, §286.

27 See, cited, § 105.

28 The Constitutional Court, with its decisions n. 212 of 1997 and n. 26/1999 recognized the judicial nature of the generic claim provided for by Article 35. A decision of the Corte di Cassazione (n. 25079 of February 26, 2003) detailed the proceedings to be followed in front of the Court: the generic complaint (Article 35), implemented by the procedure provided for by Articles 69, 71 and 14-ter, became a general remedy for all cases of violations not equipped with a specific legal remedy.

29 Cases No. 10, 1201st meeting, June 5th, 2014.

30 Decreto legge No. 92/2014, convertito. con modifiche in l. No. 117/2014.
31 See Chapter 1 in this book.
32 According to the general norms of the Italian criminal procedure code, the prisoner has to be assisted by an attorney who needs to be present, together with the Prosecutor, to the chamber audition. The proceeding follows the general rules of litigation trial and the prisoner can take part to the debate. Also, the prison administration can now participate in the debate and/or send written pleadings. The competence is given to the Surveillance Court in its monocratic composition (Surveillance Judge). The decision of the judge can be appealed to the Surveillance Court in its collegial composition (Surveillance Court) within 15 days. Lastly, the decision of the Court can be appealed to the Supreme Court (Corte di Cassazione) within 15 days. The procedure in front of the Civil Courts is the one provided by the Italian procedural civil code Article 737 (and followings). Civil judge's chamber decision can be appealed in front of the Civil Court within 10 days.
33 The misinterpretation is a consequence of the unclear distinction between the two remedies. Indeed, the preventive and compensatory remedies have different ratio and scopes, the first, aiming to stop a current damage, obviously requires an "ongoing violation" at the time of the application to the Court, while the second one aims to give a compensation when the damage is over.
34 Lasted months, sometimes more than one year.
35 The Italian political discourse has often used the idea of a mythological "Europe" in order to justify any unpopular national reforms and policies since the 90s.
36 The only two relevant reforms going in the direction suggested by Coe were the reform of preventive custody and the partial decarceration of minor drug crimes.
37 Overcrowding rate was 110 per cent on October 31, 2016 (www.giustizia.it).
38 At the time of the first reform Prison population was 66.028 (on June 31, 2013) and has decreased to the minimum level of 52.164 on December 31, 2015. Last statistics show a slow but costant increase: 55.000 prisoners on October 31, 2016, an increase of 6 per cent. (www.giustizia.it).
39 The increased early release to 75 days instead of 45 was significantly impacting on overcrowding but temporary.
40 Similar effects can be found in Countries, such as the US, which have developed litigation as a tool to protect prisoners' rights (Jacobs, 1977; Feeley – Rubin, 1992; Feeley – Swearingen 2004).
41 This system allows Prison administration to know when overcrowding in a prison is going too far from limits and to transfer prisoners to less overcrowded prisons.

References

Arnull, A. (2011). "The principle of effective judicial protection in EU law: An unruly horse." *European Law Review*, p. 51.

Bricola, F. (ed.) (1977). *Il carcere riformato*. Bologna, Il: Mulino.

Caputo, Ciuffoletti S. (2016). "Italian report." *Prison Litigation Network Research Reports*. [Electronic], Available online at: www.prisonlitigationnetwork.eu/?page_id=713 (accessed 6 March 2017).

Cojocariu, C. (2010). "Improving the effectiveness of the implementation of Strasbourg Court Judgments in light of ongoing reform discussions." *Roma Rights, 1, 2010: Implementation of Judgments*, pp. 9-16.

Della Bella, A. (2014). Il risarcimento per i detenuti vittime di sovraffollamento. *Diritto Penale Contemporaneo*, [Electronic], Available online at: www.penalecontemporaneo.it/d/3343-il-risarcimento-per-i-detenuti-vittime-di-sovraffollamento-prima-lettura-del-nuovo-rimedio-introdot (accessed 6 March 2017).

European Committee on Crime Problems. (2015). *White Paper on Prison Overcrowding*. Strasbourg: Coe.

Feeley, M. M. and Rubin, E. (1992). "Prison litigation and bureaucratic development." *Law & Social Inquiry*, 17, p. 125.

Feeley, M. M. and Swearingen, V. (2004). "The prison conditions cases and the bureaucratization of American corrections: Influences, impacts and implications." *Pace Law Review*, 24, p. 433.

Francioni, F. (ed.) (2007). *Access to Justice as a Human Right*. Oxford: Oxford University Press.

Greer, S. and Wildhaber, L. (2012). "Revisiting the debate about 'constitutionalising' the European Court of Human Rights." *Human Rights Law Review*, 12(4), pp. 654–687.

Greer, S. and Wylde, F., 2017, "Has the European Court of Human Rights become a 'small claims tribunal' and why, if at all, does it matter?", European Human Rights Law Review, vol 2017., pp. 145-154.

Jacobs, J. B. (1977). *Stateville: The Penitentiary in Mass Society*. Chicago: University of Chicago Press.

Keller, H. and Stone Sweet, A. (eds.) (2008). A Europe of Rights: The Impact of the European Convention on Human Rights on National Legal Systems. Oxford: Oxford University Press.

Lambert-Abdelgawad, E. (2011). «L'exécution des arrêts de la Cour Européenne des Droits de l'Homme (2010).» *Revue Trimestrielle des Droits de l'Homme*, 88, p. 5.

Melossi, D. and Pavarini, M. (1981). The Prison and the Factory: Origins of the Penitentiary, MacMillan, London.

Rietiker, D. (2010). "The principle of 'effectiveness' in the recent jurisprudence of the European Court of Human Rights." *Nordic Journal of International Law*, 79(2), pp. 245–277.

Santoro, E. (2015). "Contra CSM: parlare a nuora perché suocera intenda." *Diritto Penale Contemporaneo*, in [Electronic], Available online at: www.penalecontemporaneo.it/d/3604-contra-csm-parlare-a-nuora-perche-suocera-intenda (accessed 6 March 2017).

Santoro, E. (2004). *Carcere e società liberale*. Torino: Giappichelli.

Schoenfeld, H. (2010). "Mass incarceration and the paradox of prison conditions litigation." *Law & Society Review*, 44(3–4), pp. 731-768.

Shany, Y. (2014). *Assessing the Effectiveness of International Courts*. Oxford: Oxford University Press.

Simon, J. (2014). Mass Incarceration on Trial: A Remarkable Court Decision and the Future of Prisons in America. New York: The New Press.

Snacken, S. (2011). Prisons en Europe: Pour une pénologie critique et humaniste. Bruxelles: Larcier, p. 2.

Stone Sweet, A. S. (2009) *On the Constitutionalisation of the Convention: The European Court of Human Rights as a Constitutional Court*. Faculty Scholarship Series. Paper 71, [Electronic], Available online at: http://digitalcommons.law.yale.edu/fss_papers/71/ (accessed 6 March 2017).

Van Zyl Smit, D. and Snacken, S. (2009). *Principles of European Prison Law and Policy: Penology and Human Rights*. Oxford: Oxford University Press.

6 International pressure and carceral moderation

Greece and the European Convention of Human Rights

Sappho Xenakis and Leonidas K. Cheliotis

Introduction

In recent years there has been considerable scholarly debate, primarily but not solely in the fields of Law and International Relations, about the factors determining variation in state compliance with international human rights rules and norms. As we discuss in detail elsewhere (in Xenakis and Cheliotis, 2017, in press), three basic arguments have been raised to explain the ineffectiveness of international pressures in promoting national compliance with international human rights rules and norms. First, states may have signed up to the international regime but have performed insufficiently due to various 'capacity' limitations in the domestic arena.[1] Second, resistance by non-compliant states may be explained instead by reference to the fact that the social and material costs imposed by international actors have been inadequate to overcome the inertia or incentives behind non-compliance. Third, the resistance of non-compliant states to international pressure may be accounted for by the existence of a powerful normative counter-regime that serves to undermine the potency of the international human rights regime itself.

Little effort has been made so far to bring this body of research to bear on the study of human rights violations relating to conventional imprisonment and immigration detention. This is surprising, both because of the high volume of violations known to have been occurring within prisons and immigration detention centres around the world, with a parallel rise in legal and civic forms of mobilisation seeking to address the problem, and because broad recognition has been paid to the need for considering international factors and actors when accounting for national- and local-level developments in the field of incarceration.

With a view to helping fill this gap in the literature, this chapter examines the pressure exerted by the European human rights regime on Greece, assessing the efficacy of the pressure as such (both in terms of the acceptance and implementation of pertinent rules and norms) and identifying the array and relative significance of the forces that have given shape to it. In particular, the aim of our analysis is to gauge and account for the degree to which conditions of incarceration (including, for more recent years, immigration detention) in Greece have been influenced by the European Convention of Human Rights (ECHR) through derivative judicial and monitoring mechanisms: the European Court of Human Rights (ECtHR) and the Committee for the Prevention of Torture, Inhuman or Degrading Treatment or Punishment (CPT), respectively.

Greece readily lends itself as a case study through which to advance understanding of the effectiveness of pressure from the European human rights regime towards national compliance with ECHR provisions on incarceration. On one hand, as a relatively weak state within Europe, Greece might reasonably be expected to have been more likely to succumb to pressure from powerful continental actors to align its policies and practices with the Convention. On the other hand, Greece has a long and turbulent history of engagement with the ECHR, including an exceedingly poor record of compliance with a number of its provisions (see further Xenakis and Cheliotis, 2017, in press). Crucially for present purposes, Greece's non-compliance has concerned conditions of incarceration with increasing frequency over the last twenty years or so, as attested by a long series of damning reports by the CPT during this timeframe and the concurrent upsurge in the number of convictions of the country by the ECtHR for violation of Article 3 of the Convention, which prohibits inhuman or degrading treatment or punishment.

For reasons of space, this chapter's discussion of the Greek case is limited to the years that have followed the fall of the country's seven-year military dictatorship in 1974. This includes consideration of developments since 2015, when a coalition government led by the left-wing Syriza party took office, shortly after the collapse of a centrist two-party system that had been in place since the restoration of democracy (for an analysis focusing on the post-war and junta eras, see Xenakis and Cheliotis, 2017, in press; also Cheliotis and Xenakis, 2016). We conclude by summarising our findings on the causes behind Greece's longstanding non-compliance with the ECHR in the field of incarceration, also highlighting the implications of these findings for the study of international human rights regimes and the effectiveness of their interventions inside nation-states. The Greek case suggests that, in conjunction with select institutional capacity constraints, a range of domestic and international pressures, material as well as social, may combine to offset international pressure for national compliance with international human rights regimes. This not only adds impetus to warnings against mono-causal approaches that are bound to overlook the possibility of multiple forces operating simultaneously and cumulatively to produce non-compliance; it also calls attention to the diversity and potentially competing nature of influences stemming from the international sphere.

1 Greek non-compliance with the European human rights regime

In 1975, following the restoration of democracy, Greece adopted a new constitution that included an extensive bill of rights. The country went on to recognise the compulsory jurisdiction of the ECtHR in 1979 and the right of individuals to petition the ECtHR in 1985, and ratified the European Convention for the Prevention of Torture and Inhuman or Degrading Treatment or Punishment (which established the inspections monitoring regime of the eponymous Committee, known as the CPT) in 1991.

Until the 1990s, however, Greek courts usually did not cite case law emanating from the ECtHR and – reflecting their continuing subservience to domestic political leadership – tended to reject claims of ECHR violations without consideration of their merit. On occasions where such claims were given substantive consideration, Greek courts typically relied on the provisions set out by the national constitution, only rarely and fleetingly acknowledging the relevance of the ECHR. Since the late 1990s, Greek courts have demonstrated greater awareness of, and deference to, the provisions of the Convention. The number of applications lodged against Greece with the ECtHR has nevertheless risen steadily since the right to individual petition was recognised. The number of violations found by the ECtHR to have been committed by Greece has also increased steadily, with a particularly dramatic rise evident during and since the 2000s. Indeed, the country has one of the highest violation rates of states signatory to the Convention (see, e.g., Anagnostou and Mungiu-Pippidi, 2014).

Between 2001 and 2015, Greece received at least 55 convictions under Article 3 of the Convention, the overwhelming majority of which were received between 2010 and 2015 (Chatzitheodorou, 2016). Most of these cases have concerned the rights of either foreigners facing deportation or pre-trial detainees, and the majority of violations have related to the length of proceedings, the right to a fair trial, and the provision of an effective remedy. Recent years have seen a wider thematic diffusion of violations, including those relating to the right to life, freedom of expression, and the prohibition of inhuman or degrading treatment or punishment. With regard to the latter, ECtHR decisions against Greece have typically concerned minimal healthcare provision and poor material conditions (e.g., insufficient floor space, lack of ventilation and hot water, unsuitable room temperature and poor hygiene) in conventional prisons, in detention spaces inside police stations, and increasingly over recent years, in sites of administrative detention of irregular migrants (see further Cheliotis, 2012, 2013; also Chatzitheodorou, 2016).

Findings against Greece by the ECtHR – and also, in exceptional instances, by domestic courts – have involved the awarding of considerable monetary damages to victims (see further Cheliotis, 2012, 2013). According to ministerial sources, between 2011 and 2015 alone, the 16 convictions Greece received by the ECtHR involved fines totaling €1,646,000 (*Ta Nea*, 18 February 2016). Yet Greece has one of the poorest records of ECHR signatory states in implementing the judgments of the Court (Anagnostou and Mungiu-Pippidi, 2014). Indeed, the ECtHR ruled in 2011 that detention practices in Greece violated Article 3 of the ECHR and therefore that other EU Member States should cease transferring migrants to the country under the Dublin-II agreement (Cheliotis, 2013). Greece's persistent failure to improve conditions of imprisonment and immigration detention has also been subject to a long series of damning reports by the CPT, culminating in an 'exceptional public statement' in March 2011. This was only the sixth public statement to have been issued by the Committee throughout its entire 22-year existence at that juncture. Such statements are the sole form of sanction the CPT may apply when national authorities consistently fail to make the changes requested (Cheliotis, 2012), although CPT reports have also become an increasingly important source of evidence for ECtHR judgments (van Zyl Smit and Snacken, 2009). Since then, two further CPT reports have been published on Greece which have also been highly critical of persisting and worsening problems bedevilling conditions of imprisonment and detention in the country (in 2014 and 2016), alongside a host of damning reports by national and international NGOs and media organisations.

Greek governments have long responded to critical CPT reports with a combination of denial and defiance. Forms of denial in official responses to CPT reports have ranged from simply 'ignoring findings of risks of ill-treatment' (Evans and Morgan, 1998: 207) to dismissing criticisms as 'unfounded and offending [sic]' (Government of Greece, 2010: 63) – both in terms of fact (that ill-treatment occurred at all) and degree (that they were anything more than 'isolated incidents'). Greek officials have even challenged the validity of CPT criticisms by claiming that prison conditions and the treatment of prisoners are more favourable in Greece than in most of its European counterparts (see further Cheliotis, 2012). To the extent that criticisms have been accepted, responses to the CPT have commonly drawn attention to capacity limitations (from financial restrictions to staffing shortages) facing the Greek state in ameliorating conditions within prisons and immigration detention centres, whilst insisting that the country is working towards solutions to the problems at issue, whether through ongoing investigations (e.g., into allegations of abuse by staff) or planned legislative and practical interventions. Yet blame has often been deflected onto prisoners and detainees themselves and, with regard to the treatment of irregular migrants and conditions within administrative detention centres specifically, the Greek government has also complained that the CPT has failed to acknowledge the particular pressures on Greece as a major entry-point for irregular migration into the EU (Government of Greece, 2009).[2]

Notwithstanding these entrenched discourses of denial, Greece has responded at least to problems of overcrowding in conventional prisons – often prompted to do so by prisoner riots (see further Cheliotis, 2010, 2011) – through partial initiatives, including the construction of extra accommodation at existing sites and a prison-building programme. Between 1994 and 2009, the total certified accommodation in the country's prisons rose by over 130 per cent. Although during this period the ratio of prisoners to certified accommodation was thereby reduced from 1.76 to 1.28, severe overcrowding continued, especially in certain establishments (such as the male prison of Korydallos; ibid.). This was due to a combination of longer custodial sentences being handed down and limited use of early releases for prisoners, despite crime rates having risen at a significantly lower rate over the same timeframe than would plausibly justify the pace of expansion in the prison population (ibid.).

A significantly bolder step was taken in April 2015, when the Greek parliament passed a prison reform bill that sought to relieve prison overcrowding through a range of measures, such as limiting the range of imprisonable offences for young people, setting limits to the prolonged detention of foreigners facing deportation after expiry of the custody term set by courts, and most controversially, relaxing the eligibility criteria for parole, especially but not solely for disabled prisoners. One-day snapshot measurements published by the Greek Ministry of Justice itself indicate that the total prisoner population underwent a notable 18.7 per cent reduction between 1 April 2015 and 1 October 2016, dropping from 11,602 to 9,422. This constituted the largest contraction in the prisoner population in over three decades, during which ever-expanding prisoner numbers had rather been the norm (Cheliotis, 2011). It is difficult to ascertain the precise degree of responsibility that can be attributed to the European human rights regime for such steps (see further Anagnostou, 2013: 213). The regime nevertheless received considerable credit for generating the recent reforms when the Greek Minister of Justice spoke out to defend them against domestic critics, explicitly referring to 191 outstanding cases against Greece at the ECtHR over prison conditions and to continuous and expensive convictions of the country by the Court (Christou-Prentziou, 2015).

The overall picture that emerges from inside Greek prisons has remained dire (see, e.g., *Efimerida ton Syntakton*, 18 September 2016; *To Pontiki*, 9 October 2016), however, whilst conditions within immigration detention centres and other sites where irregular migrants are forcefully kept (e.g., police stations and reception centres) have continued to attract widespread infamy internationally (see, e.g., Human Rights Watch, 2016).[3]

2 Accounting for Greek non-compliance

2.1 Domestic capacity arguments

Greek non-compliance with human rights norms has been explained in official discourse and socio-legal scholarship alike by reference to 'capacity' limitations, with accounts variously stressing resource and institutional constraints.

In its official response to the CPT in 2012, for example, Greece invoked its ongoing financial crisis, stating:

> [There are] well-known fiscal problems that our country [has been] facing [over] the past 1.5 years. We will not get into details, because we think it is self-evident that the lack of financial resources implies insurmountable obstacles to the implementation of an effective correctional policy, as with any other public policy.
>
> (Government of Greece, 2012)

Financial difficulties due to economic downturn have also been evoked by Greek state authorities in an effort to explain away responsibility for the conditions in immigration detention centres across the country (Cheliotis, 2013). In fact, however, financial obstacles to Greek compliance with the ECHR have stemmed more from the way in which funding is administered than the availability of financial resources per se. Gross underfunding of the country's prison system, for instance, has a history that far exceeds the reach of the financial crisis which broke at the end of the 2000s, although knowledge of precise budget allocations has been scant (see, e.g., Dimopoulos, 1998: 205–211). Similarly, the Greek state has long made limited use of EU funds for immigration and asylum management, at least some of which could have been used to ease pressures on immigration detention centres (Cheliotis, 2013; see also *The Guardian*, 22 December 2016). Cost-free alternatives to address non-compliant issue areas, such as tackling excessive prison overcrowding by legislating to facilitate the reduced use of pre-trial detention orders and custodial sentences or the enhanced use of parole, have meanwhile been inadequately deployed; a point to which we shall return shortly.

Accounts of non-compliance privileging institutional limitations have pointed to the country's relatively weak legal infrastructure and inefficient government (as measured, for instance, by the quality of policy-making and policy implementation, the quality of public service provision, and the perceived degree of impartiality and political independence of state bureaucracy) (Anagnostou and Mungiu-Pippidi, 2014). Scholarship has specifically drawn attention to the weakness of inter-ministerial and inter-institutional co-ordination of domestic structures tasked with ensuring the implementation of ECHR requirements and ECtHR rulings, as well as the political weakness of those bodies and a broader paucity of pertinent expertise (ibid.)). It is also clear, however, that opposition by a conservative judiciary has repeatedly posed an 'institutional constraint' with which Greek government initiatives to address non-compliant issue areas relating to imprisonment have had to contend, as governments themselves have complained (see further Koulouris, 2009: 283).

Attempts by governments to relieve prison overcrowding through legislation meant to either restrict 'front-door' entries into the prison system or promote 'back-door' releases from it, for example, have usually been undermined by judicial practice. Not only have judges continued ordering pre-trial detention at excessive rates and expanded their imposition of long-term custodial sentences to the point that any gains from decarcerative reforms to other judicial procedures have been outweighed or otherwise undercut. Judges have also persisted in making limited use of options for early release, at times even in active contravention with pertinent legal reforms and at least on one occasion (in the mid-1990s) despite the threat of disciplinary proceedings by the Supreme Court (see further Massouri, 2006; Cheliotis, 2010, 2011).

This is not to imply that judicial resistance has invariably been effective in thwarting legislative reforms designed to alleviate prison overcrowding. Most notably, in March 2015, the then proposed prison reform bill, whose subsequent passage quickly brought about a drastic reduction in the prison population, was staunchly opposed by the Administrative Council of the Greek Union of Prosecutors. The latter complained that proposals contained within the bill to facilitate the early release of prisoners were 'foreign to penal doctrine' since their enactment would effectively annul judicial decisions and undermine the fair and proportionate punishment of crimes (Christou-Prentziou, 2015).

However partial, short-lived, or otherwise inadequate, the successes achieved through decarcerative legislation carry two important implications for our analysis. First, pertinent scholarship has so far given undue weight to the weaknesses of official administration as an explanatory factor for Greece's non-compliance with the ECHR. Second, and relatedly, insofar as governments have demonstrated an ability to overcome capacity obstacles, continuing failures of the Greek state to comply with its ECHR obligations cannot but also be a matter of political will (or lack thereof); a point corroborated by the array of self-defeating features found in various legislative attempts at decarceration, ranging, for example, from imposing overly restrictive definitions of parole eligibility, to introducing unrealistic conditions for the conversion of custodial sentences into monetary penalties, to leaving the discretionary powers of judges essentially untouched (see, e.g., Cheliotis, 2010, 2011).

2.2 Domestic politico-economic explanations

The failure of political will to ensure Greek compliance with the ECHR and pertinent ECtHR rulings requires explanation in turn.

As argued in detail elsewhere (Cheliotis, 2013, 2017), at least until the beginning of 2015, when a coalition government led by the left-wing Syriza party assumed power, the sustenance of carceral conditions that stand in blatant violation of the ECHR has served dominant politico-economic interests inside Greece. On one hand, in line with what has come to be known in pertinent Anglophone literature as the 'less eligibility' principle, whereby the working and unemployed poor are kept in check by being constantly threatened with a fate even worse than their poverty, the looming prospect of inhumane and degrading treatment behind bars, has functioned to enhance the exploitability of the most marginalised segments of the population in the job market, whether as wage labourers or as reserves. Whilst migrants have grown to be by far the main targets of intimidation under the pretext of political, media, and public discourses that routinely scrutinise them, so much so that they have come to outnumber Greeks in the country's crumbling prisons over recent years, the primary beneficiaries of this process have been numerous small- and medium-size enterprises profiting through labour exploitation, as well as, by extension, political elites seeking to retain and expand their electoral clienteles through sustaining the conditions for such exploitation to occur.

On the other hand, governing parties have sought to deploy incarceration as a convenient means of managing the electoral challenges of disaffection that their increasingly regressive socio-economic policies and their continuing impunity towards grand political corruption have generated amongst the broader public; disaffection that has become all the more pervasive and acute since the financial crisis hit Greece in 2009 and harsh austerity measures ensued to meet the requirements of successive bailouts. In particular, the widely publicised intensification in the use of both conventional imprisonment and immigration detention has helped to deflect and appease a range of anxieties and frustrations amongst lower- and middle-class segments of the population, from heightened concerns relating to personal and family finances, to increased anger with political elites, to a spreading sense of national humiliation before foreign audiences (Cheliotis and Xenakis, 2010, 2011; Xenakis and Cheliotis, 2013). In this case, the notoriously harsh conditions of penal and administrative detention have not just facilitated the symbolic resolution of anger diverted against out-groups scapegoated as dangerous. In accordance with what may be termed the 'more eligibility' principle, they have also become a rare source of empowerment for average Greek citizens, helping subconsciously to alleviate their pains of downward mobility and falling living standards by providing them with reassurance that they continue to enjoy material advantages at least over those on the margins of society – and over some foreign population at that, given the racialisation of custodial prisons and the proliferation of immigration detention sites around the country (see further Cheliotis, 2013, 2017).

From a domestic politico-economic perspective, then, bringing carceral conditions in line with the ECHR must have been taken to be of insufficient utility at best, whilst risking serious counterproductive effects at worst. Indeed, repeated criticisms and sanctions for non-compliant conditions of incarceration have arguably been perversely useful to the status quo insofar as they have subtly worked as powerful reminders that bolster feelings of intimidation and labour exploitability amongst those occupying the bottom of the class structure, at the same time as helping to reaffirm a sense of relative superiority amongst the mainstream public. Given the exceptionally high levels of nationalism, racism and punitiveness against foreign lawbreakers amongst Greeks (including amongst the judiciary), the fact that migrants have come to be the primary targets of state punitiveness in the country appears closely interrelated with the fact that successive governments have failed to comply with ECHR provisions regarding conditions of imprisonment and immigrant detention (see further Cheliotis and Xenakis, 2011; Cheliotis, 2013, 2017).

2.3 International drivers of Greek non-compliance

In addition to domestic politico-economic rationales, there have also been certain international pressures that have functioned to impede Greek compliance with the ECHR. The existence and role of international drivers of national non-compliance is exemplified in the crisis that has unfurled over recent years concerning conditions of immigration detention in Greece.

As a starting point, Greece's European counterparts have played a key role in making contravention of ECHR provisions on conditions of detention practically more likely. First, EU migration and border security policies bear considerable responsibility for the magnitude of irregular flows of migrants that have become concentrated in Greece given, on one hand, the European Community's long-standing efforts to tighten regular migration routes into the region (Crawley et al., 2016), and on the other hand, the area's so-called Dublin regime, which has meant that, since 1997, immigrants apply for regularisation in their first country of entry to the EU.

EU migration management has continued to channel irregular migrants to Greece despite awareness of the poor and worsening conditions of immigrant detention in the country, and without taking adequate steps to remedy them. Notwithstanding the obligation placed on EU member-states since 2011 not to return asylum seekers to Greece due to abysmal conditions of migrant detention there (European Commission, 2016a), in the face of multiplying reports by European and international monitoring bodies, as well as by NGOs testifying to these conditions, and the repeated validation of such accounts by ECtHR rulings (see, e.g., Mahammad and Others v. Greece, 2015), Greece's obligation to process new arrivals under the Dublin regime has persisted. In winter 2016, moreover, the European Commission announced that asylum seeker returns to Greece would be re-instigated as of March the following year, at the same time that the EU was coming under critical media scrutiny for its alleged gross mismanagement of funds intended to improve conditions in migrant detention sites in the country (*The Guardian*, 22 December 2016).

The EU has also contributed to poor conditions of detention in Greece by repeatedly threatening to expel the country from the Schengen area unless it immediately instigate more rigorous border control measures. In response to such threats, for example, Greece accelerated construction of prison-like asylum centres in 2012 (*Greek Reporter*, 13 April 2012) and established 'hot-spot' detention camps in 2016. Both initiatives were effectively predicated on practices of mass mandatory detention, in contravention of both regional and international human rights law (see, e.g., Boček, 2016; Human Rights First, 2012; Amnesty International, 2016a).

More generally, the EU has put pressure on Greece to manage irregular migration in ways that have lowered the standards for the treatment of migrants on Greek soil, effectively undercutting pressure from the CPT, the ECtHR and other official and non-official bodies internationally and domestically for the improved treatment of detained migrants within the country. For instance, in direct response to the EU-Turkey Statement of March 2016, which agreed the large-scale return to Turkey of irregular migrants deemed ineligible for asylum in the EU (European Commission, 2016b), and under pressure of threatened expulsion from Schengen, Greece introduced legislation in April 2016 to enable 'fast-track' deportations of irregular migrants to Turkey. This process has reportedly led to forced expulsions and bulk treatment of asylum claims without proper consideration of individual cases, thereby violating ECHR obligations (see, e.g., Amnesty International, 2016b). Even so, Greece has since been publicly chided for causing delays to the planned return of migrants to Turkey by continuing to consider asylum applications on an individual basis, despite this being a requirement under international human rights law (*Financial Times*, 28 September 2016; *The Telegraph*, 18 October 2016).

European counterparts are also reported to have informally exerted pressure on Greece to engage in illegal refoulements (or 'push-backs') of migrants' vessels at sea, a practice notorious for its wilful use of violence and reckless endangering of the lives of migrants (Migreurop, 2009). As relayed by the Greek Minister of

Migration himself in December 2015: 'They don't dare to ask us to 'drown them', but if you do push-back on a plastic boat in the middle of the sea with 50 or 70 refugees aboard, you're asking me to drown them' (*BBC News*, 27 January 2016). In sum, through the detail of their blunt and insistent official and off-the-record demands for greater border security and tighter migration controls, European political elites have exerted more effective pressure on Greece to contravene the ECHR than other CoE bodies such as the CPT and ECtHR have done in attempting to rectify Greek non-compliance.

Beyond European counter-compliance pressure on Greece, regional and international trends in compliance with human rights rules and norms have also played a tacit role in Greece's evaluation of the imperative of compliance. Whilst there is a long history of human rights non-compliance by Western states, political commitment to human rights rules and norms is today on the wane internationally, just as it was once on the ascent. As has been vividly illustrated by research into the international spread of 'clean' torture techniques that leave no physical trace, the strength of the international human rights regime and its array of monitoring bodies has correlated more with the way in which Western states and their allies have chosen to execute their abusive practices, rather than with their level of compliance per se (Rejali, 2007). Over recent years, much has been written about the rise in overt violations of human rights conventions by Western states, relating both to counter-terrorism law and practices and the treatment of immigrants (see further, e.g., Douzinas, 2007). This upsurge in unconcealed violations has gone hand-in-hand with efforts to critique and curtail the reach of international human rights law; amongst EU member-states, for example, the ECtHR has been subject to mounting criticism for its alleged activism in its interpretation of the ECHR and for over-reaching the scope of its authority in an effort to extend its influence and reputation (Flogaitis et al., 2013). As Oomen (2015) writes, 'After decades of relatively undisputed expansion of the jurisdiction, caseload and normative reach of the [ECtHR], the past years have been marked by an explicit questioning – by politicians, lawyers and opinion-makers alike – of its legitimacy.'

This discourse has not merely been mirrored in Greece, it has also been used to question the validity of ECtHR rulings against Greece and the efforts of domestic lobbies who would cite such rulings in their campaigns for human rights reform in the country. Thus, for instance, in 2012, when challenged by a Greek interviewer to account for ECtHR rulings against Greece, the then Greek Minister of Public Order Nikos Dendias responded as follows:

> The first thing we should examine is how the Court judges and what decisions it reaches. The [European] Court of Human Rights has not only convicted Greece, it has convicted countless countries countless times. It has an expansionary tendency in the application of treaties, in a totally broadened manner, while the legal adequacy of its decisions . . . opens up huge questions. . . . The expansionary way of interpreting treaties, by people who are in many cases not legal professionals, and whose legal training in the philosophy of

> law is relatively limited, generates major issues, major issues in Greek Law, European Law, and Roman Law alike.
>
> (UNFOLLOW, 2012)

The extent to which states seek to demonstrate compliance with human rights rules and norms, then, is shaped by pressures beyond the nation-state itself; pressures that may be as much nurturing of non-compliance as they may be of compliance (see further Chandler, 2004; Hopgood, 2007). Greek patterns of non-compliance therefore need to be understood within a context in which there has been substantial and increasing permissiveness towards, and even encouragement of, the forms of abuse in which Greece has been engaged, providing the country with supportive cues for continuing abusive practices.

Conclusion

This chapter shows that calculations by Greek governments of costs and benefits relating to both the domestic and international arenas, in conjunction with select institutional capacity constraints, account for Greece's longstanding non-compliance with the ECHR.

Our findings suggest that privileging national institutional capacity as the primary determinant of compliance is wanting. Taking a close look at the range of institutional obstacles to human rights reforms regarding conditions in prisons and immigration detention centres in contemporary Greece, we propose that consideration of institutional capacity extend to the stance and practices of key institutional actors themselves, such as the judiciary, whilst at the same time acknowledging the role of government in shaping institutional capacity in its various manifestations (see also Xenakis and Cheliotis, 2017, in press).

The Greek case affirms the thesis that governments engage in cost-benefit analysis when considering compliance with international human rights rules and norms, yet our findings also stress that the costs and benefits under consideration may pertain as much to the international as to the domestic arena. Clearly, significant social and material pro-compliance pressures with which Greece has had to contend at certain critical junctures have emanated from both inside the country (e.g., rioting by prisoners) and beyond (e.g., criticism and sanctions from the CPT and the ECtHR, respectively), occasionally triggering, whether singly or together, government initiatives to tackle ongoing human rights violations in sites of incarceration. The array of powerful forces that have combined to produce an overall trend towards non-compliance with the ECHR, however, have similarly spanned influences from both the domestic and international spheres.

Over recent decades, Greece's persistent failure to redress abysmal conditions of incarceration has served important politico-economic functions inside the country, from cowing disadvantaged groups into accepting exploitation in the workplace, thereby benefiting business sectors of great electoral importance to political elites, to helping successive governments limit the electoral damage wrought by their increasingly regressive socio-economic policies. At the same time, mounting criticism within Europe against the ECtHR has combined with the concurrent rise of blatant violations of international human rights conventions by various Western states to furnish Greece with ample symbolic cues towards non-compliance with the ECHR in the field of incarceration and beyond. In recent years, the EU has also set the tone for the harsh treatment specifically of migrants in carceral sites across Greece by threatening to sanction the country so as to force it into adopting stricter policies and practices of immigration control that contravene both ECHR obligations and broader international human rights legislation. With regard to immigration detention conditions as such, the international realm has even practically operated as a driver of Greek non-compliance with the ECHR, insofar as the EU has effectively fuelled overcrowding and associated problems, not least by continuing to channel large flows of irregular migration to Greece.

In sum, contrary to concerns that have been raised in scholarship on the effectiveness of international human rights regimes about the validity of causal attribution per se, our account coheres with, and provides further validation to, approaches to causation which argue not only that the identification of causal factors is a legitimate endeavour, but also that different causal factors may be inextricably bound together in a relationship of mutual constitution and cumulative efficacy (see, e.g., Kurki, 2008). What this implies is that efforts to explain national propensity towards compliance with an international human rights regime need to extend beyond considering single sets of variables (e.g., domestic capacity limitations), just as they need to extend beyond considering single variables within given sets (e.g., pro-compliance international pressures). In so doing, moreover, one needs always to remain open to the possibility that different variables within a particular set may be exerting opposing and even counter-productive effects, as our account of both pro- and counter-compliance influences stemming from the international sphere reveals.

Notes

1 We use the standard definition of the term 'regime' to denote sets of 'implicit or explicit principles, norms, rules, and decision-making procedures around which actors' expectations converge in a given area' (Krasner, 1982: 185).

2 Beyond the CPT, Greece has more generally complained in the past that her European counterparts ought to do more to mitigate the disproportionate burden placed on Greece as the principal entry-point to the EU of irregular migrants, and has also suggested that Turkey has facilitated the heavy influx of irregular migrants to the country.

3 A law that passed more recently, in late 2016, entrusted the Greek Ombudsman with the power to investigate cases of alleged abuse by staff in sites of incarceration around the country, with the proclaimed aspiration, at least in part, to promote adherence to the ECHR and ensure implementation of judgments passed on such cases by the ECtHR (see, e.g., *Avgi*, 17 November 2016). It is too early at the time of writing to ascertain whether, and the degree to which, the new law itself will be applied in practice, let alone to evaluate its effectiveness. Greece's past record in terms of investing in, or otherwise facilitating, inspection of carceral sites by domestic bodies does not allow much scope for optimism (see, e.g., Cheliotis, 2012: 6–7).

References

Amnesty International. (2016a). "Greece: Refugees detained in dire conditions amid rush to implement EU-Turkey deal." 7 April. Available online at: www.amnesty.org/en/latest/news/2016/04/greece-refugees-detained-in-dire-conditions-amid-rush-to-implement-eu-turkey-deal/ (accessed 8 November 2016)

Amnesty International. (2016b). "Greece: Reported illegal returns of Syrian refugees to Turkey 'dangerous'." *Media Advisory*, 21 October. Available online at: www.amnesty.eu/en/news/press-releases/eu/asylum-and-migration/greece-reported-illegal-returns-of-syrian-refugees-to-turkey-dangerous-1001/#.WCOV7RbWTzK (accessed 8 November 2016).

Anagnostou, D. (2013). "Politics, courts and society in the national implementation and practice of ECtHR case law." In: D. Anagnostou (ed.), *The European Court of Human Rights: Implementing Strasbourg's Judgments on Domestic Policy*. Edinburgh: Edinburgh University Press, pp. 211–231.

Anagnostou, D. and Mungiu-Pippidi, A. (2014). "Domestic implementation of human rights judgments in Europe: Legal infrastructure and government effectiveness matter." *European Journal of International Law*, 25(1), pp. 205–227.

Avgi. (17 November 2016). "The Ombudsman's scope of intervention widens" [in Greek]. Available online at: www.avgi.gr/article/10813/7653545/dieurynetai-to-pedio-parembases-gia-ton-synegoro-tou-polite (accessed 26 December 2016).

BBC News. (27 January 2016). "Belgium said 'push migrants back to sea' – Greek Minister." Available online at: www.bbc.co.uk/news/world-europe-35420967 (accessed 1 November 2016).

Boček, T. (2016). "Report of the fact-finding mission by Ambassador Tomáš Boček Special Representative of the Secretary General on migration and refugees to Greece and 'the former Yugoslav Republic of Macedonia'. 7–11 March 2016." *Report to the Committee of Ministers, Council of Europe*, 26 April 2016. Available online at: https://search.coe.int/cm/Pages/result_details.aspx?ObjectId=0900001680648495#_ftnref6 (accessed 8 November 2016).

Chandler, D. (2004). Constructing Global Civil Society: Morality and Power in International Relations. Basingstoke: Palgrave Macmillan.

Chatzitheodorou, G. S. (2016). "Contemporary conditions of detention in prisons: Between European idealism and Greek Realism." [in Greek]. In: *Crime in Crisis* [in Greek]. Athens: Ant. N. Sakkoulas.

Cheliotis, L. K. (2017). "Punitive inclusion: The political economy of irregular migration in the margins of Europe." *European Journal of Criminology*, 14(1), pp. 78–99.

Cheliotis, L. K. (2013). "Behind the veil of Philoxenia: The politics of immigration detention in Greece." *European Journal of Criminology*, 10(6), pp. 725–745.

Cheliotis, L. K. (2012). "Suffering at the hands of the State: Conditions of imprisonment and prisoner health in contemporary Greece." *European Journal of Criminology*, 9(1), pp. 3–22.

Cheliotis, L. K. (2011). "Prisons and Parole." In: L. K. Cheliotis and S. Xenakis (eds.), *Crime and Punishment in Contemporary Greece: International Comparative Perspectives*. Oxford: Peter Lang AG, pp. 557–591.

Cheliotis, L. K. (2010). "Greece." In: N. Padfield, D. van Zyl Smit and F. Dünkel (eds.), *Release from Prison: European Policy and Practice*. Cullompton: Willan Publishing, pp. 213–236.

Cheliotis, L. K. and Xenakis, S. (2016). "Punishment and political systems: State punitiveness in post-dictatorial Greece." *Punishment & Society*, 18(3), pp. 268–300.

Cheliotis, L. K. and Xenakis, S. (2011). "Crime, fear of crime and punitiveness." In: L. K. Cheliotis and S. Xenakis (eds.), *Crime and Punishment in Contemporary Greece: International Comparative Perspectives*. Oxford: Peter Lang AG, pp. 1–43.

Cheliotis, L. K. and Xenakis, S. (2010). "What's neoliberalism got to do with it? Towards a political economy of punishment in Greece." *Criminology & Criminal Justice*, 10(4), pp. 353–373.

Christou-Prentziou, C. (2015). "The 2015 Prison Reform Bill in Greece." *International Relations Quarterly*, 6(1), pp. 1–5.

Crawley, H., Düvell, F., Jones, K., McMahon, S. and Sigona, N. (2016). "Destination Europe? Understanding the dynamics and drivers of Mediterranean migration in 2015." *Final Report, Unravelling the Mediterranean Migration Crisis (MEDMIG)*. Available online at: www.medmig.info/wp-content/uploads/2016/11/research-brief-destination-europe.pdf (accessed 8 November 2016).

Dimopoulos, C. (1998). *The Crisis of the Prison Institution and Non-Custodial Sanctions*. Athens-Komotini: Ant. N. Sakkoulas Publishers [in Greek].

Douzinas, C. (2007). *Human Rights and Empire: The Political Philosophy of Cosmopolitanism*. Abingdon: Routledge-Cavendish.

Efimerida ton Syntakton. (18 September 2016). "For more human conditions of detention." [in Greek], Available online at: www.efsyn.gr/arthro/gia-pio-anthropines-synthikes-kratisis (accessed 11 November 2016).

European Commission. (2016a). "Commission adopts second recommendation identifying steps to restore Dublin transfers to Greece." Press release, 15 June. Available online at: http://europa.eu/rapid/press-release_IP-16-2182_en.htm (accessed 8 November 2016).

European Commission. (2016b). "Communication from the Commission to the European Parliament, the European Council and the Council." *First Report on the Progress Made in the Implementation of the EU-Turkey Statement*. Available online at: http://ec.europa.eu/dgs/home-affairs/what-we-do/policies/european-agenda-migration/proposal-implementation-package/docs/20160420/report_implementation_eu-turkey_agreement_nr_01_en.pdf (accessed 8 November 2016).

Evans, M. D. and Morgan, R. (1998). Preventing Torture: A Study of the European Convention for the Prevention of Torture and Inhuman or Degrading Torture or Punishment. Oxford: Oxford University Press.

Financial Times. (28 September 2016). "Merkel chides Greece for slow handling of asylum claims." Available online at: www.ft.com/content/7426f07c-8576-11e6-a29c-6e7d9515ad15 (accessed 8 November 2016).

Flogaitis, S., Zwart, T. and Fraser, J. (eds) (2013). *The European Court of Human Rights and Its Discontents*. Cheltenham: Edward Elgar.

Government of Greece. (10 January 2012). Response of the Government of Greece to the Report of the European Committee for the Prevention of Torture and Inhuman or Degrading Treatment or Punishment (CPT) on Its Visit to Greece from 20 to 27 January 2011. Strasbourg: Council of Europe.

The Guardian. (22 December 2016). "Thousands of refugees left in cold, as UN and EU accused of mismanagement." Available online at: www.theguardian.com/world/2016/dec/22/thousands-of-refugees-left-in-cold-as-un-and-eu-accused-of-mismanagement (accessed 26 December 2016).

Hopgood, S. (2007). *The Endtimes of Human Rights*. Ithaca: Cornell University Press.

Human Rights First. (2012). "Immigration detention and the Human Rights of migrants and asylum seekers: Key challenges." *Submission to UN Special Rapporteur on the Human Rights of Migrants*. Available online at: www.humanrightsfirst.org/wp-content/

uploads/pdf/Submission-Immigration_Detention-to_Special_Rapporteur_on_the_Human_Rights_of_Migrants.pdf (accessed 8 November 2016).

Human Rights Watch. (19 May 2016). *Greece: Refugee "Hotspots" Unsafe, Unsanitary*. Available online at: www.hrw.org/news/2016/05/19/greece-refugee-hotspots-unsafe-unsanitary (accessed 11 November 2016).

Koulouris, N. K. (2009). Supervision and Penal Justice: Alternative Sanctions and the Dispersion of the Prison [in Greek]. Athens: Nomiki Vivliothiki.

Krasner, S. (1982). "Structural causes and regime consequences: Regimes as intervening variables." *International Organization*, 36(2), pp. 185–205.

Kurki, M. (2008). Causation in International Relations: Reclaiming Causal Analysis. Cambridge: Cambridge University Press.

Massouri, G. S. (2006). The Introduction and Development of Conditional Release for Adults in Greece as Idiosyncratic Pardon [in Greek]. Athens-Komotini: Ant. A. Sakkoulas Publications.

Migreurop. (2016). *Europe's Murderous Borders*. Available online at: www.migreurop.org/IMG/pdf/Rapport-Migreurop-nov2009-en-final.pdf (accessed 8 November 2016).

Oomen, B. (2015). "A serious case of Strasbourg-bashing? An evaluation of the debates on the legitimacy of the European Court of Human Rights in the Netherlands." *International Journal of Human Rights*, 20(3), pp. 407–425.

Rejali, D. (2007). *Torture and Democracy*. Princeton, NJ: Princeton University Press.

Ta Nea. (18 February 2016). "At 10.287 Euros the annual cost for each prisoner in Greece, according to research." [in Greek].

The Telegraph. (18 October 2016). "EU to call on Greece to speed up migrant returns to Turkey." Available online at: www.telegraph.co.uk/news/2016/10/18/eu-to-call-on-greece-to-speed-up-migrant-returns-toturkey/ (accessed 8 November 2016).

To Pontiki. (9 October 2016). '"You come in alive, you leave dead"' [in Greek]. Available online at: www.topontiki.gr/article/188388/mpaineis-zontanos-vgaineis-nekros (accessed 11 November 2016).

UNFOLLOW. (2012). "Interview with Minister of Public Order Nikos Dendias by A. Zenakos and L. Charalampopoulos." Issue 12, December. Available online at: www.youtube.com/watch?v=IWe9lDm7wDM (accessed 8 November 2016).Van Zyl Smit, D. and Snacken, S. (2009). Principles of European Prison Law and Policy: Penology and Human Rights. Oxford: Oxford University Press.

Xenakis, S. and Cheliotis, L. K. (2017, in press). "Carceral moderation and the Janus Face of international pressure: A long view of Greece's engagement with the European Convention of Human Rights." *Crime, Law and Social Change*, forthcoming.

Xenakis, S. and Cheliotis, L. K. (2013). "Crime and economic downturn: The complexity of crime and crime politics in Greece since 2009." *British Journal of Criminology*, 53(5), pp. 719–745.

7 Assessing the role of European monitoring instruments and their impact on prison conditions in the Nordic countries

Lauri Koskenniemi and Tapio Lappi-Seppälä

Introduction

The legal systems in the Nordic countries reflect both the ideology of the social welfare state and the Nordic tradition of the rule of law. All the Nordic countries have written constitutions, the oldest dating from 1814 (Norway) and 1849 (Denmark), and the more recent from 1944 (Iceland), 1974 (Sweden) and 2000 (Finland). Prison laws in all the Nordic countries were reformed in the 2000s. All the Nordic countries were founding-members of the Council of Europe ("CoE") in 1949, except for Finland, which joined in 1989. All the Nordic countries ratified the European Convention on Human Rights ("ECHR") in 1950, except for Finland, which did so in 1989, and all have incorporated the ECHR into their national legislation (Finland in 1990, Denmark in 1992, Sweden in 1995 and Norway in 1999).

In summary, the position and rights of prisoners in the Nordic countries are defined and protected by two interacting systems of norms, at international and national levels. The implementation of these norms is monitored by organisations at international and national levels, as displayed in the figure below.

In the Nordic countries, human rights standards, as defined in international treaties (e.g. the ECHR) form a valid part of national law once incorporated into the national legal system by a separate legislative act.[1] As such, they are binding on both the legislature and the judiciary.[2] (Pellonpää, et al., 2012, and Viljanen, 2007.) Guidelines and recommendations (including the CoE Prison Rules 1987–2006) function as "soft-law" instruments. However, such soft law gains qualities usually reserved for hard-law, when used as a general standard and the basis for the recommendations of the Committee for the Prevention of Torture ("CPT") or in the judgements of the European Court of Human Rights ("ECtHR").[3]

The international monitoring instruments for human rights in the Nordic countries include the ECtHR and CPT, as responsible institutions supervising the application and implementation of the ECHR. The Optional Protocol to the 1984 United Nations Convention Against Torture ("OPCAT") established an international inspection system, consisting both of the Subcommittee on Prevention of Torture and Other Cruel, Inhuman or Degrading Treatment or Punishment ("SPT")

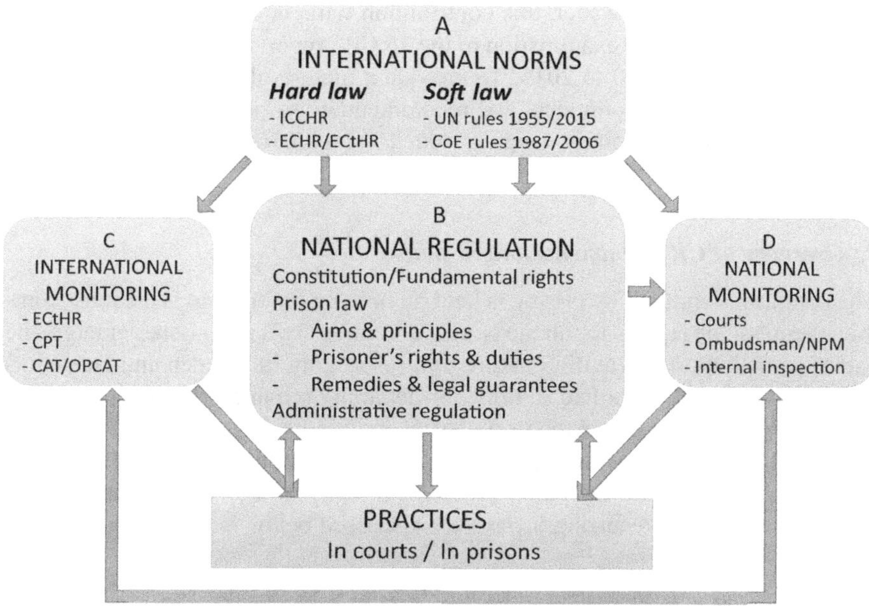

Figure 7.1 Securing the rule of law and prisoners' rights in the Nordic countries.

on the international level, and the National Prevention Mechanisms ("NPM") for the prevention of torture and ill-treatment on the domestic level.

These monitoring instruments examine and monitor prison practice, usually in the form of prison conditions or administrative procedures in prisons, and evaluate them in the light of international norms and rules. National monitoring instruments base their evaluations on both national and international norms. Their conclusions and recommendations, based on observations of practices, may target either the practices themselves or the national norms behind them (depending whether the fault is in the application of norms, or the norms themselves).

This contribution will concentrate on the role of European monitoring instruments (mainly the CPT and the ECtHR) in this setting.[4]

I. The CPT's monitoring of prisons in the Nordic countries

Since its creation, the CPT has conducted a total of twenty-six visits to Nordic countries: six each to Sweden and Denmark, five each to Finland and Norway and four to Iceland. The number of prisons visited were 24 in Denmark, 22 in Sweden, 17 in Norway and Finland and 5 in Iceland. Visits were made to larger and smaller and open and closed prisons. A list of the prisons visited per country is in the Appendix.

In addition to prisons, the CPT also visited psychiatric units, police stations, and refugee centres. However, this contribution will concentrate on prisons, and is based on a systematic examination of the 26 CPT reports from the Nordic countries, ranging from 1990 to 2015. To provide a picture of how the governments respond to the CPT's comments and recommendations, an analysis of the most recent government responses, ranging from 2012 to 2016, is also included in the article.

1. Overview of CPT comments and responses

The conditions endured by prisoners held on remand before trial is the most common theme of the reports for all the Nordic countries. Two main issues emerge: the use of court-imposed detention before trial (especially in Sweden and Denmark) and the use of cells in police stations for detaining remand prisoners (a specific problem in Finland). Other recurring issues are the use of solitary confinement, the denial of outdoor exercise, prisoner-on-prisoner violence, the need to protect "fearful prisoners", and sanitation problems (mostly in the old Finnish prisons). The most frequently recurring themes are discussed below in more detail.[5]

1.1. Remand prisoners – enforcement conditions and restrictions

SWEDEN.

The CPT conducted its first visit to Sweden in 1991 and its most recent one in 2015. According to the reports, the most problematic areas in the Swedish prison system are the conditions in which remand prisoners are kept and the frequent use of court-imposed restrictions.[6]

In its first report the CPT demanded that "urgent measures be taken to radically improve regime activities at Stockholm remand prison and the remand centre at Kumla Prison". (CPT Sweden, 1991, p. 60). Furthermore, the committee emphasised the need for remand prisoners to be allowed to spend significantly more time outside their cells. Although the wording has changed in subsequent reports, and, at times, the criticism even seems slightly softer (e.g. in the 2003 report, in which the committee requested that the then on-going developments continue) (CPT Sweden, 2003, p. 63), the problem has persisted and was once again strongly denounced in the most recent report. (CPT Sweden, 1994, pp. 13–15, 1998, p. 50, 2009, p. 65, 2015, p. 31)

In addition to insufficient activities and time outside their cells, remand prisoners are often subjected to restrictions, which limit their association with other prisoners and visitors. The CPT first commented on the issue in 1991 and has since pointed out deficiencies in both the administrative and legal procedures relating to the imposition of restrictions, and in their application in every report. (CPT Sweden, 1991, p. 29, 1994, pp. 14–16, 1998, p. 49, 2003, p. 28, 2009, pp. 26–27, 2015, p. 31) The main criticism is that remand prisoners lack sufficient access to an independent forum in which they can challenge the imposition of restrictions on them by state prosecutors. The Swedish government took note of this criticism and introduced a channel through which prisoners can seek re-evaluations of decisions to restrict their rights. However, the scope of this remedy was originally limited, until the 2010 law reform expanded prisoners' rights in this respect.[7]

This discussion appears to be continuing. In their latest response, the Swedish government made clear that it has tried, and is trying, to address the problems mentioned in the reports by producing new guidelines on restrictions and setting up working groups to review the legislation. However, the response concludes by stating that, under current legislation, restrictions are "almost without exception necessary" in large criminal cases involving many people and extensive evidence (Swedish gvt. response, 2015, pp. 23–27) and no change is therefore in sight before new, reviewed legislation is enacted. Furthermore, the committee's goal of ensuring that remand prisoners spend at least eight hours out of their cells each day is not assessed as "a realistic aim in the Swedish context". (Swedish gvt. response, 2015, p. 28)

DENMARK.

Danish prisons have been visited by the CPT regularly since the 1990s, and the sixth and most recent visit was conducted in 2014. As in the other Nordic countries, the majority of recurring issues observed and criticised by the CPT pertain to the rights and conditions of remand prisoners, especially to frequently applied restrictions and solitary confinement.

In its first report (1991), the CPT referred to the practice of placing remand prisoners in solitary confinement and it has continued to comment on this issue in every report since. (CPT Denmark, 1990, p. 59, 1996, pp. 61–63, 2002, p. 50, 2008, pp. 67–68, 2012, p. 32, 2014, pp. 24, 26 & 28) However, it seems that some progress has been made in the eyes of the committee, since the CPT's comments in its latest report are in the form of reserved praise: "The CPT welcomes the continued progress made by the Danish authorities and recommends that they pursue their efforts to ensure that remand prisoners are only placed in solitary confinement in exceptional circumstances which are strictly limited to the actual requirements of the case and last no longer than is absolutely necessary." (CPT Denmark, 2014, p. 24)

NORWAY.

The CPT has paid five visits to Norway and conducted its latest inspection of prisons in 2011. Most of its concerns pertained to the use of restrictions on remand prisoners following similar criticisms voiced in the other Nordic countries.

The issues that recur most often in the reports are the lack of human contact and out-of-cell activities available to remand prisoners under restrictions. (CPT Norway, 1993, p.61, 1999, p. 45, 2005, p. 53, 2011, p. 46) In earlier reports, the CPT's attention focused on the procedure through which restrictions are imposed (e.g. CPT Norway 1997, pp. 18–19, 1999, p. 45, 2005, p. 53), however, this issue seems to have lost its urgency, since, in its most recent evaluation of the situation, the CPT concluded that: "The information gathered during the visit would suggest that the frequency and duration of resort to court-ordered solitary confinement has diminished since the 2005 visit; this is a very welcome development." (CPT Norway, 2011, p. 31) Nevertheless, the committee still required some additional information to be provided regarding the use of restrictions. (CPT Norway, 2011, p. 31)

ICELAND

Visits in Iceland took place in 1993, 1998, 2004 and 2012. During the first visit in 1993 the CPT welcomed the changes in 1992 that ended the practice to place remand prisoners automatically in solitary confinement (CPT Iceland 1993, p. 61). However the use of restrictions placed on remand prisoners remained an issue in all reports. In 2004 the CPT remained "concerned about the fact that restrictions on contact with the outside world continue to be applied to a significant proportion of remand prisoners, for periods of usually up to two weeks." The CPT reiterated its "earlier recommendation that the police be required to record in writing the specific reasons justifying the imposition of restrictions on a remand prisoner, and that the prisoner be informed of those reasons. Further, it is again recommended that the same procedure be followed when decisions to remand in custody are reviewed by the court, and the police wish to prolong the restrictions in respect of the prisoner concerned." (CPT Iceland 2004, p.58, the critic was repeated also in CPT Iceland 2012, p.62)

FINLAND.

The issues related to remand prisoners are partly different in Finland. They concentrate on the type of prison facilities used, especially the use of police-station cells for remand prisoners, an exclusive feature of the Finnish system. By comparison, accommodation for remand prisoners in Sweden is often situated near (or even within) police stations, but it is administered by the Criminal Sanctions Agency. Remand prisoners must be transferred to this accommodation within four days of the court deciding to remand them. In Denmark, detained criminal suspects must be brought before a court within 24 hours of their arrest and judges can extend police custody for a further 72 hours, however it seems that remand prisoners rarely spend more than 8 hours in police-run facilities, and if they have to be detained overnight, they are usually transferred to the local remand accommodation. (Oikeusministeriö, 5/2016, pp. 54–55)

In contrast, the custom in Finland is to house significant numbers (around 2,000 each year) of remand prisoners in police-station cells within police establishments. On average, they spend 14 days in such accommodation, with 33% being held there for longer. (Finnish gvt. response to par. 6, 2014, p. 3) This practice has been one of the main focus points of criticism by the CPT since its first visit to Finland. The latest CPT report on Finland, published in 2015, includes a segment detailing the unsatisfactory detention conditions of remand prisoners, very similar to all the previous reports. (CPT Finland, 2014, pp. 12–19)

As the CoE's European Prison Rules clearly state, one of the main principles regarding prisoners on remand is that they should "only be detained in prisons, that is, in institutions reserved for detainees. . ."(CoE Rules, 2006, section 10.2) The underlying idea is to insulate both the police investigators and the prisoners from bribery, intimidation or violence. The use of police-station cells for holding remand prisoners thus comes with the risk of pressure and improper influence on remand prisoners from the police. As Andrew Coyle, the long-standing chairman of the CPT, puts it, "There should be a clear separation of functions between the agencies which are responsible for investigating crimes . . . and the prison administration . . . The fact that an accused person is detained may assist the investigating authorities in their work but the conditions of imprisonment should never be an element of the investigation. In other words, it is not permissible to hold pre-trial prisoners in very restricted conditions simply in order to encourage them to co-operate with investigators or to confess their guilt. The investigating or prosecuting authority should not be able to influence the prison authorities as to how they treat prisoners who are awaiting trial." (Coyle, 2002, p.117) The Finnish practice of housing remand prisoners in police-station cells breaches these requirements (as do the Swedish and Danish practices of imposing restrictions on remand prisoners at the request of public prosecutors in charge of investigations).

Over the years, the tone of the CPT's criticism has become harsher. The 2014 CPT report states that certain aspects of remand imprisonment in Finland must be rectified immediately "pending the complete and definitive end of the use of police prisons for holding remand prisoners". (CPT Finland, 2014, p. 19) Although Finnish remand prisoners have never been subject to torture or inhumane or degrading treatment (Pajuoja, 2016, p. 373), the apparent lack of interest of successive Finnish governments in improving the "unsatisfactory and inadequate" conditions in which they are held has led the CPT to expressly demand in its report that the Finnish government provide a detailed action plan to remedy the situation to the CPT within three months. In addition, the CPT gave the Finnish government one month to provide it with information about the practical steps it would take to implement the CPT report's most urgent recommendations, such as the provision of daily outdoor exercise and other activities to remand prisoners. (CPT Finland, 2014, p. 19) The request was backed up by a threat to issue a public statement about the Finnish government's failure to co-operate if an answer was not answered by the deadline. (CPT Finland, 2014, p. 10)

The issuing of public statements by the CPT is usually reserved for the denunciation of serious problems, such as severe overcrowding, ill-treatment, torture and inhuman and degrading treatment, and is thus rare.[8] Given that the main problem for Finnish remand prisoners was a lack of activities, the CPT's threat could be considered as "overkill". Nevertheless, it had the intended effect. In its initial response, the Finnish government announced that it had set up a working group in February 2014 tasked with identifying alternatives to remanding people into police custody and finding ways to improve the conditions in which remand prisoners were kept by the end of 2015. The working group's report was released in early 2016 and contains detailed suggestions on how to tackle the issues raised in the CPT report. (Oikeusministeriö, 5/2016 and Oikeusministeriö, 34/2016) The main proposals can be condensed into two categories: first of all, the number of alternatives to detention should be increased to include an enhanced travel ban, which would incorporate the use of electronic monitoring equipment into the previously known restriction to movement. Adding to this first category of proposed changes, the group also suggested limiting the maximum time in spent police prisons to seven days. Resorting to the use of police facilities would be limited to cases, where the prisoner could not be accommodated in remand prisons due to safety concerns, or when the proper investigation of the crime requires it. According to the group, the overall population increase in remand prisons, or remand wings in prisons, would amount to 25–30 prisoners a day, if the both the shortening of the maximum time in police facilities and the enhanced travel ban would be implemented. (Oikeusministeriö, 5/2016, pp. 65–66) It is quite clear, that the proposition received more positive feedback than negative from the majority of consulted experts and governmental sources. Some contrasting arguments were also made, mostly regarding the "limited scope of use" of the proposed alternatives and the fear of collusion and contamination of evidence. (Oikeusministeriö, 34/2016) At the moment amendments to the law are being drafted to the plan of the working group – whether they meet the demands of the CPT remain to be seen (see also below).

1. 2. Solitary confinement

DENMARK.

The practice of long-term solitary confinement of prisoners for security reasons in Denmark was scrutinised in the 1980s by the European Commission on Human Rights (before the establishment of the ECtHR). In three cases (one from Norway and two from Denmark) it found that periods of solitary confinement of over a year were "undesirable", but not necessarily in breach of Article 3 ECHR.[9] In its early reports on Denmark, the CPT requested that a maximum limit for solitary confinement be set in the Administration of Justice Act. (CPT Denmark, 1996, p. 62, 2002, p. 50) This was done, only for the limit to be dropped in the Execution of Sentences Act 2015. (Lov om fuldbyrdelse af straf, 2015) Before this, the CPT's general report (CPT General report, 2015, p. 28) and its country-specific report in 2014 (CPT Denmark, 2014, p. 39), reiterated its request for a maximum period of solitary confinement in Danish prisons to be reduced from 28 days to 14 days. ((Lov om fuldbyrdelse af straf, 2015, section 70) According to the CPT, some of the Danish rules governing secure detention and observation cells are still vague, but the Danish government's reply denies this, stating that these activities are regulated by Executive Orders and Acts of Parliament that over-ride the rules. (Danish gvt. response, 2014, p. 42)

1.3. Inter-prisoner violence and fearful prisoners

Inter-prisoner violence has been an issue in Finland, (CPT Finland, 1992, p. 62, 1998, p. 63, 2003, p. 65, 2008, p. 65, 2014, p. 31) Denmark (e.g. CPT Denmark, 1996, p. 61, 2012, p. 31, 2014, pp. 23–24) and Iceland. (CPT Iceland 2004, p.32–33 and 2013, p. 41) Since its first visit to Finland in 1992, the CPT has highlighted this problem, but no remedy had been found by the time of its most recent report in 2014, twenty-two years later. The 2014 report requested "more decisive and proactive steps" be taken to stop inter-prisoner violence and intimidation. (CPT Finland, 2014, p. 31) The same issue has also surfaced in the CPT's reports on other Nordic countries, but its persistence in the Finnish context is clearly visible from the recurrence, wording, and the emphasis on the lack of staff that are absent from the other reports The Finnish government's reluctance to increase staffing levels in prisons, due to economic constraints (Finnish gvt. response, 2014, p. 31) is undoubtedly one of the reasons why this problem has not been tackled.

A related issue is the need for prison authorities to categorise, protect, and isolate so-called "fearful" prisoners, who are in danger of intimidation, mistreatment and outright violence from other prisoners. This has led to such prisoners often being placed in solitary confinement for their own protection, with only very limited time outside their cells involved in activities that are already rarely available for the general prison population. (e.g. CPT Finland, 1992, p. 64, 1998, p. 63, 2008, p. 41, 2014, p. 37) Such segregation can cause considerable psychological stress, and the need for improved psychiatric and psychological care for such prisoners is highlighted in the CPT reports, particularly for judicially segregated inmates and prisoners held in high-security wings. (CPT Finland, 1992, p.31, 1998, p. 29, 2003, pp. 52 and 67, 2008, pp. 33 and 65–67, 2014, pp. 32 and 33–36) Similar problems have also been noted in Norway (CPT Norway 2005, p. 24) and Sweden, (CPT Sweden, 2003, pp. 20–21) although only in Finland and Denmark has this issue been mentioned in every CPT report. In Denmark and Sweden, segregation also is geared towards disruptive and dangerous inmates, and prisoners seeking isolation for their own protection.

1. 4. Hygiene and living conditions

The CPT reports repeatedly criticise the failure of prison authorities in the Nordic countries to provide prisoners with access to a toilet at all times. (e.g. CPT Sweden, 1991, p. 61, 1998, p. 50, 2009, p. 65, 2015, p. 34, CPT Norway 1993, p. 62, 2005, p. 53, 2011, p. 44) Finland is particularly criticised for its poor sanitary conditions for some of the prisoners, due mainly to the fact that, when the first CPT visit took place almost half (1,500) of the prison cells in the country were constructed in the nineteenth century with no toilet facilities in them. The number of these cells has steadily decreased since then as the old prisons were renovated or demolished, but the slow speed of this process has received constant criticism, as has the lack of access to toilets by prisoners at night. (e.g. CPT Finland, 1992,

p. 63, 1998, pp. 63–64, 2003, p. 32, 2014, p. 36)[10] In its latest report, the CPT denounces "slopping-out" (i.e. prisoners using buckets in cells as toilets). The most recent number of cells without toilets cited in the Finnish government's most recent response to a CPT report had fallen to 170, with a promise to eradicate slopping-out by the end of 2018. (Finnish gvt. response, 2014, p. 28) The general state of repair of Finnish prisons has also been criticised with a special emphasis on the country's largest prison in Helsinki, despite a recent major refurbishment and renovation. (e.g. CPT Finland, 1992, p. 64, 1998, p. 63, 2014, p. 36)

The poor condition of prison buildings is not only an issue in Finland, but has been commented on in all of the other Nordic country reports as well, including specific mentions of the exercise areas in Sweden and the Copenhagen Western Prison in Denmark, and the size and design of the exercise cubicles in Norwegian prisons, although Norway received less criticism overall about its prison buildings than the other Nordic countries.

1.5. Health care, medical screening and other issues

The interviewing and medical screening of prisoners entering prison have been criticised in CPT reports relating to Denmark, (CPT Denmark, 1990, p. 59, 1996, p. 63, 2002, p. 51, 2008, p. 69, 2012, p. 31, 2014, p. 34) Finland, (CPT Finland, 1992, p. 65, 1998, pp. 35 and 64, 2003, p. 68, 2008, p. 68, 2014, p. 39)[11] Iceland (CPT Iceland 2004, p.51 and 2013, p. 55) and Norway.(CPT Norway, 1993, p. 63, 2005, p. 55, 2011, p. 46) In its latest response, the Norwegian government takes note of these deficiencies and provides information on how it plans to address these issues in the next few years. (Norwegian gvt. response, 2011, pp. 14–15 and 22–23) The CPT has urged Finland to improve its prisoner healthcare facilities several times. In 2016, the responsibility for healthcare in prisons was transferred by the Finnish government from the Ministry of Justice to the Ministry of Social Affairs and Health (Finnish gvt. response, 2014, pp. 33 and 41), so we will wait and see whether or not this will produce the changes sought by the CPT.

Other issues emerging from the CPT's reports on Sweden include the quality and size of outdoor exercise facilities (e.g. CPT Sweden, 1991, p. 60, 1998, p. 49, 2003, p. 62, 2009, p. 64, 2015, p. 35) and prisoner access to telephones and other means of contacting the outside world. (e.g. CPT Sweden, 1991, p. 63, 2003, p. 65, 2009, p. 67, 2015, p. 49) Denmark has received criticism for the use of mechanical physical restraints on prisoners in a non-medical setting. (CPT Denmark, 1990, p. 60, 2008, p. 69, 2014, p. 44) In Iceland the CPT called for the discontinuation of the practice that prisoners could be prescribed medication (including neuroleptics), without being physically seen by a doctor. Medication prescribed to prisoners was frequently distributed by medically untrained custodial staff. (CPT Iceland 2004, p.46 and 47) The CPT noted also "a striking feature of Kópavogur Prison was that there was no separation of sexes during the day, male and female prisoners spending most of their time together (though they were not authorised to go into each other's rooms)." The committee did not take a definite stand on this issue, but stated: "The CPT wishes to reiterate its view that, in principle, women deprived of their liberty should be accommodated separately from men. Therefore, the Committee recommends that the Icelandic authorities ensure that all the prisoners presently accommodated at Kópavogur Prison unequivocally agree to the current arrangements; further, there should be adequate staff supervision during the day."(CPT Iceland, 2012, p. 48)

2. *Criticism and Responses – initial observations of the nature of dialogue*

Design and method.

Government responses to CPT criticisms vary. Some of them accept the criticisms and promise to take steps to tackle the problems, some are evasive and some challenge the CPT's findings. Tom Daems recently analysed the different types of Belgian government responses. (Daems, 2016) He devised ten different types of response: (1) "We fully agree and will follow up"; (2) "You're wrong"; (3) "It's not our fault"; (4) "In reality everything works perfectly"; (5) "We don't disagree with your findings, but we won't change anything"; (6) "We don't disagree with your findings, but we can't change anything"; (7) "We need to investigate this"; (8) Answer that raises new questions; (9) Partial answer, and (10) No answer.

Below, we have used Daem's categories to classify the responses from governments of the Nordic countries. We added two new types of response (1B) "We're trying" and (V) Information provided. We also combined the types into five broader categories: (I) Acceptance (types 1 and 1B), (II) Denial/Disagreement (2, 3 and 4), (III) Non-compliance (5 and 6), (IV) Evasion (7, 8, 9 and 10), and (V) Information provided.

Reading the responses to the CPT reports, it became clear that it would be difficult to fit them into the categories described above, because each response contains several elements, which, for example, could be partly accepting and partly evasive. The borderlines between options were also flexible and discretionary. To overcome this, the contents of the responses were disaggregated by analysing each element separately. Thus each response may include several elements and the analysis includes both responses and elements of responses.

Below is a brief overview of the initial results of this analysis based on the most recent government responses to the CPT reports on Denmark, Finland, Norway and Sweden. In order to maintain comparability between the countries, only comments related to prisons were included (thus comments and responses concerning police stations, psychiatric hospitals and juvenile centres are excluded). In order to widen the comparative perspective, we extended the analyses to cover also the most recent government responses from Germany (2012) and the Netherlands (2007 and 2012) to serve as the "Central European Comparison Group".

Responses.

The total number of responses from Denmark, Finland, Icaland, Norway and Sweden was 163, varying from 27 from Sweden to 41 from Iceland. Just over half (56%) of the responses included only one element and 44 % included two or more elements (two in 35 %, three in 7 %, four in 1 % and five in 2 %). On average, each response contained 1.6 elements. Counting all the elements together makes a total of 236 elements in 204 responses. No major differences could can be detected between the countries in this respect.

The distribution of response-elements across five categories is displayed in Table 7.1. Due to the small number of observations, only aggregated results are reported.

Table 7.2 gives more detailed information about the prevalence of different response-elements and their share of all response elements.

The most common response type is some sort of denial/disagreement (35% Nordic and 50 % comparison group) or acceptance (about 1/3 in both groups). Mostly denial/diasagrmeent takes form of claiming that "everything works perfectly" (or, more often, "pretty well", see below). However, the governments seldom directly refrain from any action (only 6–9 % of responses were clear statements of non-compliance). The share evasive responses was higher among the Nordic countries (23% vs 9 %).

Table 7.2 gives more detailed information about the prevalence of different response-elements and their share of all response elements.

The most common single response is aither to admit that "we fully agree and will follow up" (24% in the Nordics and 23% in the the comparison group), or the claim that "everything works perfectly/pretty well" (21% Nordic, 28% comparison). However, governments rarely claim this directly. One typical way of conveying this message is to describe current practice without any further response (this could, of course, also been interpreted as an expression of evasion). At times, the notion implies that according to the government, the practices are in line with the CPT's recommendations, although the CPT doesn't always share the government's view. More often, however, the response indicates that the government doesn't find the need to change current practices even if they don't strictly adhere to the CPT's views, albeit this is rarely stated explicitly (and in this paper is covered by other response categories).

One out of ten responses among Nordic countries, but one out of five in comparison group included statements that denied the observations ("You are wrong").

Table 7.1. The distribution of answers by response-category

	Nordic-5		*Germany & Netherlands*	
	N	%	N	%
Denial/Disagreement	71	34,8	32	50,0
Acceptance	67	32,8	22	34,4
Evasion	47	23,0	6	9,4
Non-Compliance	19	9,3	4	6,2
All	166	100,0	64	100,0
Information provided	32		10	
Total (N)	194		74	

Percentages are calculated from the total number of response-elements, however excluding answers providing only the requested information.

Table 7.2. The distribution of governments' responses by response-groups and –elements

	Nordic-5		*Germany & Netherlands*	
	N	*%*	*N*	*%*
I. ACCEPTANCE	*(67)*	*(32,8)*	*(22)*	*(34 %)*
1."We fully agree and follow up"	49	24,0	15	23,1
1B. "We are trying"	18	8,8	7	10,8
II. DENIAL/DISAGREEMENT	*(71)*	*(34,8)*	*(32)*	*(51 %)*
2. "You're wrong"	21	10,3	12	20,0
3. "It's not our fault"	8	3,9	2	3,1
4. "In reality everything works perfectly/pretty well"	42	20,6	18	27,7
III. NON-COMPLIANCE	*(19)*	*(9,3)*	*(4)*	*(6 %)*
5. "We don't disagree with your findings, but we won't change anything"	13	6,4	3	4,6
6. "We don't disagree with your findings, but we cannot change anything"	6	2,9	1	1,5
IV. EVASION	*(47)*	*(23,0)*	*(6)*	*(9 %)*
7. "We need to investigate this"	16	7,8	3	4,6
8. Answers that raise new questions	12	5,9	1	1,5
9. Partial answer	16	7,8	2	3,1
10. No answer	3	1,5	0	0,0
ALL	*(204)*	*(100,0)*	*(64)*	*(100,0)*
Only information provided	32	15,7	10	18,5
TOTAL NUMBER OF ELEMENTS	236		74	
TOTAL NUMBER OF RESPONSES			55	

In all, the Nordic countries provided more partial answers or answers that raised new questions.

Table 7.3 gives an overview of the subject of the comments and responses among the Nordic countries. The classification of the subject areas follows the structure of the CPT reports structures, with some modifications. The table also attempts to describe whether the criticisms in the reports were accepted or denied (in one way or another). Thus, the answers are divided into positive/agreeing and negative/disagreeing responses. Positive/agreeing responses are answers expressing acceptance, albeit with some forms of disagreement and evasion, but without expressions of non-compliance. The negative/disagreeing group consists of all the answers expressing non-compliance, as well as answers with clear evasive tendencies.

Table 7.3. Comments and responses by subject area. Nordic countries.

	N	*%*	*Positive/ Agreeing*	*Negative/ Disagreeing*
Physical and psychological healthcare	25	20.5	7	18
Administrative & legal procedures	19	15.6	9	10
Requests for information	16	13.1	..	..
Living conditions and hygiene	14	11.5	6	8
Discipline	10	8.2	4	6
Ill-treatment	9	7.4	7	2
Special regimes (fearful, isolation, high security)	7	5.7	4	3
Remand prisoners	6	4.9	2	4
Contacts with the outside world	6	4.9	2	4
Juveniles	5	4.1	4	1
Prison regime, work and activities	3	2.5	2	1
Prison staff	2	1.6	0	2
All	122	100.0	61	61

The largest number of comments and responses related to physical and psychological healthcare issues (21% of all responses), followed by administrative and legal procedures (16%), requests for information (13%), and living conditions and hygiene (12%, mainly criticism of slopping out).

Positive and negative responses were divided by 50/50 under a dichotomist classification. In individual items, this balance varies, even if the numbers are too small to draw any firm conclusions. However, the governments of the Nordic countries appear to protest less about criticisms of ill-treatment (7/2), whereas criticisms of physical and psychological healthcare are often contested (7/18).

The main conclusion to draw from this tentative analysis is that the governments of the Nordic countries do not seem to take the criticisms of the CPT at face value. Some sort of denial and disagreement is a typical response in about one in three cases. While these governments are less likely to say directly "you are wrong", they often imply that things are actually going pretty well. Direct statement of non-compliance were rare (but not non-existent). It also became clear that there are differences between the Nordic countries in these respects, and in order to clarify their position vis-à-vis other European countries, further research is needed. The same applies to the contents of the recommendation and the relevance of the subject under discussion. Undertaking such substantial analysis was out of the scope of this article, but preliminary comparisons to the Netherlands and Germany were made for the sake of gaining a more comprehensive picture of the governments' responses and ways of reacting to the CPT's criticism. However, no definitive distinctions could be established between the Nordic states and Central-Europe. Quite the opposite – by going through some of the more recent government responses of the aforementioned countries regarding prison conditions, it became clear that the recommendations of the CPT were not always complied with and at times actively challenged.[12]

II. The ECtHR's oversight of prisons in the Nordic countries

While there are very few ECtHR judgments related to prison conditions and the enforcement of sanctions against prisoners in the Nordic countries, it is evidently not an option for these countries to bypass or ignore these decisions, particularly those related to solitary confinement. The use of solitary confinement for a remand prisoner in Denmark was the subject of the ECtHR's judgment in *Rohde vs. Denmark* in 2005 (case ref. 69332/01, 21/10/2005). Two legal issues pertaining to Article 3 ECHR prohibiting torture and inhuman or degrading treatment or punishment were raised before the court: whether or not long solitary confinement in itself could be construed as inhuman or degrading treatment, and whether or not the Danish prison authorities had failed to adequately monitor the applicant's physical and psychological health during his detention. (ECtHR, Rohde v. Denmark, 2005, p. 27–35, sections 82–110)

The applicant was arrested on 13 December 1994 as part of a police investigation of a drug- smuggling operation. He was brought before the Copenhagen City Court the next day, which ordered him to be remanded in custody in solitary confinement. (ECtHR Rohde v. Denmark, 2005, p. 2, sections 8–10) He was detained in uninterrupted solitary confinement for almost a year, and two years after his appearance in court he suffered a paranoid psychotic episode. Although the medical expert consulted during the proceedings in Denmark stated that, in his opinion, the main cause of the episode was an underlying psychological illness (paranoid schizophrenia) rather than the lengthy solitary confinement, the court ruled that the episode was the combined result of both (ECtHR Rohde v. Denmark, 2005, p. 9 section 45 and pp. 33–34, section 107), found in favour of the applicant and awarded him compensation. This judgment was appealed to the Danish Supreme Court, which upheld the lower court's decision and increased his compensation to DKK 1,109,600 as it held that the solitary confinement was the main cause of the applicant's illness, but stopped short of holding that a breach of Article 3 ECHR had occurred. (ECtHR Rohde v. Denmark, 2005, p. 20, section 73)

The case was then appealed to the ECtHR. After citing a number of previous cases regarding the threshold of torture or inhuman or degrading treatment, the ECtHR noted the CPT's longstanding criticisms of the use of solitary confinement in Denmark. However, by a majority, the ECtHR held that the length of the solitary confinement in this case did not in itself amount to inhuman or degrading treatment, since the prisoner was not completely denied social interactions: he was allowed to meet his family, prison staff and healthcare professionals on a regular basis. (ECtHR Rohde v. Denmark, 2005, pp. 29–31, sections 89–98) Moreover, the ECtHR held that there had been no lack of effective medical and psychological monitoring or care and therefore dismissed the claim that Article 3 ECHR had been breached. (ECtHR Rohde v. Denmark, 2005, pp. 31–35, sections 91–110) However, three of the seven ECtHR judges issued a dissenting opinion, stating that a clear distinction should be made between solitary confinement on remand and as part of a sentence of imprisonment. They further stated that they had not been convinced by the Danish government's "rather general" reasoning justifying the long period of solitary confinement by saying it was necessary. They also referred to the CPT's recommendations on the use of solitary confinement. In the opinion of the dissenting judges, there had been a breach of Article 3 ECHR on this occasion. (ECtHR Rohde v. Denmark, 2005, pp. 36–38, sections 1–2)

In 2014, the ECtHR heard another case involving an applicant from a Nordic country: *Lindström and Mässeli v. Finland.* The two applicants claimed they had been subject to inhuman and degrading treatment in breach of Article 3 ECHR and that their right to privacy under Article 8 ECHR had been breached by the Finnish policy of making certain prisoners in solitary confinement wear overalls sealed with plastic strips that could not be opened, to prevent the smuggling of contraband. The applicants claimed that they had been forced to defecate inside the overalls due to the slow response of prison staff to requests for access to the toilet, and that the overalls had prevented them from washing themselves during their solitary confinement.(ECtHR, *Lindström and Mässeli v. Finland,* 2014 pp. 1–2, sections 3–4, and 6–11) Their claim had been dismissed by the Finnish courts as they had failed to prove intent in the part of prison staff deliberately delaying their responses and had provided no evidence of being unable to wash. The courts held that the use of the sealed overalls was proportionate to its objective. (ECtHR, *Lindström and Mässeli v. Finland,* 2014, pp. 2–3, sections 12–15)

The applicants then appealed to the ECtHR. In its judgment, the ECtHR stated that, although evidence of intent is not required for a measure to be considered inhuman or degrading, the lack of evidence in support of the applicants' claim tilted the balance in favour of Finnish government. By accepting the government's position, the ECtHR concluded that the use of the sealed overalls was not in breach of Article 3 ECHR. (ECtHR, *Lindström and Mässeli v. Finland,* 2014, pp. 10–11, sections 44–50) However, in a dissenting opinion, two of the seven judges stated that, in their opinion, the combination of the solitary confinement, the closed overalls and the slow response of the prison staff to toilet requests constituted a breach of Article 3 ECHR. (ECtHR, *Lindström and Mässeli v. Finland,* 2014, pp. 18–20)

Regarding the claim of a breach of the right to privacy guaranteed by Article 8 ECHR, the ECtHR held that the sealed overalls represented a significant use of public power and, as such, must be justified in law. However, the Finnish legislation regulating imprisonment did not mention the use of closed overalls, hence there had been a breach of Article 8 ECHR. (ECtHR, *Lindström and Mässeli v. Finland,* 2014, pp. 1–15, sections 55–64) Following this judgment, the Finnish government amended the Law on the Execution of Sentences to regulate also the use of sealed overalls, and the amendment entered into force in 2015.

Conclusion

International monitoring bodies have compelled the governments and prison administrations in the Nordic countries to take human rights more seriously. Although there are very few ECtHR judgments related to prison conditions and the enforcement of sanctions in the Nordic countries, it is clear that the countries cannot bypass or ignore these judgments. Indeed, Finnish law on the use of sealed overalls for prisoners in solitary confinement was changed as a direct result of an ECtHR judgment. It is interesting to note that the Finnish national ombudsman had made similar criticisms earlier, but had not been able to bring about change.[13] The CPT's criticisms have led to law reforms and changes in prison practice in the Nordic countries, for example the enactment of a specific law on remand prisoners in Finland. The adoption of court-based appeals procedures in these countries was clearly motivated by international obligations and the requirements of the ECHR.

However, the main responsibility for the day-to-day treatment and well-being of prisoners lies in the hands of national institutions, standard national appeals procedures and the national ombudsmen. The CPT visits each of the Nordic countries roughly once every 4 years, and is only able to visit 3 to 5 facilities each time. The national ombudsmen are able to visit and check between 20 and 50 closed facilities each year (depending on the country). While, the national monitoring systems (including national appeals) outnumber the international monitoring instruments, the latter speak with a "louder voice" and they often take up issues of general importance. Often, the CPT reports and ECtHR judgments bring up criticisms previously made by national ombudsmen but which only produced meagre results. However, one may assume that the establishment of the new role of the Ombudsman as the National Prevention Mechanisms under the authorization of the UN will increase the weight and impact of these recommendations.[14]

In terms of CPT report criticisms, none of the Nordic countries has a completely clean record. The CPT reports are usually 50–60 pages long and include several dozen observations (criticisms) which often remain similar in successive reports. Norway is the country with the fewest criticisms, but it has not emerged completely unscathed. The responses to criticism by the CPT range from agreement with them and promises to take action to direct denials, which are, however, fairly rare. The governments rarely disagree with criticism related to ill-treatment, safety and the well-being of prisoners, but are less likely to agree with criticism of organisational and administrative procedures. Improvement is often a slow process, but the evidence shows that the CPT and human rights (often) prevail.

The relationships and means of communication between the CPT and the governments are nuanced, and partly complicated. The effects sought after through constructive dialogue could be enhanced with more open and direct communication, which further implies the need to actively listen to the other party without resorting to obfuscating monologues or to deafening silence. This applies especially to the evasive responses, in which the governments simply describe the current situation with the hidden message that in its opinion, everything is in fact, working pretty well. It is fairly obvious that if the CPT finds an issue that it considers worth mentioning in its report, it is not satisfied with the current state of affairs. The governments should respond in detail to the CPT's questions and recommendations, but many of their responses are filled with detailed and lengthy descriptions of national legislation and institutional practices and lack concrete action plans focusing on the question or recommendation. Examples of such evasion were to be found from all countries covered in this contribution. On the other hand, a gentle perspective shift is asked also of the CPT – as the CPT adapts its level of criticism and praise to the cultural-political climate of the respective country, and although it bases its observations on legitimate concerns, sometimes issues might best be left evaluated and configured by the state in question due to its first-hand expertise on the particulars and subtleties of its penal system.

Notes

1 The Nordic countries follow a dualistic model, under which the incorporation of international treaties takes place in a form of a separate legislative act.

2 This description is greatly simplified and is only general by nature. In each country there exists rich and detailed literature about the relationship between European and national law, which I do not have space to comment on here. For Finland, see especially Pellonpää et al 2012 and Viljanen 2007.

3 For a detailed discussion of the evolvement of European prison law and policy, see van Zyl Smit & Snacken 2009, Chapter 1.

4 The role of national monitoring instruments and the Ombudsman are discussed in more detail in Lappi-Seppälä & Koskenniemi (forthcoming 2017)

5 The text concentrates on critical comments and recommendations only. The CPT reports included also several positive assessments related to overall levels of prison conditions and well-functioning co-operation, which are left aside in this report.

6 In Sweden these restrictions are imposed by the court at the request of the public prosecutor. The system is the same in Denmark and Norway, but not in Finland. Whether these differences in the procedural rules explain differences in the practice, is an issue that would require a separate analysis.

7 Nowadays the remand prisoners' right to challenge the District Court's imposition of restrictions is enshrined in the Remand Imprisonment Act and the correct procedure to be followed can be found in the Judicial Procedure Act.

8 The CPT has issued the following seven public statements to date: Prison overcrowding and ill-treatment by police and prison staff (Bulgaria 2015); The treatment of irregular migrants in detention centres where conditions may have amounted to inhuman and degrading treatment (Greece 2011); Secret detention facilities and severe and systematic physical ill-treatment of prisoners in the Chechen Republic (Russia 2001, 2003, 2007); and The lack of legal safeguards against persistent physical and psychological torture by the Anti-Terror Departments of some branches of the police (Turkey 1992, 1996). This would have indeed been harsh company for the treatment of remand prisoners in Finnish police-station cells.

9 The decision of the European Commission on Human Rights in *Rasch v. Denmark*, No. 10263/83, 11 March 1985, pp. 153–154, where a prisoner had been held in solitary

confinement for 17 months based on the risk of his escape. Although the solitary confinement was deemed to be undesirable, it was not deemed a breach of Article 3 ECHR. See the summary of cases in Ot. prp. nr 5/2001 p. As regards the Norwegian case, see: *Treholt v. Norway, No. 14610/89,* 9 July 1991, in which the European Commission of Human Rights deemed the application inadmissible, but commented on the use of solitary confinement.

10 As mentioned above, prisoner access to toilets at night is also a problem in other Nordic countries, notably Sweden and Norway. However, no mention of slopping out is made in the CPT reports for these countries.

11 As an interesting side note, initial medical screenings for prisoners can be delayed for weeks after admission to prison in the Nordic countries, and in Norway the CPT found cases where no medical examinations had been carried out at all, even though overcrowding or the lack of medical staff were only mentioned as minor issues in the reports.

12 See for example the German government's response to the CPT from 2010 and the Dutch government responses of 2007 and 2011, which include a total of 33 response-elements fitting to the category of denial/disagreement with 12 "you're wrong" –elements and 18 "everything works perfectly/pretty well" –elements out of the 65 individual critical comments pertaining to prison conditions.

13 As a result, the requirements of the legal principle are now met, but the question of whether or not the use of these overalls in the first place is in line with human and sensible enforcement principles is another matter.

14 See also the discussions in Lappi-Seppälä & Koskenniemi 2017 (forthcoming).

References

Bekendtgørelse af lov om fuldbyrdelse af straf m.v. (LBK nr 1242 af 11/11/2015). (https://www.retsinformation.dk/pdfPrint.aspx?id=170653, visited 24.03.2017)

Council of Europe: "Recommendation Rec (2006)2 of the Committee of Ministers to member states on the European Prison Rules."

(https://wcd.coe.int/ViewDoc.jsp?p=&Ref=Rec(2006)2&Language=lanEnglish&Ver=original&Site=CM&BackColorInternet=9999CC&BackColorIntranet=FFBB55&BackColorLogged=FFAC75&direct=true, visited 20.12.2016)

Coyle, Andrew 2002: "Human Rights Approach to Prison Management", *Handbook for Prison Staff,* London: International Centre for Prison Studies, 2002.

Daems, Tom 2016: "Slaves and Statues: Torture Prevention in Contemporary Europe", *British Journal of Criminology,* advance access 2016.

Lappi-Seppälä, Tapio & Koskenniemi, Lauri 2017. "National and International Instruments in Securing the Rule of Law and Human Rights in the Nordic Prisons", to be appear in Crime, Law and Social Change *2017.

Oikeusministeriö: "Tutkintavankeuden vaihtoehdot ja järjestäminen", *Mietintöjä ja lausuntoja, 5/2016,* Helsinki, 2016.

Oikeusministeriö: "Tutkintavankeuden vaihtoehdot ja järjestäminen: lausuntoyhteenveto", *Mietintöjä ja lausuntoja, 34/2016,* Helsinki, 2016.

Pajuoja, Jussi 2016: "Kansainväliset tarkastuselimet haastavat ylimmän laillisuusvalvonnan", *Edilex, 2016,* pp. 371–384.

(www.edilex.fi/artikkelit/16167, visited 24.03.2017)

Pellonpää, Matti, Gullans, Monica, Pölönen, Pasi and Tapanila, Antti 2012: *Euroopan ihmisoikeussopimus.* Talentum. Helsinki 2012

Viljanen, Jukka 2007: *The European Convention of Human Rights and the Transformation of the Finnish Fundamental Rights System: The Model of Interpretative harmonisation and Interaction*, in Scandinavian Studies of Law, Volume 52, Constitutional Law, Stockholm 2007

Zyl van Smit, Dirk & Snacken, Sonja 2009: *Principles of European Prison law and Policy. Penology and Human Rights*. Oxford University Press. Oxford 2009.

Reports:

European Committee for the Prevention of Torture and Inhuman or Degrading Treatment or Punishment: *24th General Report of the CPT,* Council of Europe, 2015.

Country Reports by the European Committee for the Prevention of Torture and Inhuman or Degrading Treatment or Punishment:

Report to the Danish Government 1990, 1996, 2002, 2008, 2012, 2014.

Report to the Finnish Government 1992, 1998, 2003, 2008, 2014.

Report to the Icelandic Government, 1993, 1998, 2004, 2012.

Report to the Norwegian Government 1993, 1997, 1999, 2005, 2011.

Report to the Swedish Government 1991, 1994, 1998, 2003, 2009, 2015.

Government Responses to the CPT's country reports:

Response of the Authorities of the kingdom of the Netherlands, 2007, Strasbourg, 2009.

Response of the Danish Government 2014, Strasbourg, 2015.

Response of the Finnish Government 2014, Strasbourg, 2015.

Response of the Finnish Government to paragraph 26 of the European Committee for the Prevention of Torture and Inhuman or Degrading Treatment or Punishment on its visit to Finland 2014, Strasbourg, 2015.

Response of the German Government, 2013, Strasbourg, 2014.

Response of the Government of the Netherlands, 2011, Strasbourg, 2013.

Response of the Norwegian Government 2011, Strasbourg, 2012.

Response of the Swedish Government 2015, Strasbourg, 2016.

Case law:

European Court of Human Rights:

Lindström and Mässeli v. Finland, 24630/10, Strasbourg, 2014.

Rohde v. Denmark, 69332/01, 21/10/2005, Strasbourg, 2005.

Appendix I:

Denmark

CPT Visits in Danish Prisons (N = 24)	*1990*	*1996*	*2002*	*2008*	*2012*	*2014*
Aarhus Remand Prison						x
Blegdamsvejen Remand Prison (Copenhagen)	x					
East Jutland State Prison				x		
Elsinore Local Jail (Remand)			x			
Esbjerg Local Jail (Remand)		x				
Horsens State Prison		x	x			
Nuuk Prison					x	
Nyborg State Prison	x			x		
Odense Remand Prison						x
Ringe State Prison						x
Sandholm Foreigners Detention Centre			x			
The Herstedvester Institution	x	x		x		
The Police Headquarters Prison (Copenhagen)	x	x		x		x
Western Remand Prison (Copenhagen)	x	x		x		x
Vridsløselille			x			x

Iceland

CPT Visits in Icelandic Prisons (N = 5)	*1993*	*1998*	*2004*	*2012*
Akureyri Prison		x		x
Kvíabryggja Prison			x	
Kópavogur Prison	x	x	x	x
Litla-Hraun Prison	x	x	x	x
Reykjavík (Skólavörðustígur) Prison	x	x	x	x

Finland

CPT Visits in Finnish Prisons (N = 17)	*1992*	*1998*	*2003*	*2008*	*2014*
Helsinki Central Prison	x	x		x	x
Hämeenlinna Central Prison	x				
Hämeenlinna Local Prison	x				
Kerava Juvenile Prison	x				x
Kuopio Prison			x		
Riihimäki Central Prison		x		x	x
Sukeva Prison			x		
Turku Prison Mental Hospital	x				
Turku Remand Prison			x		
Vantaa Prison				x	x

Norway

CPT Visits in Norwegian Prisons (N = 17)	*1993*	*1997*	*1999*	*2005*	*2011*
Bergen Prison		x	x		x
Bjørgvin					x
Bredveit Detention and Security Prison					x
Eidsberg Prison					x
Ila Prison and Security Detention Institution	x			x	x
Oslo Prison	x	x	x		x
Ringerike				x	
Skien Prison					x
Trondheim				x	
Ullersmo Prison	x				

Sweden

CPT Visits in Swedish Prisons (N = 22)	*1991*	*1994*	*1998*	*2003*	*2009*	*2015*
Falun Remand Prison						x
Gothenburg Remand Prison				x	x	
Gävle Remand Prison					x	
Hall Prison					x	
Hinseberg Prison	x					
Huddinge Unit		x				
Kronoberg Remand Prison		x				x
Kumla Prison	x				x	
Malmö Remand Prison			x			x
Saltvik Prison						x
Sollentuna Remand Prison						x
Stockholm Remand Prison	x		x	x		
Tidaholm Prison				x		
Umeå Remand Prison				x		
Växjö Remand Prison						x
Österåker Prison			x			

Part III

Refusal and strong opposition to European monitoring and absence of European monitoring due to ancient and deep national traditions and political opposition to European institutions

8 England and Wales

An uncertain relationship with European institutions

Simon Creighton, Nicola Padfield and Rosaria Pirosa

Introduction

The invitation to contribute to this book offers us an opportunity to reflect not only on the monitoring of penal and prison policies in England and Wales,[1] as the title of the book suggests, but also to explore the tensions which exist between European institutions and agencies, and domestic ones. Our focus is the uneasy and evolving relationship between the European Court of Human Rights and English domestic courts, as they both seek to 'monitor' the application of penal policies. The United Kingdom (UK), with its strong common law traditions, has always had an uneasy relationship with the European Court of Human Rights (ECtHR) and with its jurisprudence. This relationship has become more strained and these are uncertain times in the UK's relationship with 'Europe'.

The British 'establishment' thinking back in the 1950s might have been that a European Convention on Human Rights (ECHR) was necessary for those 'Europeans', but not so necessary for 'us', with our tradition of common law civil liberties. We argue, by choosing to focus exclusively on two controversial policy areas, and largely on the relationship between the domestic courts and the European Court of Human Rights (ECtHR), that today the relationship with 'Europe' remains as tense as ever. We raise at the end concerns about what 'Brexit', the British Government's commitment to leaving the European Union (EU), may mean for this relationship. From our point of view, it is a great pity that the protections of the ECHR seem to be under challenge just as much as the political might of the EU. Judge Pinto de Albuquerque has developed this theme in his dissenting judgment in *Hutchinson v UK*,[2] a case to which we will return. At a time when the UK Government seems determined to withdraw from the ECHR as well as the EU, the ECtHR has simply accepted that it already has a downgraded role.

1 A little history

In the early days of post-World War II Europe, the UK was at the forefront of drafting 'solutions' to the failure of Europeans to live in peace, such as the ECHR, under the broad umbrella of the Council of Europe (CoE), which originally had 10 members and now has 47. The role held by the UK seems to have changed over time.

Prior to the enactment of the Human Rights Act (HRA) 1998, issues that raised ECHR rights would be considered by the domestic courts against the tests for judicial review: illegality, irrationality or procedural impropriety.[3] The 'irrationality' test can be seen as one of heightened reasonableness, sometimes referred to as the 'anxious scrutiny test'.[4] Ironically, while Convention rights were not directly enforceable through domestic litigation, compliance with the obligations imposed by membership of the Council of Europe was generally taken seriously on a political level. For example, the English prison system was changed significantly following judgments of the Court, particularly in the areas of parole, prison discipline and deaths in custody. Our first example is parole. The process of judicialising the implementation of indeterminate sentences began with the ECtHR's decision in *Thynne Wilson and Gunnell v UK*.[5] This was met with almost immediate change, by means of the Criminal Justice Act 1991, with the introduction of Discretionary Lifer Panels of the Parole Board.[6] Changes to ensure compliance with subsequent judgments affecting the release of juveniles detained at Her Majesty's pleasure[7] and the mandatory adult life sentence for murder[8] followed. The House of Lords anticipated that the mandatory life sentence would inevitably be found to be in violation of Article 6 and so issued a declaration of incompatibility in the early days of the HRA 1998.[9] Our second example is the rules on prison discipline. The Court's decision in *Ezeh and Conners v UK*,[10] that prison disciplinary hearings which risked additional days being added to prisoners' release dates required the protection of Article 6, was met with a swift change to the Prison Rules in England and Wales, to make provision for these cases to be heard by independent adjudicators (district judges), also giving prisoners the right to legal representation.[11] In Scotland, the power to award additional days was simply abolished.[12]

Further evidence of the domestic acceptance of the role of the ECtHR in determining the duties and obligations of the State can be found in the incorporation of Article 2 case-law into the domestic system for investigating deaths in custody. The obligations arising following a death in custody or after contact with state agents led to fundamental reform of both the investigative procedures and the coronial system, one of the most ancient courts in the UK.[13] As Baker noted, 'the most significant changes to coronial practice in relation to cases of death after police contact have been effected not by governmental action but by precedents driven by the ECtHR'.[14] These examples of political willingness have often been matched by appropriate judicial deference to the Court's unique role in providing the proper interpretation of Convention rights. Its apotheosis can perhaps be found in the cases concerning the imposition of control orders on persons suspected of involvement in terrorism and the degree of disclosure that they should be permitted to ensure fairness in the proceedings. Cases have been batted backwards and forwards between the domestic courts, the ECtHR and the legislature, culminating in the ECtHR decision in *A v United Kingdom*[15] which found that the domestic legislation did not provide for sufficient information to be provided before the imposition of a control order. The House of Lords accepted that this provided the definitive interpretation of Article 6 in this context, with Lord Rodger reducing the legal analysis to a level of simplicity that now seems to belong to a distant past: 'Even though we are dealing with rights under a United Kingdom statute, in reality, we have no choice: *Argentoratum locutum, iudicium finitum* – Strasbourg has spoken, the case is closed'.[16]

2 The Human Rights Act 1998

The Human Rights Act (HRA) 1998 directly incorporated (the vast majority of) the ECHR into domestic law. The Act has had an important impact on the culture of public decision-making, which is now more openly harnessed to the standards of the European Convention.[17] Those who work in prisons, for example, are probably significantly more aware of the 'judge on their shoulder' than they were before the enactment of the Act. In order to maintain the constitutional sovereignty of Parliament, section 3 of the Act allows domestic courts only to issue a 'declaration of incompatibility' where they consider that primary legislation is incompatible with a Convention right – they may not actually strike down the offending law. The Act has also created tensions over the role of the judiciary, not only in traditional constitutional theory (the doctrine of Parliamentary sovereignty) but in political reality: the relationship between domestic and European judges has not been easy, and the relationship between judges and politicians often equally tense.

In this regard, we explore in particular two sensitive issues in order to consider the extent to which the UK is currently prepared to comply with judgments of the ECtHR. Both have proved controversial: whole life sentences and prisoner voting rights. We scrutinise the various cases to show how the 'relationship' between courts and Government has evolved.

3 The 'whole life' sentence

Perhaps paradoxically, the willingness of the House of Lords in *Anderson*[18] to accept that the sentencing system for the mandatory life sentence was in breach of Article 6 resulted in the passing of the legislation that introduced, for the first time, a statutory provision for the imposition of a 'whole life' sentence. Paragraph 4 of Schedule 21 of the Criminal Justice Act 2003 explicitly identifies a starting point of 'whole life' for certain categories of murder. The then Secretary of State made it clear that this was intended to be a wholly punitive sentence that would impose significant limitations on judicial discretion:

> what I want are judges who, when they mean it, ensure that the sentences are such that the perpetrators know that we mean it and the victims know that we are going to protect them. That is why I announced that life will at last mean life – no remission, no supervision, no having to join the register because they will remain in jail for the rest of their lives.[19]

The 'whole life' sentence has been much contested in both European and domestic courts' case law, which illustrates many of the tensions that exist in interpreting the 'rule of law', both in the common law and the ECtHR.[20] The landmark case in the ECtHR was the decision in *Vinter*,[21] until the Grand Chamber rolled back from its position *Vinter* in the recent case of *Hutchinson*.[22] Until *Vinter*, the caution approach of the ECtHR case-law in respect of whole life terms had been, more or less, a ratification of the domestic courts' approach in the leading English decisions from *Hindley*,[23] through *Bieber*,[24] *Wellington*,[25] and *Oakes*,[26] to *McLoughlin*.[27] It is possible to suggest that the attitude of the UK Government and judiciary today has evolved from the deference shown by the Strasbourg judges. The Grand Chamber judgment in *Vinter* may be characterised as either more principled or more confrontational and an indication that the Strasbourg Court laid down a direct challenge to the English system. It fuelled arguments for the UK to remove itself from the European parameters, given the complained lack of British "ownership".[28] The English Court of Appeal responded strongly, rejecting the Grand Chamber's analysis, in *McLoughlin*, and in Hutchinson, the ECtHR has accepted the British rejection of *Vinter*. How has this position been reached?

The key judgment of the House of Lords on the lawfulness of whole life sentences prior to *Vinter* was *Wellington* v *Secretary of State for the Home Department*,[29] which concerned a man who faced two charges of murder in the first degree in Missouri, USA, for which the mandatory penalty was imprisonment for life without parole. He unsuccessfully challenged his extradition on the grounds of Article 3 of the ECHR.[30] The majority of the court took what was called a 'relativist approach' to the scope of Article 3. In the majority, Lord Hoffmann expressed the view that, in extradition cases, the fact that extradition is being sought in order that an individual should be tried for serious crimes alleged to have been committed by him in the requesting country, and the importance of extradition in preventing fugitive offenders from evading justice (see paras. 24 and 25 of Lord Hoffmann's opinion), justifies the adoption of a 'relativist' approach to what constitutes Article 3 inhuman or degrading treatment:

> A relativist approach to the scope of Article 3 seems to me essential if extradition is to continue to function. For example, the Court of Session has decided that in Scotland the practice of 'slopping out' (requiring a prisoner to use a chamber pot in his cell and empty it in the morning) may cause an infringement of Article 3. Whether, even in a domestic context, this attains the necessary level of severity is a point on which I would wish to reserve my opinion. If, however, it were applied in the context of extradition, it would prevent anyone being extradited to many countries poorer than Scotland, where people who are not in prison often have to make do without flush lavatories.[31]

Lord Brown and Lord Scott, on the other hand, had preferred an 'absolutist approach' to what constitutes inhuman or degrading treatment.[32] If the treatment or punishment likely to be faced by an individual if extradited to the requesting country and then tried, convicted and sentenced for the crimes in question would be inhuman or degrading for Article 3 purposes in a domestic context, the treatment or punishment would, in Lord Brown's opinion, count as inhuman or degrading in a foreign context, whether as a likely consequence of extradition, or of removal from the UK on refusal of immigration consent or for any other otherwise lawful reason. Thus, if there was potentially room to extradite to a jurisdiction with the discretionary death penalty,[33] it is not surprising that, in principle, the whole life order is admissible.[34] This has some parallels with the early interpretation of the mandatory life sentence in the UK as authorising lifelong punitive detention as the price to be paid for abolishing the death penalty.[35]

The House of Lords in *Wellington*, of course, explored the ECtHR case law. Baroness Hale concluded that, 'in short, the ECtHR has not yet said, either in *Kafkaris v Cyprus*,[36] or in any other case, that all irreducible life sentences are inhuman and degrading treatment within the meaning of Article 3'.[37] She added that: 'there may come a time when it will do so and we shall then have to have regard to that view. In the meantime, it has simply said that such sentences 'may raise an issue' under Article 3'.[38] Lord Brown stated, 'What I deduce from all this is that in reality the Strasbourg Court does not consider the question of irreducibility as a matter wholly distinct from the question whether some body (judicial or not) will one day take into account of the individual circumstances of the prisoner's case'.[39] While in the Cypriot system the sentencing and review was not judicial, so that an issue of compatibility with Article 5(4) and Article 6 could potentially arise in respect of sentences that fell short of whole life, under the view expressed by Lord Brown, the Strasbourg Court had simply established a generic duty of review that does not focus on the role of the judiciary.[40] Although *Kafkaris* concerned Cyprus, in the UK the judgment could be considered to be an endorsement by Strasbourg of English case law, even if, ultimately, it affirmed the requirement for reducibility when imposing a sentence of life imprisonment.[41]

Lord Phillips was also critical of the ECtHR's approach in the Court of Appeal in *Bieber*, pointing out that the test for deciding whether a life sentence is reducible 'does not emerge with any degree of clarity from *Kafkaris*'.[42] According to the domestic courts in both *Bieber* and *Wellington*, the judicial reasoning in *Kafkaris* encompassed two questions which could be considered as strictly linked: if an irreducible life sentence is found to violate Article 3, at what point does the violation occur? Lord Phillips' view was that, the imposition of an irreducible life sentence itself does not constitute a violation of Article 3, rather the potential violation only occurs once the prisoner has been detained beyond the period that can be justified on the grounds of punishment and deterrence. It is not the sentence, therefore, but the consequent detention that is capable of violating Article 3.[43] Turning to the procedural safeguards, he held that *Kafkaris* provided authority for the proposition that an executive review was sufficient and that as the Secretary of State had a power to release in compassionate circumstances under section 30 of the Crime Sentences Act 1997, a whole life order was not irreducible and thus not in violation of Article 3. In *Wellington*, the House of Lords approved this view and concluded that the simple passing of a mandatory life sentence, even in circumstances where no satisfactory laws or procedures were in place for an individualised review to determine the actual period to be served, does not violate Article 3.[44]

Following the Fourth Chamber judgment of the ECtHR in *Vinter*[45] and immediately prior to the Grand Chamber's hearing of the case, in *Oakes*[46] the Court of Appeal affirmed the domestic interpretation that whole life orders were not incompatible with Article 3 of the Convention. The judgment focused in large part on the fact that the sentence was not mandatory and concluded that the jurisprudence of the ECtHR had established the principle that, 'a whole life order imposed as a matter of judicial discretion as to the appropriate level of punishment and deterrence following conviction for a crime of utmost seriousness would not constitute inhuman or degrading punishment. In short, it is open to the individual state to make statutory provision for the imposition of a whole life minimum term, and in an appropriate case, as a matter of judicial discretion, for the court to make such an order.'[47]

The view taken by the domestic Courts appears to be that if a whole life sentence is justified at the time it is passed, the issue of the reducibility can arise only at a *later* stage if the balance between retribution and deterrence and subsequent developments means that the penological justification for the sentence no longer exists. The judicialization in *Stafford v UK*[48] of the release procedures for mandatory life sentences where a fixed minimum term had been imposed did not address the issue of whole life sentences. The Grand Chamber judgment in *Vinter* clearly drew a distinction between the regime which governed the imposition of the sentence – which can permit the judicial imposition of a whole life sentence – and the regime for the reducibility of that sentence through review. The complaint in *Vinter* was founded on the conceptual lack of clarity in section 30 of the Crimes (Sentences) Act 1997 and the practical fact that it is applied in a very restrictive way. The dearth of certainty that limits the power of release on compassionate grounds and the absence of an effective prospect of review represent the crucial components of the irreducibility of the whole life sentence. The real innovation contained in the Grand Chamber judgment is that there must be a review mechanism in place that is not limited to compassionate grounds; that the prisoner must be told when the review will take place; and, the prisoner must be told what they must do to have a prospect of release, in particular what are the criteria that the reviewer will apply when considering release. Critically, it is the absence of these criteria at the moment the sentence is passed constitutes the breach of Article 3, refusing to allow the problem to be shunted off to some future, unspecified date. What *Vinter* failed to do was to be proscriptive about the nature of the review by, for example, transposing the *Stafford* release requirements to review of the continued penological justification for the sentence.[49]

The domestic response to *Vinter* by the Court of Appeal in *McLoughlin* was as rapid as it was uncompromising. In the first ten paragraphs, the Court of Appeal seemed to affirm the Strasbourg perspective but they then proceeded to take a hardened position against *Vinter* holding that 'the Grand Chamber were mistaken in concluding that the statutory regime for the reducibility of the sentence by review and release was insufficiently certain; and that uncertainty gave rise to a breach of Article 3'.[50] Following a direct quotation of the crucial paragraph 129 of *Vinter*, the Court commented starkly: 'We disagree'.[51] In order to remove any doubt, the Lord Chief Justice added that, 'It is important, therefore, that we make clear what the law of England and Wales is'[52] before re-stating that the decisions in *Bieber* and *Oakes* had been correct and all that *Vinter* had added was the requirement to exercise the executive power of compassionate release compatibly with the HRA in those exceptional cases where the penological justification for imprisonment may have changed:

> It is entirely consistent with the rule of law that such requests are considered on an individual basis against the criteria that circumstances have exceptionally changed so as to render the original punishment which was justifiable no longer justifiable. We find it difficult to specify in advance what such circumstances might be, given that the heinous nature of the original crime justly required punishment by imprisonment for life. But circumstances can and do change in exceptional cases. The interpretation of s. 30 we have set out provides for that possibility and hence gives to each such prisoner the possibility of exceptional release.[53]

In the subsequent report on the execution of the judgment in *Vinter*, the communication provided by the UK Government was unequivocal in its view that *McLoughlin* had settled the matter conclusively: 'The Court of Appeal has set out the operation of domestic law. That is a question which it is uniquely well placed to determine authoritatively and conclusively. . . . In those circumstances, the Government considers that no further general measures are necessary in the present case. . . . and the case should be closed'.[54] This reasoning was accepted in its entirety in the Chamber decision in *Hutchinson v UK*.[55] The Court noted that it is primarily the role of national courts to resolve issues pertaining to the correct interpretation of domestic legislation[56] and that where a national court has specifically and unequivocally stated the legal position, 'the Court must accept the national court's interpretation of domestic law'.[57] This approach was accepted by the Grand Chamber (14 votes to 3):

> In the *McLoughlin* decision the Court of Appeal responded explicitly to the *Vinter* critique. It affirmed the statutory duty of the Secretary of State to exercise the power of release compatibly with Article 3 of the Convention. As for the published policy, which it too regarded as highly restrictive (at paragraphs 11 and 32 of *McLoughlin*, see paragraph 19 above), the Court of Appeal clarified that the Lifer Manual cannot restrict the duty of the Secretary of State to consider all circumstances relevant to release under section 30. Nor can the published policy fetter the Secretary of State's discretion by taking account only of the matters stipulated in the Lifer Manual. The failure to revise official policy so as to align it with the relevant statutory provisions and case law is, the Court of Appeal explained, of no consequence as a matter of domestic law.
>
> The Court considers that the Court of Appeal has brought clarity as to the content of the relevant domestic law, resolving the discrepancy identified in

> the *Vinter* judgment. Although *Vinter* contemplated that the policy might be replaced or quashed in the course of judicial review proceedings (*Vinter and Others*, cited above, § 129), the Court notes the Government's submission that the Lifer Manual retains its validity in relation to release on compassionate (in the narrow sense of humanitarian) grounds. What is important is that, as confirmed in *McLoughlin*, this is just one of the circumstances in which the release of a prisoner may, or indeed must, be ordered.
>
> (see paragraphs 32–33 of *McLoughlin*) (at paras 39–40)[58]

Thus, the ECtHR appears to have agreed with the British Government and the Court of Appeal that the 'whole life' prisoner, at the point of the imposition of the sentence, does not need to know what he must do to have a real prospect of release. The decision provokes three dissents, including a powerful and lengthy one from Judge Pinto de Albuquerque, who passionately argues that 'the majority's ingenious effort to reconcile the letter and spirit of *Vinter* with *McLoughlin* raises not only questions of linguistic precision, logical coherence and legal certainty that were left unanswered in the present judgment, but also the fundamental issue of the compatibility of section 2 of the Human Rights Act 1998 ('the Act'), as applied in the present case by the Court of Appeal of England and Wales ('the Court of Appeal'), with the Convention'.[59]

Relying in particular on the Grand Chamber's decision in *Murray v the Netherlands*,[60] Judge Pinto comments that having established the 'relevant principles',[61] it could be expected that the Court had reached in *Murray* a point of no return in its standard-setting function for the protection of human rights of prisoners in Europe. 'Unfortunately this expectation proved to be wrong in the present case'.[62] He is deeply critical of the position taken by the British Government, the British courts and the Grand Chamber. He discusses the 'seismic consequences'[63] of the present judgment for Europe:

> The majority's decision represents a peak in a growing trend towards downgrading the role of the Court before certain domestic jurisdictions, with the serious risk that the Convention is applied with double standards. If the Court goes down this road, it will end up as a non-judicial commission of highly qualified and politically legitimised 47 experts, which does not deliver binding judgments, at least with regard to certain Contracting Parties, but pronounces mere recommendations on 'what it would be desirable' for domestic authorities to do, acting in an mere auxiliary capacity, in order to 'aid' them in fulfilling their statutory and international obligations. The probability of deleterious consequences for the entire European system of human-rights protection is heightened by the current political environment, which shows an increasing hostility to the Court.[64]

He also argues:

> The relationship between national law and the Convention is peculiarly unbalanced. The 'human rights diversity' argument reveals its real face as a

> politically unidirectional, sovereignist card, played with regard to the import of human rights and justifying the refusal of 'alien', i.e., Convention standards imposed by an international court. Of course, this also entails a biased understanding of the logical obverse of the doctrine of the 'diversity of human rights', namely the doctrine of the margin of appreciation: the margin should be wider for those States which are supposed 'to set an example for others' and narrower for those States which are supposed to learn from the example. This evidently leaves the door wide open for certain governments to satisfy their electoral base and protect their favourite vested interests. In my humble view, this is not what the Convention is all about.[65]

For Judge Pinto, *McLoughlin* illustrates the potential weakness of the Human Rights Act model, when a domestic court does not take full account of the Strasbourg case-law. The Court of Appeal did not cure the defects of the domestic law following *Vinter and Others*. Judge Sajo's dissenting opinion is also blunt:

> I could not follow the majority, for the reasons expressed in the separate opinion of Judge Paulo Pinto de Albuquerque. Even assuming that 'compassionate grounds' may mean anything a judge finds reasonable in the United Kingdom, it certainly cannot provide the specific guidance to the prisoner that was stipulated in *Murray v. the Netherlands* a mere six months ago.[66]

We quote at length from these dissenting opinions as we have considerable sympathy with them. The published criteria for release still amount to compassionate release only in highly restrictive circumstances, essentially restricted to the health of the prisoner. In practice, this presents no movement whatsoever from the law as interpreted in *Wellington*, where it was noted by Lord Brown that even if the law precludes all possibility of release or the facts demonstrate that virtually no one ever is released, 'the majority [in Kafkaris] appear to conclude no more than that it *may* raise an issue under Article 3 (not that it should be held 'in principle inconsistent with Article 3')'.[67] So, under these highly restrictive criteria, in England and Wales, the merest possibility of compassionate release at an unspecified future date means that the whole life order is not only *de jure* but also *de facto* irreducible. There are probably 70 prisoners serving a whole life sentence at the moment in England and Wales,[68] and no whole life prisoner has ever been granted compassionate release.[69] As was emphasised by counsel for Mr. Hutchinson before the Grand Chamber, 'a more compelling argument relating the real nature of the whole tariff order as conceived by the UK Government is that the number of the prisoners released is akin to zero'.[70] This is entirely consistent with the rationale outlined by the Secretary of State who introduced the legislation.[71]

Do the margin of appreciation and the need to respect domestic legal tradition give room for the domestic Court's reaction to *Vinter* and for the turn in *Hutchinson*? It is difficult to accept that the Court did not have sufficient or specific knowledge of the English system, not least because the view expressed in *McLoughlin* amounted to little more than a restatement of the earlier decisions which had been explicitly rejected by the Grand Chamber in *Vinter*.[72] The recognition that the violation of Article 3 occurs at the imposition of the sentence due to the absence of a review process also has the potential to create a tension between life prisoners who have received a very long tariff and whole life prisoners. The concept of what has been described as a '*Vinter* review' is different from the review by the Parole Board required in England and Wales after a prisoner has served a minimum period set by the sentencing court, a post-tariff review: 'The key difference is that in a '*Vinter review*' all the penological justifications for the original sentence – including the seriousness of the offence – must be reviewed to determine whether the balance between them has changed and the continued detention is justified'.[73] By contrast, the post tariff review addresses only the question of ongoing risk.

Although the Court did not endorse an 'absolutist approach' (notwithstanding even the Pope's approval of such an approach[74]), in the Grand Chamber judgment in *Vinter*, the Strasbourg position then expressed the predominance of legal principle over political expediency. The concept of a 'prospect of release' requires that the whole tariff order is reducible *de jure*, given that the judicialization of the sentence cannot be considered as an effective remedy. The practice of the Secretary of State and the domestic Court weigh on the reducibility *de facto*. In theory, the Court can order the Secretary of State to release a 'whole life' prisoner if the whole life sentence is no longer justified on legitimate penological grounds, but this is not a realistic possibility.[75] Perhaps the Grand Chamber judgment in *Vinter* simply incubated the antagonism that Westminster holds towards Strasbourg and has given fresh impetus to the Conservative Party's threat to retreat from the European Convention entirely.[76] The facts of *Hutchinson* replicate *Vinter*, so a finding of a violation of the ECHR Article 3 was likely. However, the Court effectively abandoned its previous approach and accepted that the UK is a compliant Contracting State (or, perhaps more accurately, concealing the fact that the UK is a non-complaint State). The threat to repeal the Human Rights Act, to withdraw from the European Convention and from the protections and standards of Article 3 – as the public declaration to selectively implement judgments indicates – could affect the others Members of the Council of Europe.[77]

An alternative reading of *Hutchinson* is that it does not represent a real overruling of authority, but a political insertion into the case-law of the ECtHR.[78] The Strasbourg Court not only endorsed the authoritativeness of the English Court of Appeal but also rubber stamped the UK government's position, because the *McLoughlin* decision appears as an example of 'legal formalism',[79] which neutralizes the judicialization of the sentence whole-life imprisonment. In this interpretation, the Strasbourg Court confirms the domestic Court as the authoritative interpreter of the domestic legislation, even if the statutory regime is not compliant, and moreover, as the real interpreter of the European Convention itself.[80] Under this analysis, it would be wrong to interpret *McLoughlin* as a *specimen* of 'functional disobedience'.[81] No legal change occurs in the English system, either in the law or in the practice: what has changed is the position of the European Court.

The political dimension to the decision is underlined by several judgments following *Vinter*. In *Öcalan v Turkey*[82] the ECtHR considered whether the applicant, a convicted terrorist serving a whole life sentence, was the victim of a violation of Article 3 ECHR on the ground that his sentence was irreducible. The Court observed that the Turkish President was able to order the release of a whole life sentenced prisoner on humanitarian grounds, namely where the prisoner was elderly or ill. However, they held that this discretionary power of release did not constitute a 'prospect of release' for the purposes of Article 3 ECHR. In *Murray v Netherlands*[83] there was a clear application of *Vinter* principles, with the judgment confirming that the review 'must be based on rules having a sufficient degree of clarity and certainty' and 'objective pre-established criteria'; these conditions 'must be laid down in domestic legislation'; the possibility of release on compassionate grounds such as ill-health or old age "does not correspond to the notion of 'prospect of release'; and, that the review must entail 'an actual assessment of relevant information' and be 'surrounded by sufficient procedural guarantees'.[84] Indeed, even in the extradition context the ECtHR has abandoned the relativist approach in respect of Article 3 and whole life sentences that was lighted upon by the House of Lords in *Wellington*.[85] This affirmation of the need for such sentences to be reducible both *de jure* and *de facto* affirms and develops the findings in *Vinter*, but in *Hutchinson*, the European Court seems determined to appease the British Government.

4 Prisoners' voting rights

The former Prime Minister, David Cameron, signaled the depths of his political resistance to prisoner voting with his extraordinary and ill-judged remark in the House of Commons that:

> I see no reason why prisoners should have the vote. This is not a situation that I want this country to be in. It makes me physically ill even to contemplate having to give the vote to anyone who is in prison.[86]

The background to this was the pilot-judgment[87] *Greens and M.T.*,[88] where the ECtHR held that where a breach of the Convention is identified, individuals are entitled to an effective remedy under the Article 13. So long as the UK Government continues to delay the removal of the blanket ban on prisoner voting, it risks not only political embarrassment at the Council of Europe, but also the potential cost of repeat litigation and any associated compensation. However, in *Firth and Others*[89] and *McHugh and Others*,[90] the Strasbourg Court concluded that, although there had been a violation of Article 3 of Protocol 1 of the European Convention, they declined to award any compensation or legal expenses, holding that the finding of a breach was sufficient 'just satisfaction' in itself. This position builds on the views expressed in previous judgments, especially with the minority opinion in the Grand Chamber judgment in *Hirst (2)*[91] and the majority in *Scoppola (3)*.[92] The current approach of the judiciary and legislature in the UK could be said to find endorsement from the Strasbourg court.

The joint dissenting opinion in the Grand Chamber decision in *Hirst (2)*, according to which the Court was not a legislator and should be careful not to assume legislative functions,[93] seems to echo the perspective of the Divisional Court in *Hirst v HM Attorney General*[94] concerning the reluctance to question the Representation of the People Act 1983's blanket ban on prisoner voting.[95] The minority in the Grand Chamber judgment in *Hirst (2)* accused the majority of judicial activism and intrusiveness – a reflection of the Cameron position. Cameron indicated that he would continue supporting Parliament's earlier decision against allowing prisoners to vote, arguing that this issue should be a matter for Parliament to decide, not a foreign court.[96] Regarding prisoners' voting rights, the enhancement of the doctrine of the margin of appreciation allows the UK not to consider the pressure of the issue of compatibility of the national legislation with the Article 3 of Protocol 1 to the European Convention.

Given the persistence of the disenfranchisement, in *Greens and M.T.* the position of the European Court became clear, as for the first and only time, it ordered the UK to amend its legislation, tabling proposals. After the February 2011 debate in Parliament,[97] the UK government position remained that the domestic legislation was reasonable and did not require any amendment. The Government was not alone in its view. Senior judges argued that the European Court of Human Rights should not set itself up as a national Constitutional Court because, on matters such as whole-life imprisonment and prisoners, voting rights, the sovereignty of Parliament cannot be infringed.[98]

The Grand Chamber rejected the request to refer the *Greens and M.T.* case to itself, but in *Scoppola* (3) emphasized its appeasement, confirming the finding of the incompatibility of disenfranchisement with the European Convention, but affirming that the tools to amend the legislation can be wide. As Bates concludes, 'the *Scoppola* (Grand Chamber) judgment upheld a conservative European consensus, self-restrained line, more in keeping with the approach advocated by the *Hirst* minority'.[99] It was not just a coincidence that, following this decision, the Voting Eligibility (Prisoners) Draft Bill confirmed the blanket ban on prisoners' voting rights. The UK Government had been given a further six months following the *Scoppola (3)* decision to bring forward legislative proposals to amend the law. The Voting Eligibility (Prisoners) Bill was drafted to give Members of Parliament three options on which to vote: retain the ban for prisoners jailed for over four years; retain the ban for prisoners jailed for over six months; retain the current ban.

The pre-legislative scrutiny by the Joint Committee on the Bill endorsed a rights-based approach that would abolish universal disenfranchisement of convicted prisoners.[100] They recommended that the Government introduce a Bill at the start of the 2014–15 session, to provide that all prisoners serving sentences of 12 months or less should be entitled to vote in all UK parliamentary, local and European elections; and that prisoners should be entitled to apply, up to 6 months before their scheduled release date, to be registered to vote in the constituency into which they are due to be released.[101] No Bill has been brought before Parliament.

Meanwhile, in *Chester*, *R (Chester and McGeoch) v Secretary of State for Justice*[102] seven justices of the Supreme Court unanimously maintained the position determined in Strasbourg that the UK's blanket ban on voting was contrary to the ECtHR, though it refused to make a further declaration of incompatibility. In four separate judgments, the judges explored at length both the implications of the blanket ban, and the jurisprudence of the ECtHR. Lord Mance (with whom Lord Hope, Lord Hughes and Lord Kerr agreed) declined the Government's invitation not to apply the principles in *Hirst (No 2)* and *Scoppola (No 3)* (at paras 34–35), but also decline to make any further declaration of incompatibility with the Convention rights (paras 39–42). Lord Clarke and Lady Hale (with whom Lords Hope and Kerr agreed) made separate judgments which were less critical of the Strasbourg jurisprudence. The most critical was Lord Sumption (with whom Lord Hughes agreed):

> The Strasbourg Court has arrived at a very curious position. It has held that it is open to a Convention state to fix a minimum threshold of gravity which warrants the disenfranchisement of a convicted person. It has held that the threshold beyond which he will be disenfranchised may be fixed by law by reference to the nature of the sentence. It has held that disenfranchisement may be automatic, once a sentence above that threshold has been imposed. But it has also held that even with the wide margin of appreciation allowed to Convention states in this area, it is not permissible for the threshold for disenfranchisement to correspond with the threshold for imprisonment. Wherever the threshold for imprisonment is placed, it seems to have been their view that there must always be some offences which are serious enough to warrant imprisonment but not serious enough to warrant disenfranchisement. Yet the basis of this view is nowhere articulated. It might perhaps have been justified by a careful examination of the principles of sentencing in the UK . . . However, no such exercise appears to have been carried out . . . Without the decisions in *Hirst* and *Scoppola*, I would have held that the question how serious an offence has to be to warrant temporary disenfranchisement is a classic matter for political and legislative judgment, and that the UK rule is well within any reasonable assessment of a Convention state's margin of appreciation. However, the contrary view has now been upheld twice by the Grand Chamber of the ECtHR, and is firmly established in the court's case-law. It cannot be said that the Grand Chamber overlooked or misunderstood any relevant principle of English law. There is no realistic prospect that further dialogue with Strasbourg will produce a change of heart. In those circumstances, we would be justified in departing from the case-law of the Strasbourg Court only if the disenfranchisement of convicted prisoners could be categorised as a fundamental feature of the law of the UK. I would regard that as an extreme suggestion, and in agreement with Lord Mance I would reject it. A wider and perhaps more realistic assessment of the margin of appreciation would have avoided the current controversy. But it would be neither wise nor legally defensible for an English court to say that Article 3 of the First Protocol has a meaning different from that which represents the settled view of the principal court charged with its interpretation, and different from that which will consequently apply in every other state party to the Convention.[103]

The Supreme Court in *Chester* and *McGeoch* also underlined the critical aspects of the statutory regime concerning the prisoners voting right.[104] If on one hand, the English system challenges the role of Strasbourg, on the other the Court itself seems not unequivocally to support the introduction of a more advanced standard of protection. This was further manifested in the Grand Chamber judgment in *Scoppola (3)* which perpetuated the ambiguity and did not give clear criteria regarding the criteria needed to address disenfranchisement.[105] The fundamental point of the debate on the prisoners voting right seems not to be *Greens & M.T.*, but rather the effective overturning of *Hirst (2)* through the *post-Scoppola* regime. As has been previously noted, the decisions of the European Court have been proscriptive, explaining what approaches are impermissible, but it has been less able to be prescriptive and to identify what measures must be taken. The cases on prisoners' right to vote illustrates the limitations of this approach where several years after the judgment was delivered no changes have yet been implemented.[106]

Conclusions

So, what we have learnt from our two case studies? That, despite much litigation, the British Government, supported by the domestic courts, still maintains both a 'whole life' order, without any possibility of review (except for the largely irrelevant possibility of compassionate release) and a blanket ban on all convicted prisoners registering to vote in elections. We have explored the debates, particularly between courts, between dissenting and majority judgments. Perhaps the reaction to *Vinter* would have been less strong if the ECtHR had not already handed down the decision in *Greens and M.T.* The 'whole-life imprisonment saga' and the 'prisoners voting saga' have fed each other as part of the wider 'Strasbourg and Westminster saga'. Within this drama, from a political point of view, the *Firth* and *McHugh* judgments can be viewed as the forerunners of *Hutchinson.* And so, the story continues. The current threat of upheaval is the threatened escape from the 'chains' of the Council of Europe and the Human Rights Act,[107] with the promise of a new future of a UK Bill of Rights outside of the constraints of international law.

It is ironic that the implementation of the Human Rights Act 1998, which was intended to enhance and embed Convention rights in domestic law, appears to have resulted in both a growing divergence between the UK and Strasbourg, and a weakening of the position of the ECtHR in relation to the UK. The doctrine of Parliamentary supremacy in domestic law has always raised tensions with the role of a supra-national court adjudicating on fundamental rights. The growing political mistrust of the concept of codification of rights as being contrary to the perceived flexibility of the English common law and the more fundamental concern that political issues with wider public policy issues are not amenable to simple legal solutions. These concerns are of course shared by members of the judiciary: Lord Sumption, speaking out of court but as a member of the Supreme Court, suggested that the ECtHR 'has become the international flag-bearer for judge-made fundamental law extending well beyond the text which it is charged with applying'.[108] With Judge Pinto de Albuquerque, we disagree with this interpretation. The ECtHR has emerged post-*Hutchinson* weakened.[109] Its role should be to protect human rights against the political will of government. We remain convinced that the ECtHR was acting entirely appropriately to find against both the total ban on voting, and the absence of any realistic review of 'whole life' tariffs in English law. At a time when it seems very likely that British government will seek to withdraw from the European Convention on Human Rights as well as the EU, it is particularly disappointing that the Strasbourg court in *Hutchinson* failed to stand firm in monitoring the human rights of prisoners in the UK, appearing to accept that it already has a downgraded role.

Notes

1 There are in effect four main 'nations' and legal jurisdictions within the United Kingdom: England, Wales, Scotland and Northern Ireland. We focus on legal regime applicable in England and Wales. When the term 'English' is used in this chapter, it should be taken to mean 'England and Wales'. The term 'British' is used more loosely, referring to the peoples of Great Britain or the United Kingdom.
2 *Hutchinson v United Kingdom* GC, App. no. 57592/08, 17 January 2017.
3 These heads of judicial review were explored in the classic GCHQ (Government Communications Headquarters) case, (*Council of Civil Service Unions v Minister for the Civil Service* [1985] AC 374.
4 See e.g.: R v Ministry of Defence ex parte Smith [1996] 2 WLR 305.
5 Thynne Wilson and Gunnell v United Kingdom (1990) 13 EHRR 666.
6 See N. Padfield, Beyond the Tariff: Human rights and the release of life sentence prisoners (Devon: Willan Publishing, 2002).
7 Following the judgment in *Hussain v United Kingdom* (2006) 22 EHRR 1, *interim* remedial measures were introduced within 6 months pending formal statutory change in the Crime (Sentences) Act 1997.
8 Stafford v United Kingdom (2002) 35 EHRR 32.
9 R (Anderson) v Secretary of State for the Home Department [2002] UKHL 46.
10 Ezeh and Conners v UK (2004) 39 EHRR 3.
11 These changes were inserted into the Prison Rules 1999, rules 53–56.
12 See the Prisons and Young Offenders Institutions (Scotland) Rules 2011 at rule 114.
13 R (JL) v Secretary of State for Justice [2008] UKHL 68; R (AM and others) v Secretary of State for the Home Department [2009] EWCA Civ 219.
14 D. Baker, Deaths after police contact in England and Wales: the effects of Article 2 of the European Convention on Human Rights on coronial practice, 12 International Journal of Law in Context (2016), at p. 164.
15 *A v United Kingdom* (2009) 49 EHRR 29.
16 R (AF) v Secretary of State for the Home Department [2009] UKHL 28 at para 98.
17 Irvine, Lord, 'The Impact of the Human Rights Act 1998: Parliament, the courts and the executive' [2003] Public Law 308.
18 R (Anderson) v Secretary of State for the Home Department [2002] UKHL 46.
19 David Blunkett's speech to the Police Federation, 30 March 2003. See www.ukpol.co.uk/2016/03/30/david-blunkett-2003-speech-to-the-police-federation/.
20 Judge Bratza, in an interview with the *Guardian*, on 31 January 2012 declared: "allowing states to override decisions of the Human Rights Court would be contrary to the rule of law and 'totally destructive of the system'". See www.theguardian.com/law/2012/jan/31/joshua-rozenberg-interviews-nicolas-bratza.
21 Vinter and others v The United Kingdom GC, (2013) 63 EHRR 1.
22 Hutchinson v United Kingdom (2015) 61 EHRR 13.

23 *R (Hindley) v Secretary of State for the Home Department [2001]* 1 AC 410. In the House of Lords, counsel for the Home Secretary made clear that the Home Secretary was prepared to review any whole life tariff, even in the absence of exceptional circumstances: see p. 417. Myra Hindley died, so the question of the compliance of the whole tariff order imposed on her with the ECHR Article 3 did not then go before the Strasbourg Court. This case is significantly quoted by the Court of Appeal in *Newell and McLoughlin, R v Newell and R v McLoughlin* [2014] EWCA Crim 188, para 7.

24 *R v Bieber* [2008] EWCA Crim 1601.

25 R (Wellington) v Secretary of State for the Home Department [2008] UKHL 72.

26 *R v Oakes and Others* [2012] EWCA Crim 818.

27 R v McLoughlin, supra note 23.

28 S. H. Foster, Whole Life Sentences and Article 3 of the European Convention of Human Rights: Time for Certainty and a Common Approach, 36 Liverpool Law Review, 2015, at 167–169.

29 R (Wellington) v Secretary of State for the Home Department, supra note 25.

30 After his return to the US, he agreed to plead guilty to voluntary manslaughter as part of a plea bargain and received a 15 year determinate sentence.

31 At para 20.

32 Although the ECHR Article 3 is referred to and labelled as "absolute" by domestic institutions (as we see in the quoted case within the extradition context) and by the ECtHR itself, the application of the notions of inhuman and degrading treatment can include a degree of "relativism" that calls into question the ECHR Article 3 non-derogable protection. In this chapter, we use the dichotomy absolutist-relativist approach to interpret the "relativist" tendency of the Strasbourg Court in some cases of violation of the Article 3 by a particular Contracting State such as United Kingdom.

33 Lord Brown held that "discretionary death sentences, on the other hand, are not in themselves contrary to Article 3. As the ECtHR expressly stated in *Soering v UK* (1989) 11 EHRR, 439 at para 103: 'Article 3 cannot be interpreted as generally prohibiting death penalty' (although the Court held that the extradition to Virginia to face protracted suffering on death row would breach Article 3)", ibid, para 64.

34 Concerning the ECtHR relativist approach, see also N. Mavronicola, *What is an 'absolute right'? Deciphering Absoluteness in the Context of Article 3 of the Europe Rights*, 12 Human Rights Law Review, (2012), at pp. 723–758; N. Mavronicola, *Crime Punishment and Article 3 ECHR: Puzzles and Prospects of Applying an Absolute Right in a Penal Context*, 15 Human Rights Law Review, (2015), at pp. 721–743.

35 This interpretation of the mandatory life sentence had been accepted by the ECtHR as late as 1994 – *Wynne v United Kingdom* (1995) 19 EHRR 333 and was not finally laid to rest until the *Stafford* decision in 2002 (*supra* note 8).

36 *Kafkaris v Cyprus* GC, (2009) 49 EHHR 35.

37 R (Wellington) v Secretary of State for the Home Department, para 49, supra note 25.

38 Ibid.

39 Ibid., para 78.

40 Ibid.

41 Concerning this point, M. Pettigrew, *A tale of two cities: Whole of Life Prison Sentences in Strasbourg and Westminster*, 23 European Journal of Crime, Criminal Law and Criminal Justice (2015), at 286.

42 *R v Bieber*, para 44, *supra* note 24.

43 Ibid., para 43.

44 R (Wellington) v Secretary of State for the Home Department, para 82, supra note 25.

45 Vinter v United Kingdom, (2012) 55 EHRR 34.

46 R v Oakes and Others, supra note 26.

47 Ibid., para 22.

48 *Supra* note 8.

49 See, D. Van Zyl Smit, P. Weatherby, S. Creighton, *Whole Life Sentences and the Tide of European Human Rights Jurisprudence: What is to Be Done*, 14 Human Rights Law Review, 2014, at 1–26.
50 *R v Newell and R v McLoughlin*, para 12, Lord Thomas CJ, *supra* note 23.
51 Ibid., para 29.
52 Ibid., para 30.
53 Ibid., para 36.
54 DH-DD (2014) 857: Communication from the United Kingdom concerning the case of Vinter and Others against the United Kingdom.
55 (2015) 61 EHRR 13. Referral to the Grand Chamber, 1 June 2015.
56 Para 24.
57 Para 26.
58 Hutchinson v United Kingdom GC, paras 39–40, supra note 2.
59 *Ibid.*, Dissenting Opinion of Judge Pinto de Albuquerque, para 1.
60 *Murray v Netherlands* GC, 10511/10, [2016] ECHR 408.
61 *Hutchinson v United Kingdom* GC, Dissenting Opinion of Judge Pinto de Albuquerque, para 10.
62 Ibid.
63 Ibid. para 38.
64 Ibid.
65 Ibid., para 40.
66 Ibid., Separate opinion of Judge Sajó.
67 R (Wellington) v Secretary of State for the Home Department, para 72, supra note 25.
68 Although the Government stated that as of 30 June 2016, that there were 53 'whole life' prisoners (see *Story of the Prison Population: 2013–2016 England and Wales*, July 2016, Ministry of Justice), most commentators put the figure nearer 70, and there may have been 100 since its introduction. See https://en.wikipedia.org/wiki/List_of_prisoners_with_whole-life_tariffs.
69 Including Myra Hindley who died in prison having had her applications for compassionate release refused, *supra* note 23.
70 ECtHR, Grand Chamber, *Hutchinson* hearing, Strasbourg, 21 October 2015.
71 Ibid.
72 On the claim that the European Court is changing the very nature of whole life sentences together, see S. H. Foster, *Whole Life Sentences and Article 3 of the European Convention of Human Rights: Time for Certainty and a Common Approach*?, at 165–166, *supra* note 28.
73 D. Van Zyl Smit, P. Weatherby, S. Creighton, Whole Life Sentences and the Tide of European Human Rights Jurisprudence: What is to Be Done, at 1, supra note 49.
74 See M. A. Almenara, D. Van Zyl Smit, *Human Dignity and Life Imprisonment: The Pope Enters the Debate*, 15 Human Rights Law Review, (2015), at pp. 369–376.
75 In hearing of *Hutchinson* before the Grand Chamber, the interventions of both judges and the applicant's lawyers directly addressed this issue. Interestingly, drawing on this line of jurisprudence from Strasbourg, even the Zimbabwean Constitutional Court has reached the view that not only is a 'whole life' sentence unconstitutional due to its denial of 'human dignity', but that the wholly discretionary remedy of executive pardon was insufficiently justiciable to satisfy the requirements of a review which can bear on the penological justification for the sentence to continue, *Makoni v Commissioner of Prison and another* CCZ 08–16: http://veritaszim.net/node/1745.
76 "In the event that we are unable to reach the agreement with the Council of Europe for renegotiation of terms, the UK would be left with no alternatives but to withdraw from the European Convention on Human Rights", D. Morrison, *Will a Conservative Government Withdraw from the European Convention on Human Rights?* Huffington Post, 15 October 2014, www.huffingtonpost.co.uk/david-morrison/

will-the-uk-supreme-court_b_7581174.html; See also S. Creighton, *Are Whole Life Tariffs Inhumane?*, 177, Criminal Law & Justice Weekly, 2013.

77 On this concern see M. Pettigrew, A tale of two cities: Whole of Life Prison Sentences in Strasbourg and Westminster, at 291–292, supra note 41.

78 See also N. Hart, Whole-life sentences in the UK: volte-face at the European Court of Human Rights?, 74 Cambridge Law Journal, 2015.

79 We could use this expression under the perspective of the philosophy of law, see S. J. Shapiro, *Legality*, (Belknap: Harvard 2011), at 241–243.

80 In direct contrast to the decision in *A v United Kingdom* and the deference to Strasbourg previously shown by the domestic courts, *supra* note 15.

81 See G. Martinico "Constitutional Courts (or Supreme) and 'functional disobedience'" edited by "diritto penale contemporaneo", G. Martinico, "Corti Costituzionali (O Supreme) e 'disobbedienza funzionale'": www.penaleconteporaneo.it/upload/1430150015MARTINICO_2015.pdf. This argument (what argument) has been often used by the Government in relation to both whole life imprisonment and prisoners' voting rights and it has been actually included in the Brighton Declaration 2012 High Level Conference on the Future of the European Court of Human Rights, Brighton Declaration, sections 10–11–12.

82 *Öcalan v Turkey*, 24069/03, 197/04, 6201/06 and 10464/07, [2014] ECHR 286.

83 Murray v Netherlands GC, supra note 60.

84 Ibid., para 100.

85 *Trabelsi v Belgium* (2015) 60 EHRR 21.

86 A. Hough (2011) "Prisoner vote: what MPs said in heated debate", The Telegraph, 11 February 2011, available at www.telegraph.co.uk/news/politics/8317485/Prisoner-vote-what-MPs-said-in-heated-debate.html.

87 Many of the about 74,000 cases currently pending before the ECtHR are so-called 'repetitive cases', which derive from a common 'dysfunction' at the national level. The pilot judgment procedure was developed as a technique of identifying the structural problems underlying repetitive cases against many countries and imposing an obligation on States to address those problems. See www.echr.coe.int/Documents/FS_Pilot_judgments_ENG.pdf.

88 Greens and M.T. v The United Kingdom, (2011) 53 EHRR 21.

89 *Firth and Others v The United Kingdom*, 47784/09, [2014] 874. The ECtHR having already held that the automatic ban on voting by prisoners in the UK amounted to a breach of the right to participate in free elections and that a declaration to that effect constituted just satisfaction, future applicants alleging the same breach would not receive compensation or their legal costs.

90 McHugh and Others v The United Kingdom, 51987/08 [2014] ECHR 102.

91 Hirst v The United Kingdom (No.2) GC, (2006) 42 EHRR 41.

92 *Scoppola (No. 3) v Italy* GC, (2013) 56 EHRR 19. In these proceedings, the UK intervened as third party.

93 *Hirst v The United Kingdom (No.2)* GC, joint dissenting opinion of Judges Wildhaber, Costa, Lorenzen, Kovler and Jebens, *supra* note 91.

94 Hirst v. HM Attorney General [2001] EWHC Admin 239.

95 The decision had been welcomed by Jack Straw who defined it the demonstration of how the authority of the Parliament cannot be challenged by the Courts.

96 R. Mason and T. Whitehead (2012) "David Cameron: Britain will decide on votes for prisoners not a 'foreign court'". The Telegraph, 23 May 2012, available at www.telegraph.co.uk/news/politics/9284892/David-Cameron-Britain-will-decide-on-votes-for-prisoners-not-a-foreign-court.html.

97 House of Commons Debates (2011) Voting by Prisoners, 10 February 2011, available at www.publications.parliament.uk/pa/cm201011/cmhansrd/cm110210/debtext/110210-0002.htm.

98 See L. J. Laws, "The Common Law and Europe", 27 November 2013 and Lord Judge, "Constitutional Change- Unfinished Business", 3 December 2012 in E. Bates, Analysing the Prisoners Voting Saga and the British Challenge to Strasbourg, 14 Human Rights Law Review, (2014), at p. 523.

99 E. Bates, Analysing the Prisoners Voting Saga and the British Challenge to Strasbourg, at p. 530, supra note 98.

100 Of December 2013: They reached the following conclusions on "points of basic principle":

- In a democracy the vote is a right, not a privilege: it should not be removed without good reason.
- The vote is a presumptive, not an absolute right: all democratic states restrict the right to vote in order to achieve clearly defined, legitimate objectives.
- The vote is also a power: citizens are entrusted, in voting, with an element of power over their fellow-citizens.
- There is a legitimate expectation that those convicted of the most heinous crimes should, as part of their punishment, be stripped of the power embodied in the right to vote.There is an element of arbitrariness in selecting the custody threshold as the unique indicator of the type of offence that is so serious as to justify loss of the vote.

There are no convincing penal-policy arguments in favour of disenfranchisement, but a case has been made that enfranchisement might assist prisoner rehabilitation by providing an incentive to re-engage with society.

The enfranchisement of a few thousand prisoners is far outweighed by the importance of the rule of law and the desirability of remaining part of the Convention system. See www.publications.parliament.uk/pa/jt201314/jtselect/jtdraftvoting/103/10302.htm.

101 The Committee of Ministers welcomed the Voting Eligibility (Prisoners) Draft Bill, but held that the 'no reform' option, that is retention of the blanket ban, could not be considered compatible with the ECHR. This line was approved, with 7 votes in favour, and 3 against, Decision of the Committee of Ministers, December 2012.

102 R (Chester and McGeoch) v Secretary of State for Justice [2013] UKSC 63.

103 Ibidem, paras 135, 137 and 138.

104 "The haphazard effects of an effectively blanket ban are certainly difficult to deny"; "All of this suggests an element of arbitrariness in selecting the custody threshold as a unique indicator of offending so serious as to justify exclusion from the democratic process"; "I mention these additional matters to explain why, in common with Lord Clarke, I have some sympathy for the view of the Strasbourg Court that our present law is arbitrary and indiscriminate. But I acknowledge how difficult it would be to devise any alternative scheme which not also have some element of arbitrariness about it"; *R (Chester and McGeoch), v Secretary of State for Justice*, respectively paras 35, 96 and 98.

105 Having regard to overcrowding too, the Court in the *Muršić* case abdicated its responsibility to give clear criteria related to the violation of the ECHR Article 3, overriding the restrictive impact of this decision in the domestic systems, *Muršić v Croatia*, 7334/13 [2015], ECHR 290, referral to the Grand Chamber, 6 July 2015. More broadly, the Grand Chamber decision does not completely solve the dearth of clarity regarding the parameters of violation, *Muršić v Croatia GC*, 7334/13, [2016], ECHR 927.

106 S. Creighton (2009) *No* Claim, *No Gain: Law and Litigation as Tool for Reform* Prison Service Journal, 77, 24-25. The issue of prisoners voting has now reached the Grand Chamber of the European Court of Justice. In *Delvigne* Case (Court of Justice of European Union, *Delvigne c Commune de Lesparre-Médoc*, C-650/13, 6 October 2015), a French national contested a law automatically and permanently stripping him of electoral rights, including the right to vote and stand for elections to the European Parliament, following his conviction for murder and the imposition

of a custodial sentence of 12 years. He contested the decision on the basis of two provisions of the Charter of Fundamental Rights (CFR) – Article 49 on the application of a more lenient sentence in criminal matters and Article 39 on the right to vote in European Parliament elections. The Grand Chamber of the Court found that the Charter applied but that the French law was nonetheless a permissible limitation on the rights contained in the Charter. For the Court, the matter as a whole fell within Union law following not from the existence of an interest or unexercised competence but rather from the obligation contained in Article 14(3) TEU and the 1976 Act on the elections to the European Parliament that such elections be 'universal and direct'. Hence the Charter rights were applicable. Article 39 CFR, in combination with the requirement contained in Article 14(3) TEU contained a specific right to vote in European Parliament elections. That right could be limited and the French law appeared to be proportionate (The argument based on Article 49 CFR was dismissed).

107 See A. Dyer, Irreducible Life Sentences: What Difference Have the European Convention on Human Rights and the United Kingdom Human Rights Act Made?, 16, Human Rights Law Review, (2016), at pp. 541–584.

108 Lord Sumption, *The Limits of the Law,* 27th Sutlan Azlan Shah Lecture, 20 November 2013, www.supremecourt.uk/docs/speech-131120.pdf.

109 Another weakness is the effectiveness of enforcement mechanisms: it has been proposed that the Court should, "make it the rule, rather than the exception, to set clear parameters for implementation by indicating the specific non-monetary measures and a time frame for implementation": Keller and Marti, *Reconceptualising implementation: the judicialization of the execution of the European Court of Human Rights judgments*, 26 European Journal of International Law (2015), at 850.

References

Books and Articles

Almenara, M. A. and Van Zyl Smit, D. (2015). "Human dignity and life imprisonment: The Pope enters the debate." *Human Rights Law Review*, 15, pp. 369-376.

Baker, D. (2016). "Deaths after police contact in England and Wales: The effects of article 2 of the European Convention on Human Rights on coronial practice." *International Journal of Law in Context*, 12(2), pp. 162-177.

Bates, E. (2014). "Analysing the prisoners voting saga and the British challenge to Strasbourg." *Human Rights Law Review*, 14(3), pp. 503-540.

Creighton, S. (2013). "Are whole life tariffs inhumane?" *Criminal Law & Justice Weekly*, 177(11).

Creighton, S. (2009). "No claim, no gain: Law and litigation as tool for reform." *Prison Service Journal*, 77, pp. 25-26.

Dyer, A. (2016). "Irreducible life sentences: What difference have the European Convention on Human Rights and the United Kingdom Human Rights Act made?" *Human Rights Law Review*, 16(3), pp. 541-584.

Foster, S. H. (2015). "Whole life sentences and article 3 of the European Convention of Human Rights: Time for certainty and a common approach." *Liverpool Law Review*, 36(2), pp. 147-169.

Hart, N. (2015). "Whole-life sentences in the UK: Volte-face at the European Court of Human Rights?" *Cambridge Law Journal*, 74(2), pp. 205-208.

Irvine, (Lord). (2003). "The impact of the Human Rights Act 1998: Parliament, the courts and the executive." *Public Law*, pp. 308-325.

Keller, H. and Marti, C. (2015). "Reconceptualising implementation: The judicialization of the execution of the European Court of Human Rights judgments." *European Journal of International Law*, 26 (4), pp. 829-850.

Laws, L. J. (2014). "The Common Law and Europe." 27 November 2013 and Lord Judge, "Constitutional Change- Unfinished Business." 3 December 2012 in E. Bates, "Analysing the Prisoners Voting Saga and the British Challenge to Strasbourg." *Human Rights Law Review*, 14(3), p. 523.

Martinico, G. (2015) "Constitutional Courts (or Supreme) and 'functional disobedience'" edited by "diritto penale contemporaneo." *G. Martinico, Corti Costituzionali (O Supreme) e 'disobbedienza funzionale'*. Available online at: www.penalecontepora neo.it/upload/1430150015MARTINICO_2015.pdf

Mavronicola, N. (2015). "Crime punishment and Article 3 ECHR: Puzzles and prospects of applying an absolute right in a penal context." *Human Rights Law Review*, 15 (4), pp. 721-743.

Mavronicola, N. (2012). "What is an 'absolute right'? Deciphering absoluteness in the context of Article 3 of the Europe Rights." *Human Rights Law Review*, 12 (4), pp. 723-758.

Padfield, N. (2002). *Beyond the Tariff: Human Rights and the Release of Life Sentence Prisoners*. Devon: Willan Publishing.

Pettigrew, M. (2015). "A tale of two cities: Whole of life prison sentences in Strasbourg and Westminster." *European Journal of Crime, Criminal Law and Criminal Justice*, 23(3), pp. 281 - 299.

Shapiro, S. J. (2011). *Legality*. Belknap: Harvard.

Sumption, Lord. (2013). *The Limits of the Law*, 27th Sutlan Azlan Shah Lecture, 20 November 2013, Available online at: www.supremecourt.uk/docs/speech-131120.pdf

Van Zyl Smit, D., Weatherby, P. and Creighton, S. (2014). "Whole life sentences and the tide of European Human Rights Jurisprudence: What is to be done." *Human Rights Law Review*, 14(1), pp. 59-84.

Legislation and documents

Convention for the Protection of Human Rights and Fundamental Freedoms 1950

Criminal Justice Act 1991

Crime (Sentences) Act 1997

Criminal Justice Act 2003

Prison Rules 1999

Prisons and Young Offenders Institutions (Scotland) Rules 2011

Brighton Declaration 2012 High Level Conference on the Future of the European Court of Human Rights.

Ministry of Justice, Story of the Prison Population: 2013–2016 England and Wales, July 2016.

CasesEuropean Court of Human Rights

A v United Kingdom (2009) 49 EHRR 29.

Ezeh and Connors v United Kingdom, (2004) 39 EHRR 3.

Firth and Others v The United Kingdom, 47784/09, [2014] 874.

Greens and M.T. v The United Kingdom, (2011) 53 EHRR 21.

Hirst v The United Kingdom (No.2) GC, (2006) 42 EHRR 41.

Hussain v United Kingdom (2006) 22 EHRR 1.
Hutchinson v United Kingdom (2015) 61 EHRR 13.
Hutchinson v United Kingdom GC, App. no. 57592/08, 17 January 2017.
Kafkaris v Cyprus GC, (2009) 49 EHRR 35.
McHugh and Others v The United Kingdom, 51987/08 [2014] ECHR 102.
Murray v Netherlands GC, 10511/10, [2016] ECHR 408
Muršić v Croatia, 7334/13 [2015], ECHR 290.
Muršić v Croatia GC, 7334/13, [2016], ECHR 927.
Öcalan v Turkey, 24069/03, 197/04, 6201/06 and 10464/07, [2014] ECHR 286.
Scoppola (No. 3) v Italy GC, (2013) 56 EHRR 19.
Soering v United Kingdom (1989) 11 EHRR 439.
Stafford v United Kingdom (2002) 35 EHRR 32.
Thynne Wilson and Gunnell v United Kingdom (1990) 13 EHRR 666.
Trabelsi v Belgium (2015) 60 EHRR 21.
Vinter v United Kingdom (2012) 55 EHRR 34.
Vinter and others v The United Kingdom (2013) 63 EHRR 1.
Wynne v United Kingdom (1995) 19 EHRR 333.

Court of Justice of European Union

Delvigne c Commune de Lesparre-Médoc, C-650/13, 6 October 2015.

The United Kingdom

Council of Civil Service Unions v Minister for the Civil Service [1985] AC 374.
Hirst v. HM Attorney General [2001] EWHC Admin 239.
R (AF) v Secretary of State for the Home Department [2009] UKHL 28.
R (AM and others) v Secretary of State for the Home Department [2009] EWCA Civ 219.
R (Anderson) v Secretary of State for the Home Department [2002] UKHL 46.
R v Bieber [2008] EWCA Crim 1601.
R (Chester and McGeoch), v Secretary of State for Justice [2013] UKSC 63.
R (Hindley) v Secretary of State for the Home Department [2001] 1 AC 410.
R (JL) v Secretary of State for Justice [2008] UKHL 68.
R v Ministry of Defence ex parte Smith [1996] 2 WLR 305.
R v Newell and R v McLoughlin [2014] EWCA Crim 188.
R v Oakes and Others [2012] EWCA Crim 2435.
R (Wellington) v Secretary of State for the Home Department [2008] UKHL 72.

The Zimbabwe

Makoni v Commissioner of Prison and another CCZ 08–16. Available online at: http://veritaszim.net/node/1745.

News and websites

Bratza, N., interview with the *Guardian*, 31 January 2012, Available online at: www.theguardian.com/law/2012/jan/31/joshua-rozenberg-interviews-nicolas-bratza.

Blunkett, D., *David Blunkett's speech to the Police Federation*, 30 March 2003. Available online at: www.ukpol.co.uk/2016/03/30/david-blunkett-2003-speech-to-the-police-federation/.

Morrison, D., *Will a Conservative Government Withdraw from the European Convention on Human Rights?* Huffington Post, 15 October 2014. Available online at: www.huffingtonpost.co.uk/david-morrison/will-the-uk-supreme-court_b_7581174.html.

DH-DD (2014) 857: *Communication from the United Kingdom Concerning the Case of Vinter and Others Against the United Kingdom*. On the pilot judgments. Available online at: www.echr.coe.int/Documents/FS_Pilot_judgments_ENG.pdf.

On the UK government position after the February 2011 debate in Parliament. Available online at: www.publications.parliament.uk/pa/cm201011/cmhansrd/cm110210/debtext/110210-0002.htm; www.publications.parliament.uk/pa/jt201314/jtselect/jtdraftvoting/103/10302.htm.

On the declarations of David Cameron regarding the prisoners voting right. Available online at: www.telegraph.co.uk/news/politics/8317485/Prisoner-vote-what-MPs-said-in-heated-debate.html; www.telegraph.co.uk/news/politics/9284892/David-Cameron-Britain-will-decide-on-votes-for-prisoners-not-a-foreign-court.html.

On the 'whole life' prisoners figures. Available online at: https://en.wikipedia.org/wiki/List_of_prisoners_with_whole-life_tariffs.

9 Spain as a country not being monitored by the European Court of Human Rights

Esther Pascual Rodriguez and Clara Réy Sanchez

Introduction

The monitoring exerted by the Council of Europe, particularly by the European Court of Human Rights (ECtHR), of Spain's penal and prison policies can be qualified as relatively weak when compared to the judicial supervision of the prison systems of other European countries. This lack of robust ECtHR monitoring is to be regretted since there are aspects of the domestic legislation and jurisprudence that could be improved to the benefit of prisoners and their rights. The reasons behind the weak ECtHR oversight are varied and not straightforward and the present chapter aims at shedding light on this overlooked subject matter. The first section analyses the sparse ECtHR jurisprudence regarding Spain's prison system and the domestic authorities' reaction to the obligations imposed by the Strasbourg Court. The second section of this chapter discusses the several prison supervisory bodies that exist in Spain and their effectiveness. Particular attention is given to the role of the Judge for Prison Supervision.

1 European Court of Human Rights case-law

The ECtHR has so far rendered 14 judgments on lawsuits filed against Spain by persons deprived of their liberty,[1] be it either detainees in police stations, remand or convicted prisoners. Half of these fourteen judgments refer to *incommunicado*[2] police custody. That is, complaints from detainees in police stations on whom a Court order of imprisonment has not yet been rendered, and always in the field of terrorism (since *incommunicado* detention under Spanish law is mainly, but not solely, contemplated for terrorism-related offences).

In all of these seven judgments, the applicants claimed to have suffered inhuman and/or degrading treatment during the period when they were under *incommunicado* detention, and in all of these cases the ECtHR condemned Spain for violating Article 3 – not in its substantive aspect but in its procedural aspect. The ECtHR has held Spain responsible for failing to pursue a thorough and effective examination into allegations of inhuman and/or degrading treatment perpetrated by the State Security Forces during *incommunicado* detention.

Martinez *Sala and Others,* rendered in 2004, was the judgment that triggered the ECtHR case-law condemning Spain for breaches of Article 3 in its procedural aspect. This judgment pointed to a reality already highlighted by several international organizations, including the European Committee for the Prevention of Torture and Inhuman or Degrading Punishment or Treatment (CPT)[3] and the Council of Europe Commissioner for Human Rights.[4] All of them had issued reports recommending that Spain either abrogate the incommunicado detention regime[5] or adopt a series of measures to strengthen existing safeguards for people detained incommunicado.[6]

The ECtHR has quoted the CPT reports in nearly all of its judgments on *incommunicado* detention, echoing some of the recommendations made as well as setting forth further recommendations of its own. Particular emphasis has been placed on suggesting how to carry out a thorough and independent investigation into alleged ill-treatment during *incommunicado* detention, in order for it to be considered effective under Article 3 of the ECHR. In that regard, the Strasbourg Court has stressed the need for identifying and hearing the police officers in charge of the detainees, the forensic medical experts who examined the detainees during their *incommunicado* detention and the court-appointed lawyer present during statement-taking.[7] It has also recommended that the applicant be authorised to supply evidence which might help to clarify the facts (for example: copies of the forensic reports and of statements made during *incommunicado* detention; security camera recordings of the premises where detainees were held and statements taken;[8] and new physical and psychological examinations).[9] Furthermore, the ECtHR recommended that the applicant should be heard and the forensic examination improved.[10] Finally, and in line with the recommendations of the CPT, the ECtHR has also encouraged amendments to the legal regime of *incommunicado* detention.[11]

However, the Spanish authorities still do not completely abide by the recommendations made by the ECtHR. As mentioned in the CPT reports, "whenever allegations of ill-treatment are raised by persons held under incommunicado detention, they are systematically considered as unreliable and to be part of a defence strategy . . . [designed by the terrorist group ETA] . . . to undermine the declaration drawn up towards the end of the incommunicado regime".[12] It is certainly laudable that some of the investigative judges of the *Audiencia Nacional* (the Court in charge of authorising this form of detention) do apply a series of safeguards in their personal capacity. These safeguards consist of: notifying the family of the detention and of the detained person's whereabouts; the right to be seen by a personal doctor in addition to the forensic doctor appointed by the investigative judge; 24-hour video surveillance and recording of the detention areas.[13] However, these measures are not binding and an investigative judge cannot be obliged to apply them.

Most regrettably, in 2015 the Criminal Procedure Act (*Ley de Enjuiciamiento Criminal*, LECrim) was amended by Organic Law 13/2015 but Spain missed the opportunity to bring domestic legislation in line with European standards through the introduction of the safeguards recommended by the ECtHR and international Organisations. It is true that the current law specifically prohibits applying *incommunicado* detention to juvenile offenders under the age of 16 (Article 509.4 LECrim) and limits its duration (including *incommunicado* remand prison) to a maximum of 10 days (instead of the previous 13). However, despite these improvements the new Criminal Procedure Act not only fails to provide for a number of basic safeguards[14] but also introduces further limitations to the rights of a person detained *incommunicado*. Indeed, the investigative judge may now prevent the detainee and/or his/her ex-officio lawyer from accessing the case files, except those which are essential for challenging the legality of the detention (Article 527. 1. d. LECrim).

In sum, the Spanish authorities have so far failed to properly implement the recommendations established by the ECtHR judgments on *incommunicado* detention. The clearest example of this is the fact that as recently as May 2016, Spain was condemned once again under Article 3 for its lack of an effective investigation into alleged acts of ill-treatment during *incommunicado* detention.[15] Moreover, safeguards recommended by the ECtHR which could have prevented such acts of ill-treatment being committed in future were not adopted, even though a major legal reform was recently undertaken. Instead, regulations allowing for further restrictions to the rights of *incommunicado* detainees were introduced. It is therefore highly likely that in the coming years we will see more condemnatory sentences from the ECtHR in the field of *incommunicado* detention.

As for the other ECtHR judgments regarding Spain and deprivation of liberty, three of them (*Raf*; *Scott*; and *Van der Tang v. Spain*) concerned the legality or the length of pre-trial detention pending extradition. *Mangouras v. Spain* concerned the amount set for bail, while *Tendam v. Spain* dealt with the refusal by the Spanish authorities to compensate the applicant for his pre-trial detention. All of these judgments refer to how criminal proceedings were conducted and do not strictly relate to prison issues (that is, to the experience of the detainee in prison following the enforcement of a judicial decision). *Jaurieta Ortigala v. Spain* does, as it concerns the refusal of the Spanish courts to grant the applicant ordinary temporary leave from prison. However, the ECtHR declared the application inadmissible as it did not recognize prison leave as a "right" as provided for by Article 6§1, under Spanish law or the Convention.

The judgment of *del Río Prada v. Spain* deserves a special mention given that it applied Article 46, but also because it narrowed the gap between the "sentence" and the "execution of the sentence". The case concerned postponing the final release of the applicant convicted of terrorist offences on the basis of a new approach – known as the "Parot doctrine" – which was adopted by the Supreme Court after she had been sentenced. In its judgment no. 197/2006 of 28 February 2006, the plenary Criminal Division of the Supreme Court ruled that the remissions of sentence granted to prisoners were henceforth to be applied to each of the sentences imposed and not to the maximum term of thirty years provided for in Article 70.2 of the Criminal Code of 1973 (this meant that in practice prison benefits would no longer shorten the aforementioned maximum term of thirty years).

In the *Del Rio Prada* case, the ECtHR concluded that the continued detention of the applicant beyond the 2nd of July 2008 violated Articles 7 and 5§1 ECHR. As regards Article 7, the ECtHR concluded that, although the arrangements for granting adjustments of sentence fall outside the scope of that provision, the application of the "Parot doctrine" to the applicant did not just concern how the imposed penalty was executed but, on the contrary, affected its scope (since the "Parot doctrine" deprived of any useful effect the remissions of sentence for work done in detention to which the applicant was entitled by law). In this respect, it could be argued that the Del Río Prada judgment constitutes a further extension of the concept of penalty for the purpose of extending the guarantees of the Convention.[16] Furthermore, the Court went on to argue that the applicant's continued detention after the 2nd July 2008 was not sufficiently predictable, and that this lack of foreseeability constituted a violation of Article 7. In addition, the ECtHR found that the application of the "Parot doctrine" effectively delayed the date of the applicant's release by almost nine years and concluded that since 3rd July 2008 the applicant's detention was not "lawful", in violation of Article 5 § 1 of the Convention. Finally, the Court applied Article 46 and requested that Spain ensure that del Río Prada be released at the earliest possible date. Spain released the applicant two days after the decision had been rendered. Although the ECtHR did not expressly request the release of other inmates who were in the same situation as the applicant, other prisoners affected by the Parot doctrine were also released by the Spanish authorities.

A year after the *Ines del Río* judgment, the plenary Criminal Chamber of the Spanish Supreme Court unanimously agreed that an application for review ("*recurso de revision*") provided for under Article 954 of the Criminal Procedure Act would be the most suitable procedural mechanism for implementing the ECtHR rulings which found a violation of a fundamental right affecting the innocence of the applicant.[17] Prior to this agreement the implementation of ECtHR decisions within the Spanish legal order remained uncertain.[18] The Supreme Court has already had the opportunity to implement this review procedure and has made use of it to clarify that the ECtHR judgments upholding the applicants' rights do not imply the mechanical annulment or revocation of the domestic sentence, but limit themselves to declaring the violation of a right under the Convention. The review procedure before the Spanish courts allows for the case to be reopened in order to determine the effects that must necessarily produce the ECtHR decision in the specific case under review. As explained by the Supreme Court "the violation found by the ECtHR may not have affected the entire process or all the evidence, and may therefore, subsist enough material to authorize the maintenance of the domestic sentence, in whole or in part. It is therefore necessary in each case, to determine the scope of the conclusion reached by the Strasbourg Court, taking into account the content of its judgment and of the judgment whose revision is intended".[19]

On the 1st October 2015 the amendments to the Organic Law on the Judiciary entered into force and its new Article 5 *bis* echoed the agreement reached by the Supreme Court in 2014. This provision expressly provides that for initiating the review procedure, the ECtHR must have acknowledged the violation of a right under the Convention and that such violation, due to its nature and severity, must entail persisting consequences which cannot be ceased by any other means.

Two conclusions may be drawn from our review, in this section, of the ECtHR case-law regarding Spain and deprivation of liberty. The first conclusion, with regard to the obligations imposed by the bodies of the Council of Europe, is that prison conditions and other aspects of life in Spanish prisons are not being monitored by the ECtHR. Indeed, the Court has not yet ruled on claims against Spain concerning strictly prison-related issues; that is, those relating to life in prison following the enforcement of a judicial decision and raised by remanded or convicted prisoners regarding, among other issues, material conditions of detention, access to healthcare services or their prison regime. The reasons for this lack of monitoring by the ECtHR are not straightforward. Within the framework of a research project funded by the Criminal Justice Programme of the European Union,[20] several Judges for Prison Supervision, Prison Law lawyers, Officers of the Prison Administration and prisoners were interviewed to try to ascertain why complaints on Spanish prison conditions under Article 3 ECHR do not reach the Court.

According to the Judges for Prison Supervision who were interviewed, the overall prison conditions in Spain are generally good (mainly because prisons are relatively new since most were built during the 90s) and there is a lot of judicial control, meaning that prisoners already see their requests and complaints satisfied in the domestic arena. The explanation provided by the lawyers interviewed was their lack of knowledge of both the case-law and the procedure before the ECtHR, the language barrier and the economic unattractiveness of the amount of workload not being paid off. As for the reasons provided by prisoners, they hinge around three main elements: *'litigation tiredness'* (some prisoners argued that they did not appeal before the ECtHR because they were already tired of judicial proceedings and distrusted the judicial system after having pleaded through many national judicial instances without seeing their requests satisfied), their total unawareness of the existence of the ECtHR and/or how to reach it and the lack of sufficient economic means for pleading before it. In Spain the possibility of requesting legal aid is not contemplated for the ECtHR, as none of the Bar Associations of Spain have a specific duty-lawyer's shift for the ECtHR. Moreover, access to the Legal Aid Scheme from the ECtHR is not granted immediately upon filing an application, but at a later stage. This means that prisoners have to finance by their own means the legal advice for initiating the procedure. Given the fact that many have low incomes and poor educational backgrounds, this 'gap' as regards legal aid can be a real drawback for them.

In addition to the reasons stated in the interviews, it is worth noting also that in Spain NGOs are not entitled to take part in penitentiary proceedings. Appeals must be filed by prisoners in their personal capacity and cannot be sheltered under an organization. Pursuant to the 5th Additional Provision of the Organic Law on the Judiciary only the Public Prosecutor and the prisoner him/herself may lodge appeals against the decisions of the Judge for Prison Supervision, and only they can be part of the appeals procedure. Litigating is thus vetoed for legal persons, like NGOs. They can, however, bring legal action against a Prison Administration or a prison officer for the commission of a crime in a criminal proceeding (not a penitentiary one) and request the criminal investigating judge to ascertain the facts. Therefore, Spanish NGOs that work in prisons offer mainly assistance programmes and leisure or cultural activities for prisoners, but do not actively litigate like in other European countries.

The second conclusion that can be drawn from the review of ECtHR case-law in this section, relates to how Spain has reacted to European monitoring. Strictly speaking, it has abided by the ECtHR judgments on deprivation of liberty issued so far, in that it released the applicant when it was requested to do so and paid the compensations deemed appropriate by the Strasbourg Court. Yet a deeper assessment of the overall situation reveals that Spain is reluctant to allow its policies on deprivation of liberty to be submitted to European monitoring particularly when they concern terrorist offenders. We are led to this conclusion by the fact that the recent legislative changes regarding incommunicato detention have not incorporated the recommendations included in the ECtHR judgments (the only exception being the express prohibition in Article 509.4 LECrim of detaining incommunicado people under the age of 16, which was a long-standing recommendation of the CPT); and by the fact that the procedure finally instituted to implement the ECtHR rulings which find a violation of a right enshrined in the ECHR is an application for review ("*recurso de revisión*") and that a series of requirements must be met before lodging it.

2 National supervisory bodies

The most frequently used and trusted authority for the protection of prisoners' rights in Spain is the **Judge for Prison Supervision** (Juez de vigilancia penitenciaria, JVP hereinafter). However, prisoners may also seek redress before the Prison Administration.[21] In fact, even though it is not ruled clearly in any piece of legislation, a *de facto* procedure has been developed according to which prisoners must file first a complaint or request before the Prison Director before moving to the judiciary. Nevertheless, this paper will focus solely on external means of control and will not further comment on this internal mechanism of redress.

By virtue of Article 76 of the General Organic Law on Prisons (Ley Orgánica 1/1979 General Penitenciaria, LOGP), the JVP decides on complaints and requests filed by prisoners (ranging from those referring human rights violations and other serious issues such as the application of a particular prison regime, to those referring domestic or minor matters). They also decide whether to concede or deny parole and prison leave for longer than two days (except for prisoners serving their sentence in an open regime). Furthermore, all sanctions imposed by the prison administration may also be appealed before the JVP. The control applied to disciplinary sanctions by the JVP is both substantive and formal, as the Judge controls not only whether the procedural guarantees have been observed, but also whether the sanction imposed is proportionate to the sanctioned conduct.

In addition to the complaints and requests filed by the inmates themselves before the JVP, the Prison Administration has the duty, pursuant to sentence no. 175/1997 of the Spanish Constitutional Court, to transmit some of its acts and decisions to the judiciary for judicial monitoring. In particular, the JVP controls: detainees' transfer to a closed regime (pursuant to Art. 76.2 LOGP); detainees' limitations under their regime (pursuant to Art. 75 of the Prison Rules, i.e. inmates who request to be held in isolation because their life is at risk); use of coercive means (pursuant to Art. 45.2 of the LOGP); interception of communications (pursuant to Art. 51.5 of the LOGP); and application of the following measures or sanctions: remaining at the arrivals units for over 5 days (Art. 20.3 Prison Rules), transfers (pursuant to art. 34 Prison Rules), suspension of oral communications (pursuant to art. 44 Prison Rules), and transfer to a closed regime (pursuant to art. 95.3 Prison Rules). Finally, in all cases in which an injury report is drawn up in prison (irrespective of whether injuries are due to the application of coercive means or internal fights or self-harm, or whether they were already present at the time of the imprisonment or transfer from another prison) the medical staff must (in accordance with Article 262 of the Criminal Procedure Act) systematically draw up a report and submit it, within the shortest delay possible, to the competent judicial authority (that is, to the criminal judge assigned to its investigation). Notice should also be given to the JVP so that all measures necessary to prevent the commission of further acts of ill-treatment against the prisoner-claimant inside prison may be adopted.

It can be therefore concluded, in light of the above, that the supervisory powers of the JVP are broad and thorough. This, combined with its independence and the binding force of its decisions,[22] make it an appropriate external supervisory organ. In practice however, they handle a total of 34,000 cases a year, which means that each individual JVP initiates an average of 640 files per year[23] and does not have the means to give them the attention they deserve. They receive complaints on fundamental issues as well as on more superficial ones. However, they are required to study every one of them and so lack the time to carry out effective investigations and in-depth analysis, and to provide well-grounded arguments.[24]

There are specific proceedings for requesting parole, applying for temporary leaves, appealing the application of a prison regime and for filing complaints and requests. All these proceedings are very similar in terms of procedure, but differ mainly in their time-limits and the judicial authorities before which the decision of the JVP must be appealed. Yet, a common feature to all the proceedings is that legal assistance is not provided when inmates first reach the JVP, and so they must lodge their applications on their own behalf. There is no sample-form to be used as a template, and all kinds of written submissions are accepted. It suffices for prisoners to identify themselves and state their willingness to appeal. However, at this stage prisoners can rely on the so-called Service for Legal Advice in Prison (*Servicio de Orientación Jurídica Penitenciaria*),[25] which is free of charge for prisoners (since it is either subsidised by the Bar Association or offered voluntarily by lawyers) and consists of providing legal advice from lawyers who are experts on Prison Law. These lawyers conduct interviews with inmates in prison every week and answer their queries. They also help prisoners fill in their requests for a duty-lawyer. However, they do not formally file applications before judicial authorities; they only answer questions (such as those inmates may have when filing complaints and requests before the prison administration or the JVP). It is a highly-requested service which, regrettably, is not available in every prison in Spain. Legal assistance by a lawyer only becomes mandatory when appealing a JVP's decision, sometimes it is provided too late to allow for a proper defence and in particular, appropriate means of proof. Once prisoners reach the procedural stage where legal advice is foreseen, they can request free legal aid[26] in which case they will not have to pay the duty-lawyer's fees.[27]

Inmates appear exceptionally before the Judge for Prison Supervision upon the Judge's request. It is not the general rule, but the exception and it is done mainly through videoconference. The decisions handed down by the JVP must be reasoned and are subject to appeal, either before the same JVP (through an action for reform, "*recurso de reforma*") or directly before a higher judicial instance, like the Province Court (through a direct appeal "*recurso directo de apelación*"). There is no urgent procedure. Usually, the procedure that follows since the first inmate's request until the Province Court renders its final decision and notifies it to the Prison may last, on average, from 6 to 8 months. All judicial decisions must be notified to inmates through a court officer who comes to Prison and inmates must sign a receipt.

The general rule on the burden of proof for inmates who complain before the JVP is summarised by the aphorism *affirmanti incumbit probatio*. This may be excessive for inmates who claim to have been subjected to acts of ill-treatment, especially as they may have difficulties in gaining access to evidence when they report mistreatment by Prison Officers. Indeed, the access by inmates who request the injury report drawn up by the prison medical staff continues to be an issue of concern for the Ombudsman,[28] as well as the lack of thoroughness of this report (which should be more in line with the so-called Istanbul Protocol).[29]

Finally, it is to be noted that there is no specific compensatory remedy for prisoners. Therefore, when claiming compensation they must first address the General Secretariat for Prison Administration (i.e. they must exhaust administrative remedies before turning to the Judiciary). At this stage, regulations do not provide for legal assistance by an ex-officio lawyer. This can be a disadvantage for most prisoners, given the technicalities of this administrative process. Following the dismissal or the implied rejection of the claim for compensation by the General Secretariat of Prison Administration, the prisoner can then turn to an Administrative Court judge, not to the JVP, and will now be assisted by a duty lawyer (and could be granted free legal aid if requested). Here too the burden of proof may be excessive as it is the claimant who must prove the damage, the failure of the Administration and the causal link between the two. The causal relationship must be direct, immediate and exclusive (STS 2500/2000, 28 March 2000) and in the event that the causal link is not proven, the Prison Administration is not held responsible (STS 7764/2005, 18 October). The proceedings usually last a year and the judicial decision can be appealed before a higher administrative court.[30]

The other external supervisory mechanism worth mentioning is the **Ombudsman**. In Spain, the Ombudsman is elected by the Congress of Deputies and the

Senate by a three-fifths majority. His mandate lasts five years and does not seek or receive orders from any authority. He discharges his functions with neutrality, independence and impartiality; and enjoys full immunity and inviolability in the performance of his duties.[31] As a result of the entry into force of the *Optional Protocol to the Convention against Torture and Other Cruel, Inhuman or Degrading Treatment or Punishment*, the Spanish Ombudsman acts as the so-called National Mechanism for the Prevention of Torture (hereafter NMPT).

In addition to launching investigations ex-officio, the Ombudsman in its NMPT capacity can also act when prisoners file complaints before it in cases of ill-treatment. These complaints are filed free of charge. Prisoners address it by letter in their own handwriting and on their own behalf. Complaints must be signed by the party concerned, providing a name and address in a document stating the grounds for the complaint, and within a maximum of one year from the time of the underlying events. Once the complaint has been presented to the Ombudsman's Office, it is registered and the signatory is sent notice of its reception. If the issue at stake falls within the scope of the Ombudsman's competencies and there is evidence for the alleged infringement or administrative irregularity, then an investigation is launched. If not, the complaint's signatory is informed in writing of the reasons for this rejection and, if possible, of the most appropriate channels for vindicating his or her right. The reality, however, is that complaints are sent by prisoners directly from the prisons where they are serving sentences and this complaint cannot be anonymous, and so many inmates are discouraged from filing complaints about ill-treatment. A further drawback of the Ombudsman is that its activities may be classified generally as a form of non-jurisdictional, and therefore non-binding, supervision. Indeed, the Ombudsman is not empowered to overrule acts and decisions of the Public Administration, and limits itself to suggesting modifications to the guidelines used to apply them. This is done by providing reports on the results of its investigations. These reports include a series of resolutions and are sent to the public authorities and the civil servants involved in the case as well as to the interested party.

Conclusion

In light of the above, it can be concluded that European monitoring of the Spanish prison system is limited as no ECtHR judgment deals *stricto sensu* with Spanish prison conditions. Spain is nevertheless equipped with national supervisory mechanisms for the oversight of its prison system, with the Judge for Prison Supervision being the core figure. In general terms, it is a rights-based system and the fact that the main supervisory body is independent from the Prison Administration is one of its strengths. Yet the lack of a robust European monitoring, particularly by the ECtHR, is to be regretted since the national supervisory mechanisms and procedures could be enhanced to the benefit of prisoners and their rights if it were aligned with some of the criteria set forth by the Strasbourg Court. In this regard, there are many potential areas for improvement, particularly as regards the burden of proof, the availability of compensatory remedies more in line with the specifications of the ECtHR case-law, the provision of legal aid from the very outset, the thoroughness of the investigations of ill-treatment and the hearing of prisoners during proceedings.

Notes

1 As of September 2016, the following judgments from the ECtHR relate to Spain and deprivation of liberty (judgments referring to *incommunicado* police custody are in bold): 1.) ***Beortegui Martinez v. Spain*, 36286/14, ECtHR 2016;** 2.) ***Arratibel Garciandia v. Spain*, n° 58488713, ECtHR 2015;** 3.) ***Extebarria Caballero and Ataun Rojo* v. *Spain*, n° 74016/12 and 3344/13, ECtHR 2013;** 4.) *Del Río Prada v. Spain*, n° 42750/09 ECtHR 2013; 5.) *Jaurrieta Ortigala* v. Spain, n° 24931/07 ECtHR 2013; 6.) ***Otamendi Egiguren v. Spain*, n° 47303/08, ECtHR 2012;** 7.) ***San Argimiro Isasa v. Spain*, n° 2507/07ECtHR 2010;** 8.) *Tendam v. Spain*, n° 25720/05 ECtHR 2010; 9.) *Mangouras v. Spain*, n° 12050/04 ECtHR 2010; 10.) ***Beristain Ukar v. Spain*, n° 40351/05, ECtHR 2005;** 11.) ***Martinez Sala and others v. Spain*, n° 58438/00, ECtHR 2004;** 12.) *Raf v. Spain*, n° 53652/00, ECtHR 2003; 13.) *Scott v. Spain*, n° 21335/93, ECtHR 1996-Reports 1996-VI; 14.) *Van der Tang v. Spain*, n° 19382/92 ECtHR 1995-A32.

2 A brief explanation of *incommunicado* detention seems appropriate. Under Articles 384 bis and 509–520 of the Criminal Procedure Act, investigative judges may authorise that a person suspected of "membership or relationship with armed groups or terrorist or rebellious individuals" be detained *incommunicado*. This form of detention may be imposed for an initial period of up to five days in police custody and may also be applied during remand custody in prison for a maximum period of five days (after the enactment of the Organic Law 13/2015 modifying the Criminal Procedure Act) depending on the circumstances and the nature of the criminal offence. Incommunicado detention is intended as an exceptional measure to preserve evidence which is crucial to the ongoing investigation. It must be authorized by a judge on the basis of a reasoned decision, and the personal situation of the detainee must be subject to an ongoing, first-hand supervision by the judge who authorized the *incommunicado* detention or by the examining judge of the judicial district in which the detainee is being held. Report to the Spanish Government on the visit to Spain carried out by the European Committee for the Prevention of Torture and Inhuman or Degrading Treatment or Punishment (CPT) from 31 May to 13 June 2011, CPT/Inf (2013) 6, pp. 14–16.

3 In fact, incommunicado detention and its regulation in Spain are issues on which the CPT has been making recommendations throughout its periodic visits. *Op Cit.* CPT/Inf (2013) 6, pp. 15–24.

4 Report by Niels Muiznieks, Council of Europe Commissioner for Human Rights, following his visit to Spain from 3 to 7 June 2013, pp. 19 et seq.

5 "Since incommunicado detention creates conditions that facilitate the perpetration of torture and can in itself constitute a form of cruel, inhuman or degrading treatment or even torture, the incommunicado regime should be abrogated" A/HRC/10/3/Add.2, *Op. Cit.* § 66.

6 Notably, the prohibition of incommunicado detention for minors; the necessity for a detained person to be brought physically before the competent judge prior to any decision to extend the detention period beyond 72 hours; the right to meet and talk in private with an ex officio lawyer; the right of access to a doctor of one's choice; the right to have a third person informed of one's detention at the earliest possible time and in no case later than 48 hours following the deprivation of liberty; the adoption of a code of conduct on questioning and interrogation; and the full video and audio recording of all aspects of incommunicado detention. *Op. Cit.* CPT/Inf (2013) 6.

7 Etxebarria Caballero v Spain, Op. Cit., § 47.

8 SanArgimiro Isasa v. Spain, Op. Cit. § 42.

9 Ataun Rojo v. Spain, Op. Cit., § 36.

10 Beristain Ukar v. Spain, Op. Cit., § 33.

11 So as to ensure rights such as: being assisted by a lawyer of the prisoner's choice; being examined by a forensic doctor of the prisoner's choice from the public health system, in addition to the State-appointed forensic doctor; notifying a family member or person of one's choice of the fact of the arrest and the place of detention; and meeting in private with the duty lawyer appointed to assist them. *Beortegui Martinez v. Spain, Op. Cit.*, § 46.

12 *Ibíd*, p. 6 § 16.

13 *Ibíd*, p. 6 § 18.

14 Above all, the right to consult a lawyer of one's own choice or to consult the court-appointed lawyer in private (even after the formal statement to the law enforcement officials has been made); the right to have the fact and place of one's detention notified to a person of one's choice (or in the case of a foreign national, to inform the Consular Representation of their country); or the right to be examined by a doctor of one's own choice (only a doctor from the public health system is in charge of the examination, and will proceed to examine the detainee twice every 24 hours if deemed necessary).

15 Beortegui Martinez v. Spain, 36286/14, ECtHR, 2016.

16 "The court would emphasise that the term 'imposed', used in the second sentence of Article 7 § 1, cannot be interpreted as excluding from the scope of that provision all measures introduced after the pronouncement of the sentence. It reiterates in this connection that it is of crucial importance that the Convention is interpreted and applied in a manner which renders its rights practical and effective, not theoretical and illusory". Del Rio Prada v. Spain [GC], no. 42750/09, § 88, 21 October 2013.

17 Acuerdo del Pleno No Jurisdiccional de la Sala Segunda del Tribunal Supremo de 21 de octubre de 2014, available at: www.poderjudicial.es.

18 See for example, Bujosa Vadell, L, Las Sentencias del Tribunal Europeo de Derechos Humanos y el Ordenamiento Español, (Tecnos: Madrid 1997); Celdrán Kuhl, España y el Tribunal Europeo de Derechos Humanos, (Ministerio de Asuntos Exteriores, Escuela Diplomática: Madrid 2004); Ruiz Miguel, C., La ejecución de las sentencias del Tribunal Europeo de Derechos Humanos, (Tecnos: Madrid 1997).

19 Judgment of the Spanish Supreme Court n° 330/2015, of 19 May 2015, FJ° 3.

20 Prison Litigation Network JUST/2013/JPEN/AG www.prisonlitigationnetwork.eu/

21 It is to be noted that in Spain there are two Prison Administrations: The Central Government Prison Administration, under the jurisdiction of the Ministry of Home Affairs, which supervises prisons located throughout the entire Spanish territory, except Catalonia; and the Catalan Prison Administration, under the jurisdiction of the Department of Justice of the Government of Catalonia, which supervises prisons located in that territory. These two administrations are independent in the sense that each has its own personnel, with its own budget.

22 According to Article 117 of the Spanish Constitution, judicial authorities (including JVP) are independent and impartial and their decisions are binding and directly enforceable.

23 The list of items in descending order are as follows: 35 per cent of court orders issued concern permissions; 30 per cent concern prison classification; 25 per cent have to do with conditional release; and the remaining 10 per cent concern complaints and requests. www.cgpj.es/datosactividadjudicial.

24 During the interviews held within the framework of the Prison Litigation Network Project, some JVPs suggested that in order to avoid the clogging up of the judiciary it would be useful to have a sort of filter allowing complaints on domestic or minor matters to be separated from those regarding human rights violations and other serious issues, and to introduce fast-track proceedings for the latter cases.

25 The Web page of the Bar Association of Pamplona offers detailed information and keeps track of how other Bar Associations from other cities in Spain provide this Service www.derechopenitenciario.com/SOAJP/index.asp.
26 To apply for legal aid the prisoner must fill in an application form for legal aid authorizing the Autonomous Community to consult their tax data, which replies within two months, either granting or denying the requested free legal aid. Almost all prisoners are granted legal aid since they usually earn very little money, either because they have no job or one with low pay.
27 The fees for duty-lawyers are set and paid by the Legal Aid Committee of each Autonomous Community through the Bar Association. The costs of litigating prison-related issues are always allocated ex-officio; that is, prisoners are always levied even if they do not win the appeal.
28 Informe del Defensor del Pueblo: "Estudio sobre los partes de lesiones de las personas privadas de libertad" 17 June 2014.
29 Office of the United Nations High Commissioner for Human Rights, Manual on the Effective Investigation and Documentation of Torture and Other Cruel, Inhuman and Degrading Treatment or Punishment, "*Istanbul Protocol*", 1999, HR/P/PT/8/Rev. 1.
30 The amount of compensation awarded is usually tempered by the Courts based on the conduct of the prisoner himself and/or third parties' intervention. Guillén Navarro, N.A. "Análisis Actual de la Responsabilidad Patrimonial en el ámbito Penitenciario", *Revista Aragonesa de Administración Pública*, nums. 39–40 (2012), p. 439.
31 Articles 1–4 of the Organic Law 3/1981, of 6 April, on the Ombudsman.

References

Books and articles

Almeda, E., Di Nella, D. and Navarro, C. (2012). "Mujeres, cárceles y drogas: datos y reflexiones." *Oñati Socio-Legal Series*, 2(6), pp. 122–145.

Beltrán Verdes, E. (2009). Derechos torcidos: tópicos, medias verdades y mentiras sobre pobreza, política y derechos humanos. Barcelona: Debate.

Bujosa Vadell, L. (1997). *Las Sentencias del Tribunal Europeo de Derechos Humanos y el Ordenamiento Español*. Madrid: Tecnos.

Carrillo Salcedo, A. (2003). *El Convenio Europeo de Derechos Humanos*. Madrid: Tecnos.

Celdrán Kuhl, C. (2004). *España y el Tribunal Europeo de Derechos Humanos*. Madrid: Ministerio de Asuntos Exteriores, Escuela Diplomática.

Cid Moliné, J. (2008). "El incremento de la población reclusa en España entre 1996–2006: Diagnóstico y remedios." *Revista Española de Investigación Criminológica*, 6, pp. 2–31.

De Miguel Calvo, E. (2014). "Encarcelamiento de mujeres: El castigo penitenciario de la exclusión social y la desigualdad de género." *Revista de Servicios Sociales*, 56, pp. 75–86.

Drd, O. and Nedelcu-Surdescu, O. (2010). "Brief analysis of the operation of the pilot judgment procedure before the European Court of Human Rights (ECHR)." *Journal of European Studies and International Relations*, I(1).

El Sistema Penitenciario Español. (2014). Madrid: Ministerio del Interior, Secretaría General de Instituciones Penitenciarias.

Escobar Hernández, C. (1992). "Problemas planteados por la aplicación en el ordenamiento español de la sentencia Bultó (Comentario a la STC 245/1991, de 16 de diciembre)." *Revista de Instituciones Europeas*, 19(1), pp. 139–164.

Gallego Díaz, M., Cabrera, P. J., Segovia Bernabé, J. L. and y Ríos Martín, J. (2010). *Andar 1 km en línea recta. La cárcel del siglo XXI que vive el preso* (3rd Ed.). Madrid: Biblioteca Comillas Derecho, Universidad Pontificia Comillas.

Garberí Llobregat, J. and Morenilla Allard, P. (1999). Convenio europeo de Derechos Humanos y jurisprudencia del Tribunal Europeo relativa a España, Textos, Protocolos, Nuevo Reglamento del Tribunal, Normas complementarias y Formulario de Demanda. Barcelona: Bosch.

García Arán, M. and Botella Corral, J. (Dir.) (2009). *Malas noticias, medios de comunicación, política criminal y garantías penales*. Valencia: Tirant lo Blanch.

García de Enterría, E. (2004). "La Sentencia del TEDH de 28 de octubre de 2003, Stone Court Shipping Company, S.A. c/España, y las prácticas judiciales españolas para inadmitir recursos: Una censura expresa a la doctrina del Tribunal Constitucional sobre el derecho a la tutela efectiva: Necesidad de una rectificación radical de las posiciones restrictivas del Tribunal Constitucional y del Tribunal Supremo en cuanto al ámbito del derecho fundamental a la tutela judicial efectiva." *Revista de Administración Pública*, no.163(enero-abril 2004), pp. 169–195.

Garland, D. (2005). La cultura del control: Crimen y orden social en la sociedad contemporánea. Barcelona: Gedisa.

Gerard, J. (2012). "The pilot judgment procedure before the European Court of Human Rights as an instrument for dialogue". In: M. Claes, P. Popelier, eds, Constitutional conversations. Antwerp: Intersentia, pp. 371–395.

Guillen Navarro, N. A. (2012). "Análisis actual de la Responsabilidad Patrimonial en el ámbito Penitenciario." *Revista Aragonesa de Administración Pública*, (39–40), pp. 425–442.

Hierro Romero, M. J. (2009). "Responsabilidad de la administración Pública Penitenciaria." *Diario La Ley n° 7157, Sección Dossier*.

Informe de Amnistía Internacional. (2009). España: salir de las sombras: Es hora de poner fin a la detención en régimen de incomunicación.

Informe de Humans Rights Watch. (2005). "¿Sentando ejemplo?" *Medidas antiterroristas en España*, 17(1), p. D.

Informe de la Coordinadora para la Prevención y Denuncia de la Tortura. (2013). *La Tortura en el Estado Español, Informe de 2012*. Barcelona: Mayo de.

Informe relativo a España del Comité contra la tortura de 19 de noviembre de 2009 en su 43° período de sesiones del 2 al 20 de noviembre de 2009 (CAT/C/ESP/5).

Juanete y Dorado, C. (2016), *Manual de Derecho Penitenciario* (3rd Ed.). Madrid: Iustel.

López Barja de Quiroga, J. (2004). *Tratado de derecho procesal penal*. Navarra: Thomson Aranzadi.

López Bofill, H. (2011). "Prohibición de tortura, violación del artículo 3 del Convenio Europeo de Derechos Humanos desde el punto de vista procedimental." *Revista Aranzadi Doctrinal*, (10), pp. 85–94.

Matthews, R. (2003). Pagando tiempo: Una introducción a la sociología del encarcelamiento. Barcelona: Bellaterra.

Miralles Ruiz-Huidobro, R. and Saura Estapá, S. (2013). "La jurisprudencia del Tribunal Europeo de Derechos Humanos relativa a España por torturas: Del terrorismo a la criminalización de la disidencia." *Informe n° 31 El tiempo de los derechos Instituto de Derechos Humanos de Cataluña*. Available online at: www.idhc.org

Morenilla Rodríguez, J. M. (1989). La eficacia y ejecución de las Sentencias del Tribunal Europeo de Derechos Humanos. Madrid: Poder Judicial.

Moreno Catena, V. and Cortes Dominguez, V. (2015). *Derecho Procesal Penal* (7th Ed.) Valencia: Tirant lo Blanch.

Ríos Martín, J. (Coord.) (2014). *Manual de ejecución penitenciaria: Defenderse de la cárcel* (7th Ed.). Madrid: Colex.

Ríos Martín, J. and Cabrera Cabrera, P. (2002). *Mirando el abismo: el régimen cerrado*. Madrid: Universidad Pontificia Comillas.

Ríos Martín, J. and Cabrera Cabrera, P. (1998). *Mil voces presas*. Madrid: Universidad Pontificia Comillas.

Ruiloba Alvariño, J. (2005). "La sentencia del TEDH en el asunto Martínez Sala y otros c. España, de 2 de noviembre de 2004: Crónica de una muerte anunciada." *Revista Española de derecho internacional*, 57(1), pp. 209–220.

Ruiz Miguel, C. (1997). La ejecución de las sentencias del Tribunal Europeo de Derechos Humanos. Madrid: Tecnos.

Sáez Arnáiz, A. (1999). La apertura constitucional al Derecho Internacional y Europeo de los derechos humanos: El artículo 10.2 de la Constitución Española. Madrid: Consejo General del Poder Judicial.

Sarmiento Ramirez-Escudero, D., Mieres Mieres, J. and Presno Linera, M. A. (2007). *Las sentencias básicas del Tribunal Europeo de Derechos Humanos*. Pamplona: Civitas.

Legislation and documents

Optional Protocol to the Convention against Torture and Other Cruel, Inhuman or Degrading Treatment or Punishment (OPCAT) A/RES/57/199

Constitución Española, BOE-A-1978–31229

Real decreto de 14 de septiembre de 1882 por el que se aprueba la Ley de Enjuiciamiento Criminal (Criminal Procedure Act) BOE-A-1882–6036

Ley Orgánica 13/2015, de 5 de octubre, de modificación de la Ley De Enjuiciamiento Criminal para el fortalecimiento de las garantías procesales y la regulación de las medidas de investigación tecnológica, BOE-A-2015–10725

Ley Orgánica 10/1995, de 23 de noviembre, del Código Penal (Criminal Code) BOE-A-1995–25444

Ley Orgánica 1/1979, de 26 de septiembre, General Penitenciaria (Prison Act) BOE-A-1979–23708

Real Decreto 190/1996, de 9 de febrero, por el que se aprueba el Reglamento Penitenciario (Prison Rules) BOE-A-1996–3307

Real Decreto 840/2011, de 17 de junio, por el que se establecen las circunstancias de ejecución de las penas de trabajo en beneficio de la comunidad y de localización permanente en centro penitenciario, de determinadas medidas de seguridad, así como de la suspensión de la ejecución de las penas privativas de libertad y sustitución de penas, BOE-A-2011–10598

Ley 50/1981, de 30 de diciembre, por la que se regula el Estatuto Orgánico del Ministerio Fiscal (Organic Statutes of the Public Prosecution Services) BOE-A-1982–837

Ley Orgánica 6/1985, de 1 de julio, del Poder Judicial (Organic Law on the Judiciary) BOE-A-1985–1266

Ley Orgánica 3/1981, de 6 de abril, del Defensor del Pueblo (Organic Law on the Ombudsman) BOE-A-1981–10325

Estudio sobre los partes de lesiones de las personas privadas de libertad. Defensor del Pueblo. 17 junio 2014. Available online at: www.defensordelpueblo.es/wp-content/uploads/2015/05/2014-06-Estudio-sobre-los-partes-de-lesiones-de-las-personas-privadas-de-libertad.pdf

Manual on the Effective Investigation and Documentation of Torture and Other Cruel, Inhuman and Degrading Treatment or Punishment, "Istanbul Protocol", Office of the United Nations High Commissioner for Human Rights, 1999, HR/P/PT/8/Rev. 1, Available online at: www.ohchr.org/Documents/Publications/training8Rev1en.pdf

Report by Niels Muiznieks, Council of Europe Commissioner for Human Rights, following his visit to Spain from 3 to 7 June 2013

Report of the Special Rapporteur on the question of torture, Theo van Boven, on his visit to Spain from the 5th to the 10th October 2003 (E/CN.4/2004/56/Add.2)

Report of the Special Rapporteur on the promotion and protection of Human Rights and fundamental freedoms while countering terrorism, Martin Scheinin, 16 December 2008 (A/HRC/10/3/Add.2)

Report to the Spanish Government on the visit to Spain carried out by the European Committee for the Prevention of Torture and Inhuman or Degrading Treatment or Punishment (CPT) from 31 May to 13 June 2011, CPT/Inf (2013) 6

Report to the Spanish Government on the visit to Spain carried out by the European Committee for the Prevention of Torture and Inhuman or Degrading Treatment or Punishment (CPT) from 19 to 22 June 2012, CPT/Inf (2013) 8

Report to the Spanish Government on the visit to Spain carried out by the European Committee for the Prevention of Torture and Inhuman or Degrading Treatment or Punishment (CPT) from 19 September to 1 October 2007, CPT/Inf (2011)11

Cases

European Court of Human Rights

Beortegui Martinez v. Spain, 36286/14, ECtHR 2016

Arratibel Garciandia v. Spain, n° 58488713, ECtHR 2015

Extebarria Caballero and Ataun Rojo v. *Spain*, n° 74016/12 and 3344/13, ECtHR 2013

Del Río Prada v. Spain [GC], n° 42750/09 ECtHR 2013

Jaurrieta Ortigala v. Spain, n° 24931/07 ECtHR 2013

Otamendi Egiguren v. Spain, n° 47303/08, ECtHR 2012

San Argimiro Isasa v. Spain, n° 2507/07ECtHR 2010

Tendam v. Spain, n° 25720/05 ECtHR 2010

Mangouras v. Spain, n° 12050/04 ECtHR 2010

Beristain Ukar v. Spain, n° 40351/05, ECtHR 2005

Martinez Sala and others v. Spain, n° 58438/00, ECtHR 2004

Raf v. Spain, n° 53652/00, ECtHR 2003

Scott v. Spain, n° 21335/93, ECtHR 1996-Reports 1996-VI

Van der Tang v. Spain, n° 19382/92 ECtHR 1995-A32

Spain

STC 245/1991, 16 de diciembre [BOE n° 13, de 14 de enero 1992]

STC 175/1997, 27 de octubre [ECLI:ES:TC:1997:175]

STS 330/2015, 19 mayo 2015 [ECLI:ES:TS:2015:2493]

STS 197/2006, 28 febrero 2006 [ECLI:ES:TS:2006:753]

STS 2500/2000, 28 marzo 2000 [ECLI:ES:TS:2000:2500]

STS 7764/2005, 18 octubre [ECLI:ES:TS:2005:7764]

Acuerdo del Pleno No Jurisdiccional de la Sala Segunda del Tribunal Supremo de 21 de octubre de 2014

Jurisprudencia penitenciaria (de 1982 a 2014) (Ministerio del Interior, Secretaría General de Instituciones Penitenciarias: Madrid)

10 Conclusion

The European monitoring of national penal and prison policies as a dynamical system

Gaëtan Cliquennois and Hugues de Suremain

Introduction

There is no book that really engages with this major monitoring process within penal and prison policies in Europe. Yet state reactions to such interventions have remained relatively understudied to date. Relevant scholarly research has been mainly preoccupied either with the scope and validity of criticisms raised against given states or with the specific structure and operations of the institutions that raise criticisms in the first place. Much less is known about the nature of reactions from the states concerned, the forces that determine them, and their respective influence on the effectiveness of criticisms and subsequent censures. But thanks to the contributions to this book, we are able to shed light on these forces, on the nature of reactions from national states to this European monitoring and on the interplay between the European and national legal orders in order to explain the recent evolutions of penal and prison policies in Europe in times of austerity.

Our ambition in this book was therefore to fill the gap in the litterature by focusing on the historical development of European control over prisons and the relations between the European and national structures of control. A reinforcement of the influence of the EU and the CoE and the interactions between their organs has been observed over the last twenty years. This is why we shed light on these interacting European bodies to analyse their impact on the evolution of penal polices. We have assumed thus that the strengthening of the relationships between the EU and the CoE has increased the pressure and control over national penal and prison administrations. Moreover, the positive procedural obligations imposed by the ECtHR on the Member States have led to legal, administrative, judicial and practical changes, such as the adoption of domestic penal and prison legislation enforcing the effective implementation of policies to prevent deaths in custody; to provide healthcare services to prisoners; to assess prisoners' ability to serve custodial sentences and their right to apply for parole; to limit overcrowding and improve the conditions of detention; to offer prisoners the right to effective remedies and compensation; to enhance rehabilitation programmes and to develop family visits.

Regarding the development of these European controls over penal and prison policies, we have questioned whether it has contributed to the shaping of prison policies and the creation of a monitoring system based on human rights, which has forced national prison administrations to develop political, legal and organisational responses. Indeed, this "panopticon" based on human rights seems to be inverted in the sense that the supervision exerted by the CoE and EU judicial and institutional bodies over the prison administrations is influenced by the complaints by prisoners and NGOs to them. In other words, is there any evidence in addition to the constant multifaceted supervision of prisoners (as in the hypothesis of Foucault, 1975), that national Ministers of Justice and prison administrations are now also monitored and supervised by the European bodies?

In this respect, this conclusive chapter draws together and compares the key contributions that this mapping of monitoring activities across Europe has produced. The aim of this conclusion is threefold: first, to provide an overview of what is European about modernisation through European monitoring and what is local and distinct within the history and political system of the nation state; second, to make a contribution to penal and prison studies through developing innovative, critical and robust approaches to major monitoring strategies and their impacts on national states, not least through respecting the continued resistance of the nation states within an European policy context; and third, to reflect on the future perspectives of the European monitoring and the evolving reactions that it is generating at a national and local level. In this regard, it is necessary to take into account the monitoring of penal policies and prisons exerted by the CoE and in particular by (1) the CoE and the ECtHR and its impacts on national penal and prison policies (2) to underline the limits of this "inverted panopticon".

1 The monitoring of national penal and prison policies exerted by the CoE and the ECtHR

The substantial changes to the CoE and ECtHR's architectures and political roles (see chapter 1) and the fact that the Strasbourg Court spends more than a third of its time examining complaints by prisoners (Sauvé, 2009) have led, over time, to the recognition by Member State governments of many rights for prisoners, such as the right to life (Cliquennois and Champetier, 2013), the right to health, the right to protection against torture, inhuman and degrading treatment, the right to family contacts, the right to marry, the right to some cultural and social activities, the right to education and the right to social reintegration (Snacken and Dumortier, 2012). Particularly in cases brought by human rights groups, the ECtHR's jurisprudence, combined with the recommendations issued by the CM, has constrained its Member States to adopt progressive penal and prison policies which respect prisoners' human rights.

1.1 The theoretical requirements from the council of Europe and the Strasbourg court

Particularly in cases brought by human rights groups, the ECtHR's jurisprudence, combined with the recommendations issued by the CM, has constrained its Member States to adopt progressive penal and prison policies which respect prisoners' human rights.

These European organs, and in particular the Strasbourg Court, require notably Member States to:

(i) limit overcrowding[1] and poor conditions of detention,[2] situations which, according to the ECtHR, limit to a certain measure the degree of discretion that Member States enjoy in developing their criminal policies.[3]
(ii) create a mechanism guaranteeing regular judicial reviews for prisoners serving very long sentences,[4] in the sense that life-sentence prisoners must have the right to request (but not the right to be granted) parole, and not to be subjected to solitary confinement,[5] disciplinary sanctions and repeated transfers.[6]
(iii) apply and implement a risk-based approach to prisoner suicides and homicides through prevention programmes and adequate staff training and surveillance.[7]
(iv) introduce procedural guarantees before imposing disciplinary sanctions.[8]
(v) introduce regular evaluations of the risk of recidivism[9] using risk management techniques.[10]
(vi) regularly assess the mental health of prisoners[11] serving long sentences or subject to indeterminate preventive measures.
(vii) establish independent parole boards and judicial processes for deciding on conditional releases (at least regarding convict serving long-life or indeterminate sentences) and recalls to prison.[12]
(viii) empower courts to release detainees whose state of health is exceptionally serious.[13]
(ix) develop healthcare structures,[14] particularly the provision of appropriate psychiatric treatment for mentally ill prisoners[15] by significantly improving medical structures in the psychiatric wings of prisons, by building psychiatric facilities, and by increased use of existing psychiatric and hospital facilities.[16]
(x) Implement effective domestic remedies to give access to justice and the opportunity to complaint about conditions of detention for prisoners. According to the ECtHR, this last objective can be achieved by equipping the courts with appropriate legal tools allowing them to consider the problem underlying an individual complaint and effectively deal with situations of massive and concurrent violations of prisoners' rights resulting from inadequate detention conditions in a given facility.[17]

By requiring, among other things, Member States to set up independent mechanisms and procedural guarantees before imposing disciplinary sanctions on prisoners, and by considerably strengthening the role of the national courts through the obligation to afford an effective remedy to enforce the ECHR rights,[18] these rulings have limited the discretionary powers of Ministers of Justice in the Member States.

In parallel, the ECtHR has endorsed CM Recommendations in its rulings, such as Recommendation 98(7) on healthcare in prison and the European Prison Rules (2006), to exert external control over prison and medical staff. In this sense, the ECHR requires Member States to carry out independent investigations[19] into all deaths in custody. These independent investigations are conducted by various bodies, including judges, the police and members of the CPT and have led to some Member States being found guilty of breaching the ECHR by the ECtHR. They have also contributed to the increased transparency of the decisions made by the prison authorities and also to the widening of Member States' liability[20] (Cliquennois and Champetier, 2013).

The standards and public reports released by the CPT for each Member State and the Recommandations issued by the Committee of Ministers, such as the European Prison Rules, have served as evidence and standards for the ECtHR. Conversely, the rulings made by the ECtHR have inspired and enforced the Recommandations and the standards issued by the CM as well as the reports released by the CPT (van Zyl Smit and Snacken, 2009; Snacken, 2011; Snacken and Dumortier, 2012).

1.2 National responses to the European monitoring

This is why the European monitoring has deeply impacted penal and prison policies conducted by some national states such as Germany. While for many years European influences, and in particular the jurisprudence of the European Court of Human Rights, have been of minor importance, this changed considerably in 2009 with the case of "M vs. Germany" that had significant impact on legislation and practice concerning preventive detention in Germany. The German Federal Constitutional Court in recent years also not only sought to incorporate the jurisprudence of the European Court of Human Rights in its judgments concerning prison matters but also "soft law" recommendations by the Council of Europe, mainly the European Prison Rules. Even if high court case law has an indirect preventive effect by setting precedents and shaping the overall prison culture, other preventive mechanisms that function in addition to the retrospective review of potential violations of prisoners' rights have influenced prison law and practice in Germany more recently. This is primarily the case for the work of the CPT, which is generally acknowledged by the German authorities and has impacted at least discreetly on new prison legislation. In a similar way, the Netherlands belong to the few countries where the complaint and appeal system has gotten a high approval rating by the ECtHR and the CPT except the fact that not all complaints and appeals can be settled within the prescribed time limits. The procedure is indeed smart, easily accessible and based on confidentiality. It provides a preventive and compensatory remedy because the grievances are dealt with by an external, independent body that has the competence to issue binding and enforceable decisions and the power to redress complainant's situation or – if that is not possible anymore – to provide financial or other forms of compensation. It is also an effective remedy because of the effective participation of the prisoner in the complaint and appeal procedure and because of his entitlement to assistance of a lawyer and – if needed – an interpreter.

By contrast, the European oversight has more mixed records and results in certains countries such as France and the Nordic countries although the ECHR and the ECtHR jurisprudence have played a wide role in the transformation of the "structure of political conflicts" in criminal detention since the end of the twentieth century. European standards in effect have constituted a regulatory horizon, which is largely shared, and against which national prison policies are promoted, criticised and measured. Beyond this place in the regulatory landscape, litigation before the ECtHR has accompanied the developments in French prison law in the last twenty years. In particular, the development of the jurisdictional control of the acts and actions of the prison authorities has led to a corpus of jurisprudence which to a certain extent defines the reach of the rights of prisoners. Nevertheless, the potential for transformation that comes with European law must be assessed through the prism of the professional and institutional resistance which oppose it. The case of body searches as such raises the question of its capacity to put an effective end, within a reasonable time, to clearly intrusive and humiliating practices, when prison union organizations throw all their weight behind maintaining them. The provisional assessment of a ten-year legal and political battle reveals that internal social dialogue had prevailed here over the European regulatory requirements. French prison law still bears the marks of the conditions of its emergence, namely a patchwork progression, lacking in structured ambition and unable to deal with structural problems such as the material conditions of detention or overpopulation. Whereas the hopes raised by an increasing political desire to reduce the number of people in prison have disappointed, it is the ECtHR, and the prospect of a pilot judgment, that a proportion of the actors in the prison sector are relying on to bring about a reorientation of criminal policy. European law is but an ambiguous resource for the rationalities which it conveys, likely to reinforce the liberties of the prison population as much as the discretionary scope of the prison authorities, and is dependent on the social forces which interpret it, resist it or feed it.

In the same manner, the European monitoring bodies have compelled the governments and prison administrations in the Nordic countries to take human rights more seriously. Although there are very few ECtHR judgments related to prison conditions and the enforcement of sanctions in the Nordic countries, these countries cannot bypass or ignore these judgments. Indeed, Finnish law on the use of sealed overalls for prisoners in solitary confinement was changed as a direct result of an ECtHR judgment. The CPT's criticisms have led to law reforms and changes in prison practice in the Nordic countries, for example the enactment of a specific law on remand prisoners in Finland. The adoption of court-based appeals procedures in these countries was clearly motivated by the requirements of the ECHR. However, the main responsibility for the day-to-day treatment and well-being of prisoners lies in the hands of national institutions, standard national appeals procedures and the national ombudsmen. Often, the CPT reports and ECtHR judgments bring up criticisms previously made by national ombudsmen but which only produced meagre results. In terms of CPT report criticisms, none of the Nordic countries has a completely clean record. The responses to criticism by the CPT range from agreement with them and promises to take action to direct denials, which are, however, fairly rare. The governments rarely disagree with criticism related to ill-treatment, safety and the well-being of prisoners, but are less likely to agree with criticism of organisational and administrative procedures. Improvement is often a slow process, but the evidence shows that the CPT and human rights often prevail. The dialogue between the CPT and the governments of the Nordic countries could be improved by using more open and direct communication. This applies especially to the evasive responses to CPT reports where governments simply describe the current situation, implying that everything is, in fact, working pretty well. Many of the responses offered by the Nordic governements are filled with detailed and lengthy descriptions of national legislation and institutional practices and lack concrete action plans focusing on the question or recommendation.

The CoE and EU monitoring has led also in certain countries to minor changes in their penal and prison policies as the Italian case reveals. One of the limits of this European oversight is its temporary character and short duration of this monitoring (as the Committee of Ministers is obliged to close a case once the states having been condemned by the European Court have replied and complied), and the resistance opposed by national judiciary systems on the long term. For instance, while Italy has been compliant from a political and a cultural point of view, the Italian government has implemented a twofold strategy. The Italian authorities have aimed on the external front, at answering to the European condemnations in a very prompt way, but on the internal front, the government has justified the prison reforms aiming at improving prison conditions, as an irrefutable "European" request. In this manner, this process has minimised the scope of changes as the latter were characterised by their temporary dimension. In this regard, the answers offered by the Italian government have been inadequate to improve the prison condition. Overcrowding was only faced through deflating and temporary measures, not pursuing decarceration and decriminalization policies as recommended by the Coe. Thus overcrowding has never been totally solved and prison population has started to increase again in Italy since one of the most relevant deflating measures adopted has not been extended by the Government, after the positive evaluation of the execution procedure in the Torreggiani case. Aftermaths, not so much has been done to solve the structural and endemic problems of Italian prisons and the Italian prison administration has only introduced an electronic system to monitor overcrowding in the prisons and a semi-open-regime that allows prisoners to spent from 6 to 8 hours out of the cells, in the corridors of the prison or, rarely, in common rooms. This policy has been positively ratified by the Committee of Ministers in the execution procedure against Italy, without any further considerations concerning the effectiveness of the Italian model. The Italian case shows therefore clearly the limits of the execution procedure of the ECtHR's judgments.

The European monitoring also faces strong political opposition in some countries. For instance, the Greek case suggests that, in conjunction with select institutional capacity constraints, a range of domestic and international pressures, material as well as social, may combine to offset European pressure for national compliance with international human rights regimes. This not only adds impetus to warnings against mono-causal approaches that are bound to overlook the possibility of multiple forces operating simultaneously and cumulatively to produce non-compliance; it also calls attention to the diversity and potentially competing nature of influences stemming from the European sphere.

In a different way and despite much litigation and judgments delivered by the Strasbourg Court, the British Government, supported by the domestic courts, has still maintained both a "whole life" order, without any possibility of review and a blanket ban on all convicted prisoners registering to vote in elections. The current threat of upheaval is the threatened escape from the "chains" of the Council of Europe and the Human Rights Act with the promise of a new future of a UK Bill of Rights outside of the constraints of European law. The implementation of the Human Rights Act 1998, which was intended to enhance and embed Convention rights in domestic law, appears to have resulted in both a growing divergence between the UK and Strasbourg, and a weakening of the position of the ECtHR in relation to the UK. The doctrine of Parliamentary supremacy in domestic law has always raised tensions with the role of a supra-national court adjudicating on fundamental rights. The growing political mistrust of the concept of codification of rights as being contrary to the perceived flexibility of the English common law and the more fundamental concern that political issues with wider public policy issues are not amenable to simple legal solutions.

The absence of a real European monitoring in Spain shows also the interest and the necessity of this transnational oversight. The Spanish supervisory mechanisms and procedures could be enhanced indeed to the benefit of prisoners and their rights if it were aligned with some of the criteria set forth by the Strasbourg Court. In Spain, there are many potential areas for improvement, particularly as regards the burden of proof, the availability of compensatory remedies more in line with the specifications of the ECtHR case-law, the provision of legal aid from the very outset, the thoroughness of the investigations of ill-treatment and the hearing of prisoners during proceedings.

2 The limits of the CoE and EU monitoring of penal and prison policies

While European-level monitoring has become stronger over time, it also has a negative side as it relies mainly on the principle of subsidiarity that gives the leadership to national governments to implement changes in their legislation and case law. Therefore, compliance with ECtHR requirements depends on the national governments' will and their attitudes (from acceptance and co-operation to defiance, strong opposition and refusal) towards the CoE and the ECtHR. Moreover, the strategy pursued by the CoE and the EU implies effective domestic remedies, strong NGOs litigating in domestic courts, legal aid schemes, networks of barristers, and connections between NGOs, barristers, ombudsmen and international and national authorities responsible for human rights protection. In many countries, knowledge and access to law and to the authority(ies) by prisoners and NGOs are not sufficient to litigate successfully. This is especially the case in Spain which is not targeted by the ECtHR jurisprudence.

2.1 The importance of NGOs and legal aid in litigation activities

Contrary to what some expect, most part of the litigation before the European Court is indeed carried out by NGOs that prolong their litigation efforts undertaken first on their national level. In this regard, Hodson analysing specifically the European context has highlighted the impact that NGOs have had on the case law of European courts, something which in her view proves that we should better get rid of the idea that litigation aims at achieving individual justice (Hodson, 2011). This is why NGOs play a very important role in defending prisoners' interests against prison administrations. Therefore, the influence NGOs can exert on a national level deeply influences the way they can litigate and protect prisoners' rights. This phenomenon totally overlooked by the ECtHR case law constitutes one of its major black hole. We could thus partly explain both the lack and absence of the ECtHR monitoring of certain countries such as Spain as the result of poor influence of NGOs in these countries. The recognition by each national judicial of the role played by NGOs in litigation constitutes also an essential part. For instance, the Italian judicial system for prisoners' rights protection neither before nor after the reform followed to Torregiani's case has recognized any role to NGO in litigation. Italian NGOs are therefore not entitled to seize the surveillance court and cannot be called to testify. Also if there is any legal impediment, reports provided by NGO have never been used by Courts in any case.

In the same manner, competences of barristers appear also to be crucial in litigation and in connection with legal aid. For instance, the number of appeals to the Deutch administrative courts remains low overall. Another likely contributing factor is that these appeals demand considerable amounts of time and require lawyers to be versed in administrative, prison and adjective law for judiciary system divided into administrative and civil justice like in France and the Netherlands. Even in different and less complex judiciary systems, compensation and human resources in taking prison cases are generally of concern to lawyers and their clients. Money is not sufficiently attractive for lawyers and barristers in many countries.

The European justice pushing the development of domestic remedies is also limited by poor access to justice for prisoners in the context of the economic crisis. More precisely, we can underline two types of hindrances to the access to justice for prisoners. First, the poor social and economic resources of detainees and the austerity policies of national governments under the supervision of the European Commission have made it harder for prisoners to access legal remedies. In this regard, main social characteristics influence the will or capability to litigate (through criterion as age, sex, diploma, curriculum, social position in the prison hierarchy, kind of condemnations, prison past. . .). For instance, in France, a structural reason to explain the lack of litigation from prisoners arguably lies in the fact that the underprivileged background of prisoners works against them in a system where administrative courts favour those who have the necessary social, cultural and economic dispositions (Spire and Weidenfeld, 2011). Due to the combination of these factors, prison authorities have considerable discretion to deal with internal prison matters. Moreover, access to justice for prisoners depends above all on the level of legal aid available to them and the support they can receive from NGOs for litigation, and in particular their ability to mobilise at a European level.[21] For instance, in the UK, the Legal Aid, Sentencing and Punishment of Offenders Act 2012 (LASPO) set out the new rules on referral fees which are paid by lawyers who take on new cases, by prohibiting referral fees and cutting the legal aid. The LAPSO has therefore limited massively the access to justice for prisoners, law firms and NGOs.

Second, detainees do not often bring complaints before the courts because they fear retaliation from prison staff, which can result in violence, harassment, hindrances to sentence implementation and prison leave and removal of sentencing credits (Steiner and Cain, 2017). Both these issues seem to be overlooked, or at least neglected, by the ECtHR, even though prisoner litigation remains the main vehicle for transformation of national legislation.[22] Another hindrance to seize courts is the pressure (both psychological and physical) exerted by the prison system and staff on prisoners undertaking litigation. Barristers and Prison Law lawyers do recognize that inmates who file many complaints are placed in a disadvantage by the Prison and/or the officers in many countries. For example, in Spain, some prisoners who frequently denounce are ranked first grade on the grounds that they do not fit the ordinary regime of prison life and hinder the normal functioning of prison (9 per cent of prisoners are ranked first grade due to this reason[23]). Several reports that analyze prison life offer information in this regard. Another hindrance is related to the kind of organisation of remedies inside jails and prisons among prisoners. Some prison litigation systems seem to favour centralization (one or several inmates are the key litigants and centralize complaints, being the go-between barristers, NGOs and prisoners) such as in France, others are characterized with dispatching individualism and absence of organisation such as in Germany.

Lastly, we must also point out that litigation has its own limits and cannot on its own completely change domestic legislation and practices as judicial power has only a limited influence on society and its social structures. This is particularly the case in penal and prison matters in which many national prison administrations often derogate and violate both European and national laws. For instance, the French prison administration has obtained a moratorium on the obligation of individual cells. In this regard, European and national laws are not able to constraint national prison administrations to respect and comply with their content. In addition, these limits are reinforced by the judicial translation and filtering effects of prisoners' concerns and complaints (Schoenfeld, 2010) and the increasing dependency of NGOs on private funding for litigation (Cliquennois and Champetier, 2016). This limited influence of law on society is not only specific in the field of prison. More broadly speaking, Confucius already considered at his time in his Analects that the world is ruled by symbols, neither by words nor by law (Creel, 1949). Perhaps, the efficiency of law is optimal when it relies on symbols and not only on social norms and values. In this respect, we must also recognize and acknowledge that many social domains are governed by exceptions and derogations to the law. This is, for instance, the case of legislation on terrorism that relies on symbols, exception and emergency concepts that constraints and frames penal and prison policies.

2.2 The limits of the ECtHR jurisprudence and its punitive aspect

The ECtHR jurisprudence relies notably on the development of domestic complaints systems to reinforce the compliance of national states with the ECHR. However, many domestic complaints systems suffer from weaknesses, especially their complexity, effectiveness, preventive and compensatory dimensions, promptness and speed, independence, contradictions, access and establishment of facts, burden of proof, power of decision-making by judges and some overlaps in the field of disciplinary sanctions and conditional release.[24]

In addition, some aspects of European jurisprudence have had negative effects in the field of death prevention (entailing both suicide and homicide prevention), long and life sentences and conditional release. Not only the impacts of law seem to be limited but the European jurisprudence when ruling and relying on Article 2 of the European Convention on Human Rights could also induce bad effects on prison practices applied by national prison administrations to comply with the European case law. This is especially the case in the field of death prevention covering both the suicide and homicide prevention and also in long and life sentences and conditional release matters. These domains are governed by risk management and assessment and reinforced surveillance that could be considered in certain cases as bad and inhumane treatment.

The surveillance measures (such as permanent CCTV for prisoners facing suicide crisis, special cells with no anchor points, fireproof mattresses and tearproof sheets, reinforcement of physical surveillance, removal of all objects or substances that could be used to commit suicide or murder including scarves and bed sheets, particularly intense surveillance. . .) imposed by the Strasbourg Court on national states could be considered to be inhumane and degrading treatment. In particular, the Strasbourg Court stipulated that the right to life should not only be passively respected, but that the prison administration had an obligation to take practical, suitably adapted steps to protect this right when the risk of suicide was known or foreseeable on the basis of Article 2 and Recommendation 98(7) of the Committee of Ministers of the Council of Europe (ECHR, Ketreb v. France[25]).[26] These new measures included daily medical supervision and intensive surveillance with direct visual contact (ECHR, Keenan v. United Kingdom). By requiring prisons to take these kinds of measures, the ECHR placed recognition of the right to life above that of self-sufficiency considerations; prison authorities now have to decide on measures and general precautions that reduce the risk of self-harm without totally ending individual autonomy (ECHR, Keenan v. United Kingdom). A compromise between the right to life and the principle of autonomy was found by the ECHR when it required prisons to have established a previous risk of suicide before rendering them liable. Nevertheless, the ECHR gave priority to the right to life when it stated, in Tanribilir v. Turkey and Renolde v. France, that the prison authorities had a positive obligation to take practical preventive measures to protect the right to life of individuals. This court decision even requires these measures to be applied in constraint of the inmate himself.

As a result, a new punitive approach in the French and British prison sector has emerged as a result of the European Court of Human Rights and the French administrative courts and British courts exerting pressure on prison governors in response to the complaints made by prisoners' families, barristers, the demands of human rights groups, and the requirements of human-rights-protection bodies. By publicising cases of suicide and using strategic litigation based on the right to life, human rights groups and barristers have put the French and British prison administrations under pressure. All these courts exert pressure on prison governors, fuelled by complaints from prisoners' families, the demands of prisoner-welfare groups, and the requirements of the British and French human-rights-protection bodies. By publicising prisoner suicides and murders, these bodies have forced the prison administration to change its regulations to comply with the European Convention on Human Rights. The emergence of a rationale that combines a risk management approach with a death-prevention policy shapes the interactions between the prisons, the European Court of Human Rights and the French and British courts and tribunals. These pressures have resulted in a model of prison administration where punitive practices and actuarial risk-management thinking have been both sharpened and intensified. Gathering statistics and information, both systems attempt to identify risky inmates, places and times, often creating different scales for treating those considered at risk of suicide or self-harm (Liebling, 1992, 1995, 2001; Liebling and Arnold, 2005; Cliquennois and Champetier, 2013; Cliquennois, 2010). These prevention systems reinforce the punitive approach to prison since prisoners registered on the "suicide watch list" and designated as "high risk" are transferred for at least 24 hours to special cells with no anchor points and equipped with video-surveillance, fireproof mattresses and tear-proof sheets. The prisoners at high risk are also dressed in special tear-proof clothes and are observed by prison staff around the clock.[27] Even prisoners assessed at medium risk of suicide are placed under enhanced surveillance by prison staff and offered psychiatric counselling.[28] Prison officers are also required to complete observation forms about each medium-risk prisoner.[29]

In the UK, following the rulings by the ECtHR (*Keenan v the UK*, 2001; *Osman v the UK*, 1998; *L.C.B. v the UK*, 1998; *Mc Cann and others v the UK*, 1995), the recommendations 98(7), 2003(23) and 2006(2) of the Committee of Ministers and the CPT standards, HM Prison Service priorities were seriously reoriented since 2004 towards prison health issues and death avoidance which became for the first time a key performance indicator (*Annual Report and accounts 2004–2005; 2006–2007*, HM Prison Service). In this perspective, HM prison service established a range of Prison Service Performance Management Standards contributing to the management of ten key risks (among which self-inflicted deaths and offending behaviour) through audit and corporate assurance. The Prison Service developed government and actuarial risk management arrangements which were applied across the organisation. In this sense, the OASys[30] risk assessment tool has been applied with full connectivity across prison and probation since 2006–2007 (*Annual Report and accounts 2004–2005* and *2006–2007*, HM Prison Service).

Helped by the Head of Internal Audit, the Prison Service further developed and strengthened its risk management framework as a mean of reaching its targets and objectives. This risk management framework has been extended to suicide prevention through the development of the ACCT (Assessment, Care in Custody & Teamwork), a monitoring system for care of at-risk prisoners. The ACCT approach replaced the F2052SH care-planning system for prisoners identified as at-risk of suicide or self-harm, considered as inefficient. The ACCT aimed to provide individualised care in accordance to need backed by suitably trained staff and to reduce the number of self-inflicted deaths in custody through better risk management of those who self-harm. This implementation of suicide risk assessment has been controlled by the Committee for the Prevention of Torture (CPT). The CPT has during its visits observed the identification of inmates at risk of self-harming and those attempting to commit suicide under the ACCT scheme and considered that is was overall satisfactory (CPT/Inf (2009)30 §64; CPT/Inf (2014)11 §61). The CPT has also observed with satisfaction the UK suicide prevention approach implying the placement of the at risk inmate in an anti-ligature observation cell, provision of rip-proof clothing and close monitoring ranging from 15 to 60 minute intervals (CPT/Inf (2014)11 §61). However, the CPT has identified some defects in the system since some inmates known to have mental health issues and being at risk of self-harming have committed suicide, putting some doubts on the effectiveness of the ACCT monitoring system. According to the CPT, a better training of staff should be provided to identify prisoners at risk of committing acts of self-harm or suicide (CPT/Inf (2009)30 §64; CPT/Inf (2014)11 §61). This monitoring exerted by the CPT reinforces therefore the risk management approach to suicide and self-harm.

In this manner, this actuarial rationale forges a new punitive approach to imprisonment: to be alive is a condition of the expression of the power of the state to punish "living bodies". Punishment puts living bodies and souls in a confined space; it is ended by death. This nature of the sentence (affliction of the body) and its condition (the living body) raises questions about the death of people while under the state's protection, and thus under the rule of law. On this regard, death prevention promoted by the European Court is a way of continuing to punish prisoners (Cliquennois and Champetier, 2013; Cliquennois, 2010).

Conclusion

The strengthening of the relationships between the CoE and the EU and the increasing power of the ECtHR have increased their pressure on, and control over, national penal and prison administrations. The positive and procedural obligations imposed by the ECtHR on the Member States have thus led to legal, administrative, judicial and practical changes such as the adoption of domestic penal and prison legislation enforcing the effective implementation of death prevention in custody policies; the provision of healthcare services; the assessment of prisoners' ability to serve custodial sentences and their right to apply for parole; reductions in overcrowding; improvements in conditions of detention; the right to effective remedies and compensation; the enhancement of rehabilitative programs and the development of family visits. Nevertheless, we can also note the limits of this European monitoring, which has been unable so far to improve access to justice for prisoners and ensure effective domestic legal remedies in certain countries.

Notes

1 ECtHR, *Torreggiani and others v. Italy*, 8 January 2013, No 43517/09.
2 ECtHR, *Canali v. France*, 25 April 2013, No 40119/09.
3 See, in particular, ECtHR, *Ananyev and others v. Russia*, 10 January 2012, No 42525/07 and 60800/08, §197; ECtHR, *Norbert Sikorski v. Poland*, 22 October 2009, No 17599/05, §158.
4 ECtHR, *Vinter v. UK*, 9 July 2013, No 66069/09.
5 ECtHR, *Ramirez Sanchez v. France*, 4 July 2006, No 59450/00.
6 ECtHR, *Khider v. France*, 9 July 2009, No 39364/05; *Payet v. France*, 20 January 2011, No 19606/08.
7 ECHR *Osman v UK*, 28 October 1998, No 23452/94; *Keenan v UK*, 3 April 2001, No 27229/95; *Paul and Audrey Edwards v UK*, 14 March 2002, No 46477/99; *Trubnikov v Russia*, 5 July 2005, No 49790/99; *Taïs v France*, 1 June 2006, No 39922/03; *Renolde v France*, 16 October 2008, No 5608/05; *De Donder and De Clippel v Belgium*, 6 December 2011, No 8595/06; *Ketreb v France*, 19 July 2012, No 38447/09.
8 ECtHR, *Campbell and Fell v. UK*, 28 June 1984, 7819/77; *Payet v. France*, 20 January 2011, 19606/08; *M. v. Germany*, 17 December 2009, 19359/04.
9 ECtHR, *Stafford v UK*, 24 April 2002, No 46295/99.
10 ECtHR, *Stafford v UK*, 24 April 2002, 46295/99; *Clift v UK*, 13 July 2010, 7205/07.
11 ECtHR, *Weeks v UK*, 2 March 1987, No 9787/82; *Thynne Wilson and Gunnel v UK*, 25 October 1990, No 11787/85; *Murray v. the Netherlands (GC)*, 26 October 2014, No 10511/10.
12 ECtHR, *Thynne Wilson and Gunnel v UK*, 25 October 1990, No 11787/85.
13 ECtHR, *Gülay Çetin v. Turkey*, 5 March 2013, No 44084/10.
14 ECtHR, *Aerts v. Belgium*, 30 July 1998, No 61/1997/845/1051; *De Donder and De Clippel v Belgium*, 6 December 2011, No 8595/06; *L.B. v. Belgium*, 2 October 2012, No 22831/08; *Claes v. Belgium*, 10 January 2013, No 43418/09; *Dufoort v. Belgium*, 10 January 2013, No 43653/09; *Swennen v. Belgium*, 10 January 2013, No 53448/10.
15 ECtHR, *Aerts v. Belgium*, 30 July 1998, No 61/1997/845/1051; *Mouisel v. France*, 14 November 2002, No 67263/01; *Rivière v. France*, 11 July 2006, No 33834/03; *G. v. France*, 23 February 2012, No 27244/09; *Lankaster v. Belgium*, 9 January 2014, No 22283/10.
16 ECtHR, *L.B. v. Belgium*, 2 October 2012, No 22831/08; *Claes v. Belgium*, 10 January 2013, No 43418/09; *Dufoort v. Belgium*, 10 January 2013, No 43653/09; *Swennen v. Belgium*, 10 January 2013, No 53448/10.
17 ECtHR, *Ananyev and others v. Russia*, 10 January 2012, No 42525/07 and 60800/08, §219.
18 The implementation of effective domestic remedies for breaches of the ECHR has been a long-standing concern of the CoE, repeatedly considered a priority at the

highest political level, notably at the High-Level Conferences on the Future of the Court (Interlaken, February 2010; Izmir, April 2011 and Brighton, April 2012).

19 ECtHR, *Troubnikov V. Russia*, 5 July 2005, No 49790/99, §95.

20 See for example ECtHR, *Novosselov v. Russia*, 2 June 2005, No 66460/01, §45.

21 Report of the Prison Litigation Network to the European Commission (2016).

22 Report of the Prison Litigation Network to the European Commission (2016).

23 "Mirando el abismo. El régimen cerrado", Julián Ríos Martín y Pedro Cabrera Cabrera, Ed. Universidad Pontificia Comillas y Fundación Santa María (2002) p. 54, Table 17

24 Report of the Prison Litigation Network to the European Commission (2016).

25 , Ketreb v. France, 19 July 2012, Req. 38447/09.

26 The recommendation states that: "The risk of suicide should be constantly assessed both by medical and custodial staff. Physical methods designed to avoid self-harm, close and constant observation, dialogue and reassurance, as appropriate, should be used in moments of crisis." (Recommendation R (98)7, III.D.58.)

27 Memorandum, 15 June 2009; Memorandum, 17 December 2009.

28 Memorandum, 7 July 2009.

29 Ibid.

30 OASys (Offender Assessment System) is based on a series of computer-based forms on which clinical offenders' evaluations are made by staff. It comprises also supervision and sentence plans which are recorded on a periodic basis: generally 16 weeks for offenders in the community and less frequently for imprisoned offenders.

References

Cliquennois, G. (2010). "Preventing suicide in French prisons." *British Journal of Criminology*, 50(6), pp. 1023–1040.

Cliquennois, G. and Champetier, B. (2016). "The economic, judicial and political influence exerted by private foundations on cases taken by ngos to the European Court of Human Rights: Inklings of a new Cold War?" *European Law Journal*, 22(1), pp. 92–126.

Cliquennois, G. and Champetier, B. (2013). "A new risk management for prisoners in France: The emergence of a death-avoidance approach." *Theoretical Criminology*, 17(3), pp. 397–415.

Committee of Ministers of the Council of Europe (2006). European Prison Rules. Strasbourg, Rec(2006)2.

Creel, H. G. (1949). *Confucius, the Man and the Myth*. New York: The John Day Company.

Hodson, L. (2011). NGOs and Litigation Before the European Court of Human Rights. Oregon: Hart Publishing.

Liebling, A. (1992). Suicide in Prison. London: Routledge. Liebling, A. (1995). "Vulnerability and Prison Suicide." British Journal of Criminology, 35(2), pp. 173–187.

Liebling, A. (2001). "Suicides in Prison: Ten Years On". Prison Service Journal, 138(7), pp. 35–41.

Liebling, A. and Arnold, A. (2005). Prisons and their Moral Performance: Study of Values, Quality and Prison Life. Oxford: Oxford University Press.

Sauvé, J.M. (2009). "Le contrôle de l'administration pénitentiaire par le juge administratif. Institut d'études judiciaires de Lille 2, 24 Bebruary 2009.

Schoenfeld, H. (2010). "Mass incarceration and the paradox of prison conditions litigation." *Law & Society Review*, 44(3), pp. 731–768.

Snacken, S. (2011). Prisons en Europe: Pour une pénologie critique et humaniste. Brussels: Larcier.

Snacken, S. and Dumortier, E. (2012). Resisting Punitiveness in Europe: Welfare, Human Rights and Democracy. Abingdon: Routledge.

Spire, A. and Weinefeld, K. (2011). "Le tribunal administratif: une affaire d'initiés ? Les inégalités d'accès à la justice et la distribution du capital procédural." Droit et Société, 79(3), pp. 689–713.

Steiner, B. and Cain, C. (2017). "Punishment within prison: An examination of the influences of prison officials' decisions to remove sentencing credits." Law & Society Review, 51(1), pp. 70–98.

Van Zyl Smit, D. and Snacken, S. (2009). *Principles of European Prison Law and Policy: Penology and Human Rights*. Oxford: Oxford University Press.

Index

Bold page references indicate tables and graphs.

Made in the USA
Middletown, DE
18 October 2024

62864793R00117